the language of graphic design

ROCKPORT

pointlineshapeformlightcolortexturescale

closureexpressionabstractiontonecontra

gridpointlineshapeformlightcolortexture

First published in the United States of America
by Rockport Publishers, a member of Quayside Publishing Group
100 Cummings Center
Suite 406-L
Beverly, Massachusetts
01915-6101
Telephone: (978) 282-9590
Fax: (978) 283-2742
www.rockpub.com

Library of Congress Cataloging-in-Publication Data
Poulin, Richard.
 The language of graphic design : an illustrated handbook for
understanding fundamental design principles / Richard Poulin.
     p. cm.
Includes bibliographical references and index.
ISBN-13: 978-1-59253-676-4
ISBN-10: 1-59253-676-X
1. Graphic arts. 2. Design. I. Title.
NC997.P63 2011
741.6--dc22

                                    2010049318
                                        CIP

ISBN-13: 978-1-59253-676-4
ISBN-10: 1-59253-676-X

Digital edition published in 2011
eISBN-13: 978-1-61058-0359

10 9 8 7 6 5 4 3 2

Design: Poulin + Morris Inc.

Printed in China

Richard Poulin

movementspacebalancesymmetryasymmetryt
figure-groundframeproportionimagepatternt
calemovementspacebalancesymmetryasymme

BEVERLY MASSACHUSETTS

An
Illustrated
Handbook
for
Understanding
Fundamental
Design
Principles

the language of graphic design

ROCKPORT
PUBLISHERS

contents

lan·guage \ˈlaŋ-gwij, -wij\ *n*
1 a: the words, their pronunciation, and the methods of combining them used and understood by a community
2 b: form or manner of verbal expression; *specif*: style

Anyone trying to communicate in a new language has to first gain a complete understanding of its fundamentals; the ABCs of that language—definitions, functions, and usage. *The Language of Graphic Design* provides graphic design students and practitioners with an in-depth understanding of the fundamental elements and principles of their language—graphic design—what they are, why they are important, and how to use them effectively.

Similar books on the market today limit their focus and content to a student audience, using their work only to demonstrate a premise. This book goes beyond the student experience. It includes work by some of the most successful and renowned practitioners from around the world and how they have applied these fundamental principles to their work. By examining both student and professional work, this comprehensive handbook is a more meaningful, memorable, and inspiring reference tool for novice design students as well as young designers starting their careers.

The foundation of any successful graphic designer relies upon an understanding of the fundamentals of graphic design. Throughout a designer's education and career, these basic tenets are constantly referred to for inspiration and provide the basis for designing meaningful, memorable, and communicative work.

To understand visual communications, a graphic designer has to first understand by "seeing." To develop this discipline or visual sense is similar to learning a new language with its own unique alphabet, lexicon (vocabulary), and syntax (sentence structure). This book provides clear and concise information that will enhance visual literacy, while using dynamic, memorable, visual references to inform, inspire, and reinforce a sense of "seeing."

> **"It's not what you look at that matters, it's what you see."**
>
> HENRY DAVID THOREAU (1817-1862), *American, Author, Naturalist, Poet*

The Language of Graphic Design is organized in twenty-six chapters with each chapter defining a fundamental element (basic building blocks of the graphic designer's vocabulary) and principle of graphic design. Please note that the inclusion of twenty-six elements and principles should not be interpreted as a definitive number—they are solely a reference to the standard alphabet; the building blocks for Western language.

Each chapter includes a narrative and visual sidebar referencing a historical graphic design benchmark to further illustrate each element or principle being explored, while continuing with an in-depth, illustrated overview of what it is, why it is important, and how to use it effectively.

Additionally, dictionary definitions begin each chapter to illustrate one of my convictions as a teacher. I have always reinforced to my students the value of the written word. Furthermore, I have stressed that words should never be taken for granted. Graphic designers are visual interpreters; however, we can't be effective communicators without first having a deep and continued appreciation and respect for narrative form. To further this point, I insist that my students always refer to a dictionary to remind themselves of the meaning of words (familiar or not). I believe this strengthens their understanding of what they ultimately need to interpret visually. With this book, I hope to achieve the same with you—the reader.

Visual communications, like written and verbal communications, involve analysis, planning, organizing, and, ultimately, problem solving. When you write or speak, you intuitively choose which words to use and how to use them together to effectively communicate your message. In visual communications, the same end result can be achieved; however, the graphic designer needs to be as intuitive.

"The challenge is for the graphic designer to turn data into information and information into messages of meaning."
KATHERINE McCOY (B. 1945), *American, Educator, Graphic Designer*

The principles of graphic design are the framework for using elements in the most appropriate and effective manner to create meaningful and understandable visual communications. Elements are the "what" of a graphic designer's visual language, and principles are the "how." When carefully considered and utilized together, they allow graphic designers to "speak" in an accessible, universal, visual language. We never think of writing a sentence as an unusual or extraordinary act. We are taught at an early age about the principles and elements of written and verbal communications. Unfortunately, the same cannot be said for visual communications. However, as we were taught the basics of spelling, grammar, and syntax, we can also be taught the same fundamentals of visual communications.

"Creativity . . . involves the power to originate, to break away from the existing ways of looking at things, to move freely in the realm of the imagination, to create and recreate worlds fully in 'one's mind—while supervising all this with a critical inner eye."

OLIVER SACKS (B. 1933), *British, Author, Educator, Neurologist*

The elements and principles of graphic design such as point, line, shape, light, color, balance, contrast, and proportion are a graphic designer's vocabulary for giving voice and, ultimately, meaning to any visual communication. Without a reliance on these fundamentals, visual communications will be ineffective, non-communicative, and will not "speak" to any audience.

"The hardest thing to see is what is in front of your eyes."
GOETHE (1749-1832), German, Author

My goal for this design reference book is that the reader will be able to refer back to the contents of it on a regular basis for essential information, inspiration, and guidance. Design students, as well as practitioners, are in dire need of a comprehensive reference book that provides them with essential information and inspirational resources on the basic tenets of visual communications and graphic design fundamentals.

Hopefully, *The Language of Graphic Design* will become one of the few primary resources and references that will be referred to time and time again.

point \\'pȯint\\ *n*

4 a: a geometric element that has zero dimensions and a location determinable by an ordered set of coordinates

point.

1

"An idea is a point of departure and no more. As soon as you elaborate it, it becomes transformed by thought."
PABLO PICASSO (1881-1973), *Spanish, Painter, Sculptor*

A point is the fundamental building block of all visual communication elements and principles. It is also the simplest and purest of all geometric elements in a graphic designer's vocabulary and used as an essential element in geometry, physics, vector graphics, and other related fields.

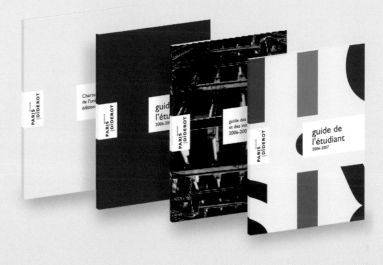

Paris Diderot Université's logotype is literally based on an "**X** marks the spot" graphic representation or, in this case, the intersection of two visual elements or lines creating a singular point. Additionally, the dots of the lowercase *i*'s in the words *Paris* and *Diderot* are shared to create a visual focal point and integration between the two words, providing a much stronger and cohesive unity to the overall message.

CATHERINE ZASK
Paris, France

Definitions

A point has many definitions. It is often considered within the framework of Euclidean geometry, where it is one of the fundamental objects. Euclid (325–625 BC), creator of modern geometry, originally defined the point vaguely, as "that which has no part."

It is an abstract phenomenon indicating a precise location; however, it cannot be seen or felt. It is a location or place without area. In typography, a point is a period. It is a dot character such as a full stop, decimal point, or radix point. It is also the smallest

(continued on page 16)

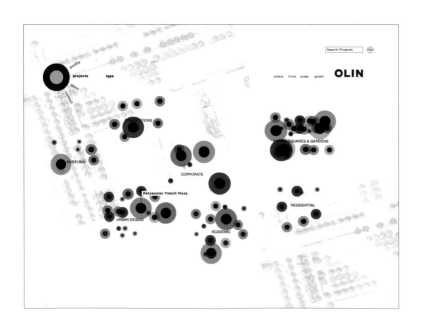

The website for Olin, a landscape architecture, urban design, and planning firm, relies solely upon varied size points, or dots, as the primary navigational tools for accessing specific information, such as profile, project types, and news on the firm. It also visually symbolizes the macrocosm and microcosm of the organization through the fluid, kinetic movements of the site's interface, further conveying Olin as an organic, living entity.

PENTAGRAM
New York, New York, USA

AEG Lamp Poster
PETER BEHRENS
Munich, Germany

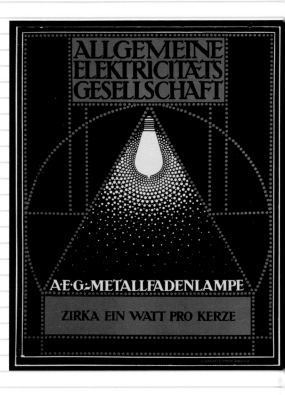

PETER BEHRENS (1868–1940) was a true visionary and the first Renaissance designer of the modern age, moving with ease from one discipline to another—painting, architecture, product design, furniture design, and graphic design. His creative interests were boundless. Behrens was the first to pursue a seamless integration of visual communications and architecture and was an inspiration to the founders of the modernist movement.

As a young man, he worked as a fine artist, illustrator, and bookbinder in his native Hamburg. In 1899, Behrens became the second member of the recently created Darmstadt Artists' Colony, where he designed and built his own house as well as everything inside it—from furniture and textiles to paintings and pottery. While at Darmstadt, he realized that he was more interested in simplified geometric forms than the more organic and curvilinear forms of the current Jugendstil (New Art) or art nouveau. In the early 1900s, he became one of the leaders of architectural reform in Germany and one of the first architects of factories and office buildings utilizing a modernist materials palette of brick, steel, and glass.

As a teacher, his ideas and teachings on design for industry, as well as everyday objects and products, influenced a group of students that would ultimately alter the direction of twentieth-century architecture and design worldwide, including Ludwig Mies van der Rohe, Le Corbusier, Adolf Meyer, and Walter Gropius, founder of the Bauhaus school in Dessau, Germany.

In 1907, Allegemein Elektricitäts-Gesellschaft (AEG), Germany's largest electrical utility and industrial producer, hired Behrens as their new artistic consultant. It was at AEG that he created a unified brand for every aspect of the company's visual environment—office buildings, factories, and visual communication materials.

A primary example of Behrens's design philosophy at AEG was a promotional poster he designed advertising AEG's newest product in 1910—a technologically advanced lamp or lightbulb. The design of the poster is clearly based on fundamental modernist design elements and principles. Its orthogonal graphic composition is organized with an articulated grid and comprises basic geometric shapes—a continuous frame or square, a circle, and an equilateral triangle. The triangle provides a focal location for the lightbulb and a simplified, abstract dot pattern represents brilliance and illumination. The pattern and lines framing and dividing the composition of the poster, as well as the outline of the circle and triangle, are all composed of a series of dots or points, which symbolize and communicate light.

In defining his approach, Behrens stated, "Design is not about decorating functional forms—it is about creating forms that accord with the character of the object and that show new technologies to advantage."

His visionary approach not only influenced the entire AEG corporate culture, it became the first seminal example of corporate identity and branding that would inevitably become a primary force within the design professions in the later part of the twentieth century.

Peter Behrens and the AEG Brand

14

15

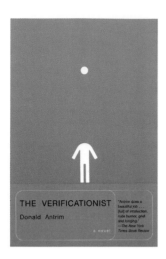

THE VERIFICATIONIST
Donald Antrim

a novel

This book cover for *The Verificationist* uses a diminuitive-scaled, universal symbol of man as a visual metaphor that supports the book's title and main character—a middle-aged psychotherapist in the midst of a midlife crisis. The head of the symbol—a point represented in a larger scale—is divorced and distant from its body, creating an immediate and jarring focal point to an otherwise restrained graphic cover composition.

JOHN GALL
New York, New York, USA

unit of measurement, being a subdivision of the larger pica—one point is equal to 0.0148 inches, 1/72 of an inch, whereby twelve points equals one pica. It also describes the weight or thickness of paper stock.

Visual Characteristics

In visual communications, a point takes the form of a visible mark or dot. It can stand alone, identified solely by its own presence, or become an integrated element of a larger collective whole. A point can be realized in many ways and take on many graphic forms. A series of points can create a line. A mass of points can create shape, form, texture, tone, and pattern. While it is a visible mark, it has no mass. It is a design element that has a location in space but has no extension. It is defined by its position in space with a pair of *x*- and *y*-coordinates.

Every shape or mass with a recognizable center is also a point, no matter what its size. A point simultaneously radiates inward and outward. An infinite set of points is also a line. Any two points can be connected by a straight line. A plane or shape with a center is a closed form and can also be described as a point. Even when its size is increased, it still retains its essential identity as a point.

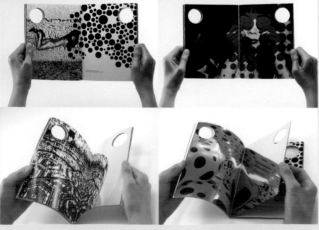

Point—or dot—is shown in a variety of different forms, scales, and configurations throughout this monograph brochure on the work of Japanese avant-garde artist Yayoi Kusama. Dot matrix letterforms, die-cut circles, varying-scale dot patterns, dot-patterned images, and linear dotted frames juxtaposed with black and white, as well as saturated, intense color fields, all add to the visual celebration of this artist's work.

SANG LEE JIN, Student
TRACY BOYCHUK, Instructor
School of Visual Arts
New York, New York, USA

This assignment requires sophomore students to consider fundamental design elements—in this case, point—found in their environment and in everyday objects. With photography they explore their surroundings and document examples of point found in surprising and intriguing situations. The final images are cropped to a 3 X 3-inch (7.6 X 7.6 cm) square and then composed in a 3 X 3 nine-square composition, further communicating the student's examination of interrelationships in form, color, texture, scale, and contrast between the various images. This visual exercise helps design students increase their understanding of fundamental design elements, increase their awareness of the natural and built environment, become more comfortable with a camera and with composing compelling and communicative photographic images, crop images to create interesting and dynamic compositions, identify visual relationships between seemingly disparate images, and become familiar with image software such as Camera Raw, Adobe Photoshop, and Adobe Bridge.

NEIL AGUINALDO, Student
ANNABELLE GOULD, Instructor
University of Washington
Seattle, Washington, USA

Conventional offset printing is also solely based on a point, since it is the single common denominator for creating color, tone, value, gradients, and halftones. A spatial point describes a specific object within a given space that consists of volume, area, length, or any other higher dimensional form. It is an object with zero dimensions.

While it can be defined in many ways and take on a variety of visual realities, when used in a meaningful scale and in an appropriate context, a point can communicate a multitude of visual meanings.

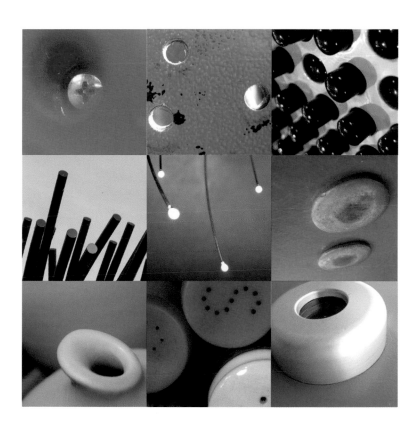

A free-form mass of minuscule, graphic points is the primary visual element on this identity program for the Museum of the African Diaspora (MoAD), a first-voice museum that explores and celebrates the history, culture, and contributions of the people of the African Diaspora around the world. These graphic points, in this context, communicate the brand and mission of the institution and can be found in the building's architecture, exhibition design, graphic identity, collateral materials, and environmental graphics. Here, the museum's acronym and logotype comprise thousands of points, further reinforcing that the MoAD is about the individual and their own unique experiences.

SUSSMAN/PREJZA
& COMPANY
Los Angeles, California, USA

This simple, iconic eclipse logotype represents summer as well as the elements of risk and mystery found in the diverse work of the performing artists appearing at this independent theater and arts festival in Toronto, Ontario. An organizational grid of different suns based on a common graphic point and juxtaposed on an intense, neon-yellow background further reinforces this message, as well as creates an eye-catching and memorable visual for the festival.

MONNET DESIGN
Toronto, Ontario, Canada

This information-based poster titled *The Shape of Globalization: World Auto Industry* and designed for the U.S. Department of Energy documents the designer's analysis of the global auto manufacturing industry and its impact on sales and use throughout the world. The poster is composed of a series of points—dots and circles of varying scale, used as primary identification elements for specific auto types, manufacturers, brands, and subsidiaries. Adjacent and overlapping circles communicate statistical data relating to the collaborative partnerships between two or more automakers. Color is used as a codification for the six primary countries that produce automobiles and trucks worldwide.

CHRISTINA VAN VLECK
Lexington, Massachusetts, USA

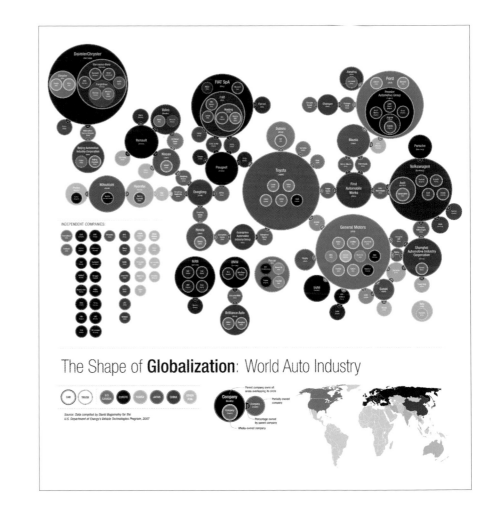

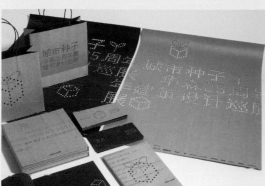

This visual identity system for Huasen Architecture Company's touring exhibition titled *Seeds of the Cities* relies solely on perforated letterforms derived from a series of **LED** indicator displays found throughout the traveling exhibition. These dot-based characters and symbols are either printed or literally punched through various paper stocks for the project logotype, promotional posters, exhibition catalog, invitations, and shopping bags. In some situations, the dot-based characters are composed as a visual continuum, similar to a typical **LED** zipper display, where the information is literally traveling from one surface to another.

SENSE TEAM
Shenzhen, China

The visual branding program for **AOL** reflects the fluid, flexible, and ever-changing content of the digital media world. The program's only stable, rigid, and consistent element is its logotype—a bold sans serif acronym followed by a period or point. The counter of the lowercase *o* in **AOL**, as well as the period at the end of the acronym, reinforces this logotype's singular clarity and focus. Its asymmetrical placement and juxtaposition to various photographic and graphic images, such as a set of black balloons, the extended wing of a hawk, or an expressive texture of colorful brushstrokes, further enhance its unique and unconventional visual characteristics.

WOLFF OLINS
New York, New York, USA

line \ˈlīn\ *n*

1: the path traced by a moving point

2: a thin, continuous mark, as that made by a pen, pencil, or brush applied to a surface

2

"The geometric line is an invisible thing. It is the track made by the moving point . . . . Here, the leap out of the static into the dynamic occurs."

WASSILY KANDINSKY (1866-1944), *Russian, Painter*

One of the most basic and pervasive visual elements of a graphic designer's visual vocabulary is a line.

A line's functions are limitless. It can join, organize, divide, direct, construct, and move other graphic objects. A line can be read as a positive mark or a negative gap. Lines can be actual or implied.

This brand design standards guide for Point Loma Nazarene University, a liberal arts teaching university in San Diego, California, uses a singular, free-flowing line (made of string) as a youthful, energetic, authentic, and fun information element for the reader. It literally is "a common thread" to follow for the reader and functions as a visual information cue and guide throughout the various sections of this user reference guide.

MIRIELLO GRAFICO
San Diego, California, USA

They can be realized as edges or boundaries to objects as well as contours to shapes and forms. A line can lead the reader's eye as well as provide movement and energy to any composition. When used properly, a line can improve readability, immediacy, and the ultimate meaning of any visual message.

Historical References

We are taught "a line is the shortest distance between two points." While this fact is true, we have never been taught to appreciate the other inherent characteristics and qualities of a line. Since man felt the need to visually (continued on page 24)

Kinetic, fluid lines used in this logotype and environmental graphics program play multiple roles. First, they convey Signature Theatre Company's brand and mission to provide a venue for an evolving series of diverse voices and visions in the theater. The logotype's linear composition is constructed of layered, handwritten signatures of the company's history of playwrights-in-residence. They also create a cloud of signatures that serves a myriad of uses such as a frame, backdrop, and even as a container to hold photographs or artwork. The relationship between the logotype's linear elements and the vibrant color palette used in various applications creates a dynamic and memorable identity.

C+G PARTNERS LLC
New York, New York, USA

1955

Zurich Tonhalle Concert Poster
JOSEF MÜLLER-BROCKMANN
Zurich, Switzerland

JOSEF MÜLLER-BROCKMANN (1914–1996), designer, writer, artist, and educator, was one of the pioneers of functional, objective graphic design and the Swiss International Typographic Style. His poster series for the Zurich Tonhalle is a seminal example of this modernist, constructivist style and set the standard for the use of pure geometry, mathematical systems, and the grid in visual communications.

During the 1950s, he explored various theories of nonrepresentational abstraction, visual metaphor, subjective graphic interpretation, and constructive graphic design based on the sole use of elements of pure geometry without illustration, nuance, or embellishment.

Each poster in the Tonhalle series uses geometric elements such as circles, squares, arcs, and lines as visual metaphor and is visually orchestrated with rhythm, scale, and repetition. Müller-Brockmann said that these posters were "designed in which the proportions of the formal elements and their immediate spaces are almost always related to certain numerical progressions logically followed out."

For example, the Zurich Tonhalle poster he designed for a concert featuring the work of Igor Stravinsky, Alan Berg, and Wolfgang Fortner was based on a series of photographic studies he had been working on earlier. One study was composed of intersecting lines of varied thickness and lengths, where the dimensions of each line were determined in relationship to each adjacent line. These spatial relationships were also used in defining the spaces between each line. The overall composition is angled by 45 degrees so that each line appears to move diagonally in two directions across the poster.

This approach supported Müller-Brockmann's interpretive view that visual form is comparable to nonrepresentational structures and mathematical systems found in all musical composition. Here, the structural and compositional framework of lines expresses the true nature of the composer's music. At the time, it was said that Müller-Brockmann was a musician composing without an instrument.

All of his work can be analyzed in a similar manner. A precise mathematical plan, logically constructed, is always employed. Every element has a reason for its size, placement, and position.

In reviewing the poster series, Paul Rand said, "They reveal an artist at work, as well as one who fathoms the world of communication, the particular audience for a particular function. These posters are comfortable in the worlds of art and music. They do not try to imitate musical notation, but they evoke the very sounds of music by visual equivalents."

Müller-Brockmann's integration of typography and pure geometry illustrates a timeless relationship between image and music—vocabulary and message.

Josef Müller-Brockmann and the Zurich Tonhalle Posters

The exhibition Brno Echo: Ornament and Crime from Adolf Loos to Now is a lively dialogue between historical and contemporary design on "modern ornament." Adolf Loos's 1908 manifesto "Ornament and Crime" serves as the conceptual foundation for this exhibition, which looks at the recurrence of lines and patterns that constitute a fundamental grammar of modern ornament, connecting everything from the Wiener Werkstätte through pop art to current variants of retro-futurism. Here, geometric striping and concentric forms are a type of ornamentation that is acceptably modern. This, in turn, leads the viewer through an archaeology of concentric striping that links early modernism with other stylistic visual languages throughout the last century. The exhibition's graphic identity is based on the *B* designed for the original Brno Biennial identity, and these posters utilize this line-composed letterform to create "**BRNO ECHO.**"

PENTAGRAM
New York, New York, USA

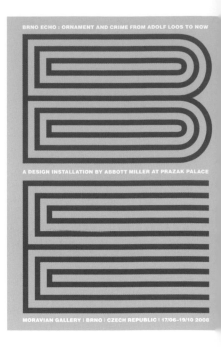

This promotional poster for Design UK, one component of a comprehensive public awareness and branding program for the British Embassy in Tokyo, is based on an abstract Union Jack created from red and white illuminated neon tubes attached to a blue background. The resulting linear construction, symbolically British with futuristic Japanese overtones, was used to brand the entire event and appeared on a diverse set of collateral print materials and websites.

FORM
London, United Kingdom

communicate his day-to-day experiences by making marks on cave walls, he has unconsciously relied upon line. This fact is evident in cave paintings in southern France, burial messages in Egyptian hieroglyphics, inscriptions on Roman tribunal arches, and medieval crests adorning castle walls. Line has always been a fundamental element of our visual communications palette.

In reexamining these historical references, we can further identify the many functions that man has given to line.

Character and Meaning

A line is composed of a number of points located next to one another in one direction; the number of points can be infinite or there can be two endpoints—a beginning point and an endpoint—or a vector. Its path defines the quality and character of the resulting line. It can be straight, meander, or curve across itself or it can follow the precise arc of a circle segment. The end result gives specific character and meaning to each line.

A line is elemental in visual communications. It is also a fundamental element of visual geometry. Without it, the circle, square, and triangle would not exist, nor could we visually represent them. As an elemental geometric form, a line always has length, but never breadth. When this proportional relationship occurs, a line inevitably becomes a plane or surface.

The primary function of a line in visual communications is to connect or separate other elements in a composition. A line's inherent nature is directional. When it is articulated as a smooth gesture, the eye follows it in an easy and unconscious manner; when it is rough or irregular, it impedes movement, thereby slowing the eye's connection with it. Lines create boundaries and ultimately define shape and form. They are inherently dynamic gestures as opposed to points that are always static. Lines communicate movement because they move in two directions.

Man created line as the simplest means to visually communicate. We see lines as boundaries in objects and are initially taught to draw lines as a way to convey or communicate naïve shapes and forms.

Tone and Message

A line communicates division, organization, emphasis, sequence, and hierarchy. These inherent functions can change in tone and

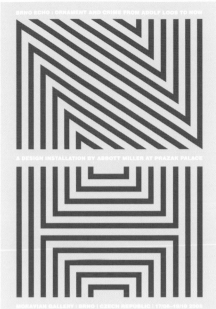

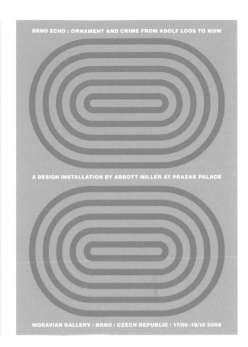

Stories from the Field

The United Nations
Documentary Film Festival

This logotype and promo-
tional poster use a series of
dramatic calligraphic lines
rendered in bold, kinetic
brushstrokes to represent
the Asian influences of this
documentary film festival's
program offerings to the
general public.

TAKASHI KUSUI, Student
JI LEE, Instructor
School of Visual Arts
New York, New York, USA

This logotype for the
restaurant Txikito Cocina
Vasca, featuring cuisine
from the Basque region of
Spain, is based on curvilinear
wrought-iron signs found
throughout the region and
was reproduced in gold leaf
on its entrance doors.

LOUISE FILI LTD.
New York, New York, USA

The Prix Émile Hermès competition focuses on young European designers and rewards them for their creative and innovative contributions to the functionality of designed objects. The awards program is named in honor of Émile Hermès, a creative visionary and pioneer who recognized the value of form and function in design as well as the relationship between craftsmanship and the end product. The logotype for the prize captures the spirit of function, craft, and innovation through the use of line, letterform, and metaphor.

CATHERINE ZASK
Paris, France

PRIX
ÉMILE
HERMÈS

LE SENS DE L'OBJET

message through the tool used to articulate a line. Lines are expressive. They can be long, short, thick, thin, smooth, or irregular and can convey a wide range of emotions. A straight line is mechanical and cold; a curvilinear line is natural and approachable; a thin line is soft and restrained; a bold line communicates strength and power. If a line is drawn with a brush, it conveys a more fluid and undisciplined message as opposed to a line created with a mechanical pen that conveys precision and a disciplined message.

Another aspect of line quality is determined by the tool that makes it; for example, the sketched quality of a charcoal pencil line, the precision of a line drawn with a digital pen tool, or the organic quality of a line brushed with ink. Again, history confirms this to be true. From the naïve nature of a line drawn by a hand's finger or a branch from a tree to a metal scribe or a calligraphic pen nib, the communicative nature of the line has evolved over time at the same pace as man's reliance on different tools and technologies.

Graphic Forms
The orientation and position of a line can also further influence a visual message. A horizontal line is calm, quiet, and serene; a

This exercise requires sophomore graphic design students to consider fundamental design principles—in this case, line found in the environment. With photography, they explore their surroundings and document examples of line found in surprising and intriguing situations. The final images are cropped and composed in a unique and compelling manner, further communicating the students' exploration of line, color, form, and contrasts between images. This exercise helps students increase their understanding of fundamental design principles; increase their awareness of the natural and built environment; become more comfortable with a camera and with composing compelling and communicative photographic images; crop images to create interesting, dynamic compositions; find visual relationships between seemingly disparate images; and become familiar with image software such as Camera Raw, Adobe Photoshop, and Adobe Bridge.

AMBER JOEHNK, Student
ANNABELLE GOULD, Instructor
*University of Washington
Seattle, Washington, USA*

The identity and collateral material for a fund-raising event, Safe Horizon, was based on work contributed by a number of artists who created their own interpretations of the word *safety*. The majority of art was based on line, as well as form, texture, and pattern created by line. The art was displayed and auctioned at the event.

ROGERS ECKERSLEY
DESIGN
New York, New York, USA

vertical line communicates strength, height, and aspiration. Vertical lines appear more active and communicate a more powerful and immediate message than a series of horizontal lines. Diagonal lines are much more suggestive, energetic, and dynamic.

While we have always been told to "color within the lines," we should consider that lines can be realized in a variety of different graphic forms. They can be straight, curvilinear, thin, thick, solid, and dotted. Multiple lines, whether parallel or juxtaposed at right angles, create texture, movement, tension, pattern, tone, value, perspective, and structure.

This poster is from an exercise, "Visual Storytelling and Narrative Form," and requires a student to read, analyze, and visually interpret the narrative themes of the Pulitzer Prize–winning play *Angels in America*. Each student conceptualizes and photographs imagery that visually communicates his or her point of view. Here a loose, frayed thread on the verge of breaking is a metaphor for the main characters of the play undergoing extreme challenges in their lives. The purity of the image, as well as the supporting typography, allows the line to be emotional, provocative, and highly communicative.

MIKIHIRO KOBAYASHI,
Student
RICHARD POULIN, Instructor
*School of Visual Arts
New York, New York, USA*

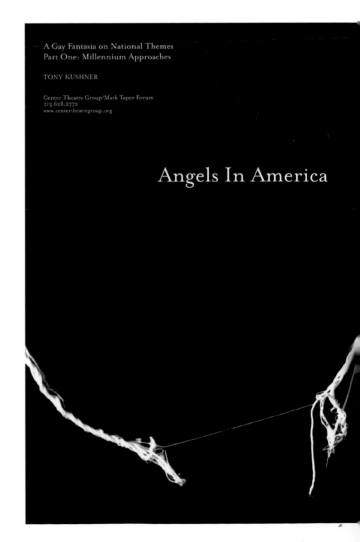

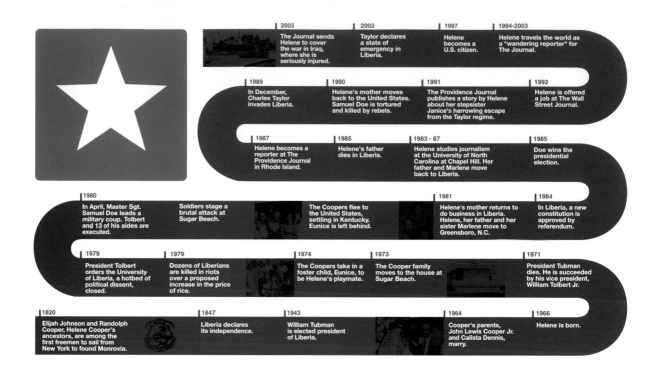

2003 The Journal sends Helene to cover the war in Iraq, where she is seriously injured.

2002 Taylor declares a state of emergency in Liberia.

1997 Helene becomes a U.S. citizen.

1994-2003 Helene travels the world as a "wandering reporter" for The Journal.

1989 In December, Charles Taylor invades Liberia.

1990 Helene's mother moves back to the United States. Samuel Doe is tortured and killed by rebels.

1991 The Providence Journal publishes a story by Helene about her stepsister Janice's harrowing escape from the Taylor regime.

1992 Helene is offered a job at The Wall Street Journal.

1987 Helene becomes a reporter at The Providence Journal in Rhode Island.

1985 Helene's father dies in Liberia.

1983 - 87 Helene studies journalism at the University of North Carolina at Chapel Hill. Her father and Marlene move back to Liberia.

1985 Doe wins the presidential election.

1980 In April, Master Sgt. Samuel Doe leads a military coup. Tolbert and 13 of his aides are executed.

Soldiers stage a brutal attack at Sugar Beach.

The Coopers flee to the United States, settling in Kentucky. Eunice is left behind.

1981 Helene's mother returns to do business in Liberia. Helene, her father and her sister Marlene move to Greensboro, N.C.

1984 In Liberia, a new constitution is approved by referendum.

1979 President Tolbert orders the University of Liberia, a hotbed of political dissent, closed.

1979 Dozens of Liberians are killed in riots over a proposed increase in the price of rice.

1974 The Coopers take in a foster child, Eunice, to be Helene's playmate.

1973 The Cooper family moves to the house at Sugar Beach.

1971 President Tubman dies. He is succeeded by his vice president, William Tolbert Jr.

1820 Elijah Johnson and Randolph Cooper, Helene Cooper's ancestors, are among the first freemen to sail from New York to found Monrovia.

1847 Liberia declares its independence.

1943 William Tubman is elected president of Liberia.

1964 Cooper's parents, John Lewis Cooper Jr. and Calista Dennis, marry.

1966 Helene is born.

The graphical articulation of a line also impacts its presence, subtle or obvious, on any given surface. Shaded lines recede as they change from thick to thin, creating a subtle illusion of space. The thicker the line, the more it comes forward or advances.

Another way to think of line is as an edge. When it is given this function, it allows the eye to perceive an object from its background. We also immediately understand line as edge when a horizontal line distinguishes land from sea or land from sky. A linear edge can also exist along the side of any straight or curved shape or as the result of shapes sharing the same edge.

A line can also be implied, meaning it occurs as the result of an alignment of shapes, edges, or even points. Implying the existence of a line in that way can be very engaging for the viewer. Implying lines also activates the compositional space.

This dramatic three-dimensional, textural wall mural for PMP Limited Melbourne is composed of horizontal lines dimensionalized in an abstract manner symbolizing the activities of this media production and magazine distribution company. Spectrum-colored up-lighting and an exaggerated bas-relief of each horizontal band further create a spatial and ascending focal point to this two-story, double-height office reception space.

EMERYSTUDIO
Victoria, Australia

This information graphic for the *New York Times Book Review*'s *The House at Sugar Beach: In Search of a Lost African Childhood*, by Helene Cooper, visually highlights specific developments and dates found throughout her emotional memoir. The graphic is composed of a serpentine bold stripe chronologically identifying key dates in her country's development as well as her own life, finally arriving at a symbolic star or home. The graphic composition is based on the Liberian flag and shows the circuitous route that the reader will travel when reading her book.

JULIA HOFFMANN
New York, New York, USA

This information graphic, titled "The Bilbao Effect" from *Metropolis* magazine, contains a list of cultural institutional buildings conceived since 1991—the year that the Guggenheim in Bilbao, Spain, opened. Line weights and line lengths vary based on the specifics of each building project, which is further identified at the end of each line graphic: commission, completion date, location, architect, and time span of project. The lines are organized in a curvilinear manner, evoking the forms and massing of the Bilbao building, and further create a unified and cohesive message. Each individual line is coded with specific building project information: new museum/institution (green), new building (pink), expansion or addition (blue), canceled (red), and in progress (orange).

PURE + APPLIED
New York, New York, USA

The Quality of a Line

Lines have a variety of functions in visual communications. They can serve as the contour of an object or human figure or exist purely to serve themselves as elements used to separate information, lead the eye in a particular direction, or imply alignment. Lines can also become textures or patterns. The quality of a line can communicate the nature of what is being described; for example, delicate, precise, angular, architectural, chemical, anatomical, fluid, or awkward.

One of the most prevalent uses of line is in print material, such as newspapers, magazines, publications, and websites. Here, lines are used to organize information, separate and emphasize content, and direct the eye to specific areas of interest. In all of these situations, line is used primarily to improve readability, allow easy access to information, and reinforce the immediacy of any visual message.

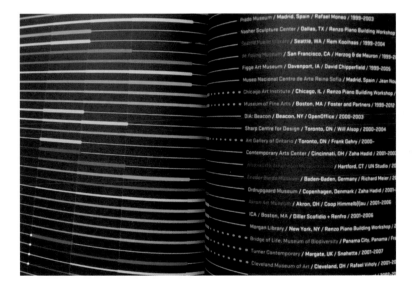

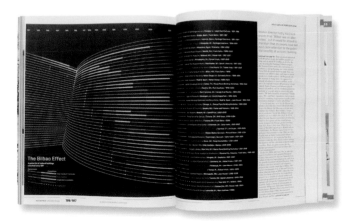

shape \\'shāp\\ *n*

1: spatial form or contour, or the characteristic surface configuration of a thing; an outline or a contour; see *form*

"The object of art is to give life a shape."

JEAN ANOUILH (1910-1987), *French, Dramatist*

From ancient glyphs to contemporary symbols, shape is one of the fundamental elements of a graphic designer's vocabulary. Generally, *shape* is defined by boundary and mass. It refers to a contour or an outline of a form. A plane or shape is a point or dot that has become too large to

retain its pure identity due to its weight or mass, even if it still has a flat appearance. When this transformation occurs, a dot becomes a shape.

A shape is a graphic, two-dimensional plane that appears to be flat and is defined by an enclosing, contour line, as well as by color, value, texture, or typography. It is the external outline of a plane that results from a line that starts at one point and continues back to its beginning, creating an enclosed space or shape. It is composed of width and height but never depth. It is a line with breadth. Shapes are used to define layouts, create patterns, and compose countless elements in a composition.

Basic Characteristics

Examples of basic shapes are the circle, square, and triangle. All other complex shapes, such as an oval, rectangle, trapezoid, pentagon, hexagon, and octagon, are derived from these three elemental shapes. A shape can be solid or outline, opaque or transparent, smooth or textured.

Basically, shapes are either geometric, organic, or random. Their overall configura-

(continued on page 34)

The playful and unconventional shapes for the Museum of Arts and Design (MAD) identity program are reminiscent of forms evident in the building's original interior architecture and represent the museum's unique home, expanded collections, and diverse program offerings. A broad and visually diverse set of colors, textures, materials, forms, and images allows the museum's acronym to constantly evolve and change from application to application, furthering the eclectic nature and public message of this institution's mission.

PENTAGRAM
New York, New York, USA

1928

The Sold Appetite Poster
**VLADIMIR AND GEORGII STENBERG
(STENBERG BROTHERS)**
Moscow, Russia

VLADIMIR STENBERG (1899–1982) and GEORGII STENBERG (1900–1933), also known as the Stenberg brothers, were Soviet artists and designers who came to renown following the Russian Revolution of 1917.

After an initial interest in engineering, the Stenbergs attended the Stoganov School of Applied Art (later renamed the State Free Art Workshops) in Moscow from 1917 to 1922, where they designed the decorations and posters for the first May Day celebration of 1918. In 1919, the Stenbergs along with a group of comrades founded the OBMOKhU (the Society of Young Artists) and participated in its first group exhibition in May of 1919. During the 1920s and '30s, they were well established and members of the avant-garde community, collaborating with other artists, architects, and writers such as Alexandr Rodchenko, Varvara Stepnova, and Kasimir Malevich.

They worked in a wide range of media, initially as sculptors and then as theater designers, architects, and draftsmen, designing everything from clothing and furniture to costumes and stage sets. However, their greatest achievement was in graphic design, particularly with the design of mass-produced posters used to advertise a new and powerful form of universal communication—film.

In the early 1900s, the commercial film poster provided artists and designers, such as the Stenbergs, with new and uncharted approaches for communicating a diverse range of visual themes. Up to this point in time, film posters usually relied upon a narrow point of view for communicating their story—either a single scene from the film or an image of the featured star of the film—to gain the public's attention.

The Stenbergs were at their prime during this revolutionary period of politics, propaganda, and artistic experimentation in Russia. They started to experiment with collage, photomontage, and assemblage, as well as portions of photographic images and preprinted paper created by others. They realized a new approach and methodology for creating imagery and compositions that were no longer connected to conventional realism.

While the visual characteristics of their posters included perspective, texture, scale, contrast, and movement as well as an innovative use of color, pattern, and typography, shape was a primary compositional element used in all of their work. Whether its scale is exaggerated, its graphic form distorted, or its visual composition jarring, the Stenbergs used shape to create identity and visual immediacy, as well as to reinforce a poster's story. Their posters were groundbreaking, abstract studies of line, plane, and shape composed in space and reflected a kinship to Suprematist painting, Russian Constructivism, and the work of El Lissitzky, Vladimir Mayakovsky, and Wassily Kandinsky.

The majority of their posters, radical even by contemporary standards, were produced within a nine-year period from 1924 to 1933, the year of Georgii's untimely death at age 33. Vladimir continued to design film posters and organized the decorations of Moscow's Red Square for the May Day celebration of 1947.

The Stenberg Brothers and the Russian Avant-Garde Film Poster

The soft inviting shape of this four-sided wine label for Terrazzo Prosecco provides an appropriate frame and background for its delicate, linear border, as well as for its symmetrical typography and fluid script lettering of the wine name.

LOUISE FILI LTD.
New York, New York, USA

tion can determine their inherent message and meaning. For example, a soft, curvilinear shape may appear warm and welcoming, whereas a sharp, angular shape may appear cold and threatening.

Straight lines and angular corners create rectilinear, geometric shapes. Curvilinear lines create amorphous, organic shapes. Circles, squares, triangles, and rectangles are geometric shapes that are crisp and mathematically precise with straight lines and consistent, curved profiles. A natural or organic shape can either be irregular or regular.

The pairing of these two pure geometric shapes provides a strong visual counterpoint for this identity for the University of Kentucky's Arts in HealthCare program. The dynamic juxtaposition of the shapes fully depends upon the visual clarity of the square representing the institution, combined with the imperfect dots of the concentric circles symbolizing the human connection of the visual and performing artists represented in this program.

POULIN + MORRIS INC.
New York, New York, USA

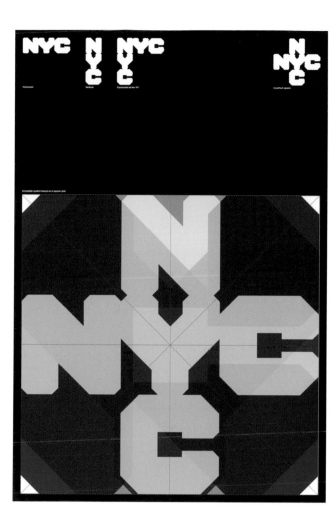

Three thick, sturdy, and bold custom letterforms are composed as one shape to further communicate the strength and power of New York City's branding and identity program. Used alone or collectively as a visual texture and pattern, this unique mark is designed as one continuous shape, organized in a variety of compositional configurations. Due to the shape of this logotype, it is still immediately understood as three separate and distinct letterforms with an unmistakable visual characteristic that is immediate, durable, impactful, and strong.

WOLFF OLINS
New York, New York, USA

A bold, six-sided, vertically proportioned shape functions as a distinctive frame and containment element for the name and logotype of Darden Studio, a type foundry housed in a historic building in downtown Brooklyn. Framed on a black field and outlined with a thin, white hairline, this shape communicates a strong sense of craft in the studio's aesthetic, is rooted in centuries of type founding, and is reminiscent of historical board and flag signs found in the area.

MUCCA DESIGN
New York, New York, USA

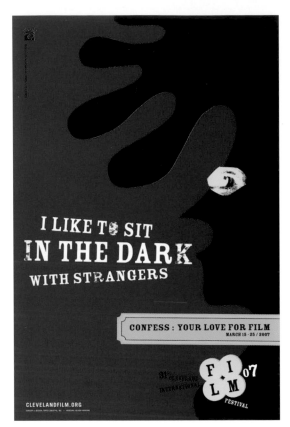

This poster series for the
Cleveland International Film
Festival relies upon unusual,
random, free-form shapes
representing the festival's
attendees. Overscale, bold,
black shapes set against
vibrant color backgrounds
strengthen the overall identity of these memorable and
eye-catching profiles and are
further married with smaller
dynamic shapes containing
typographic information
and visual textures for added
nuance and character.

TWIST CREATIVE INC.
Cleveland, Ohio, USA

The stylized, machinelike, curved shape of this *M* represents Mac Industries, a precision machining and fabrication company, and the image is further conveyed with a corner of the *M* separated and set apart from the body of the letter functioning as a dotted *i*. This dynamic void creates a visual intersection within the stylized shape of the letterform, reinforcing **a level of detail and precision in the firm's identity and secondary descriptive line.**

INFINITE SCALE DESIGN
Salt Lake City, Utah, USA

Categories of Shape

There are three categories of shape, each with their own unique visual characteristics and criteria:

Geometric

The most familiar shapes are geometric in character—circles, squares, rectangles, and triangles. They are based on mathematical formulas relating to point, line, and plane. Their contours are always regularized, angular, or hard edged. We are most familiar with geometric shapes because they are the first shapes we tend to encounter when we are small children.

Organic

Shapes that are created or derived from nature and living organisms are organic. These shapes are used more freely than geometric shapes are usually irregular and soft.

Random

Shapes created from invention and imagination are random and have no sense of order, semblance, or relationship to geometric or organic shapes.

The amorphous, free-form shape of a stylized window, projected back in space and framed with soft corners, symbolizes a youthful appeal for this Seattle-based boutique urban realtor named Funky Lofts.

URBAN INFLUENCE DESIGN STUDIO
Seattle, Washington, USA

These letterforms are unconventional not only in their shape, but also in their subtle variations in profile, proportion, counter, and stroke thickness. Reinforced with nonalignment to a common baseline and a pronounced dot over the letter *i*, the active and lyrical typographic statement is unique and memorable. Color is also used as an alternating, pulsating visual element to further unify the varying shapes and meaning of the logotype.

WINK
Minneapolis, Minnesota, USA

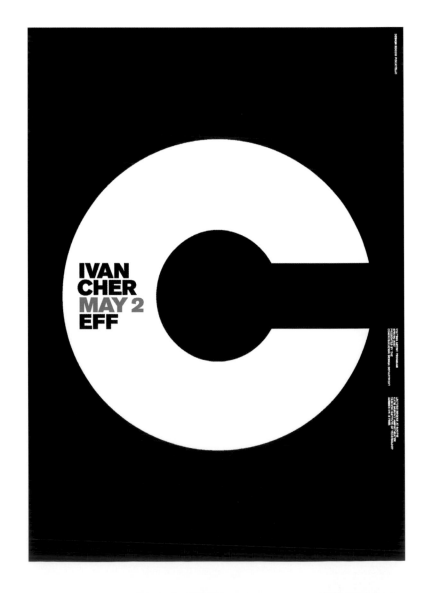

The visual strength, immediacy, and simplicity of a pure geometric-shaped letterform is the central focal point and singular message of this lecture-series poster. A large-scale, sans serif, white *C* centered within the vertical composition of this poster and contrasted against a dramatic black background further reinforces the purity and beauty of this geometric shape, as well as the design philosophy and career of the designer, Ivan Chermayeff.

PISCATELLO DESIGN CENTER
New York, New York, USA

The fluid profile of the black letter *T* and star ligature combined with the purity of the starlike, circular seal for this identity and stationery program creates a strong visual integrity and counterpoint between an organic shape and a geometric-based shape that become one and the same with the firm name of Thomas & Star.

MARKATOS MOORE
San Francisco, California, USA

This promotional poster was part of a series that was developed by Scholastic, Target, and AIGA to help educators introduce design to their K–8 curriculums. The pro-bono project invited designers to "respond" to an art piece by creating a poster that celebrates its themes or formal elements. The dual nature of Picasso's painted terra-cotta piece titled

Vase-Bird inspired the random, half animal, half object, and hybrid shapes evident in this poster. These playful, whimsical letterforms are further strengthened by an intense two-color palette, a strong figure–ground relationship, and an unusual overall texture that is engaging to the viewer.

ALFALFA STUDIO LLC
New York, New York, USA

Shape versus Form

The terms *shape* and *form* are commonly used interchangeably; however, they have two separate and distinct meanings. A shape has a two-dimensional character, whereas a form is perceived to have a three-dimensional character. Other terms commonly used for form are *mass* and *volume*.

A form, mass, or volume is a three-dimensional shape because it has height, width, and depth.

In compositional terms, a shape functions as a figurative element in or on a ground, surrounding background, or space. It is a positive element within a negative space. This is a fundamental principle of figure-ground and an integral characteristic of balance in a visual composition.

The traditional, cruciform shape of this symmetrical, ornamental medallion is derived from unique architectural features of the Old Police Headquarters building, a renovated, historic, mixed-use real estate development in downtown San Diego.

URBAN INFLUENCE
DESIGN STUDIO
Seattle, Washington, USA

form \\'fȯrm\ *n*

1 a: the shape and structure of something as distinguished from its material, or the shape and structure of an object

form

4

"Art is nothing without form."
GUSTAVE FLAUBERT (1821-1880), *French, Novelist, Playwright*

Basic forms are derived from basic shapes—a square becomes a cube, a circle becomes a sphere, a triangle becomes a pyramid. The terms *shape* and *form* are often confused with one another as if they meant the same thing. In chapter 3, criteria and characteristics that define shape were

The CNN Grill was a "wired hub of political activity" for journalists, political operatives, and celebrities during the national political conventions. Bold, illuminated geometric forms and typography, coupled with patriotic colors, created a strong and memorable identity for this temporary gathering venue.

COLLINS
New York, New York, USA

explained. Form is achieved by integrating depth or volume to the equation of shape. It is a three-dimensional element of design that encloses volume. It has height, width, and depth. For example, a two-dimensional triangle is defined as a shape; however, a three-dimensional pyramid is defined as a form. Cubes, spheres, ellipses, pyramids, cones, and cylinders are all examples of geometric forms.

Form is always composed of multiple surfaces and edges. It is a volume or empty space created by other fundamental design elements—points, lines, and shapes. *(continued on page 44)*

The paper slit of this magazine cover for *Camera Work* creates a three-dimensional, concave surface on a two-dimensional plane that is furthered strengthened by the asymmetrical placement of typography on the cover.

MENDE DESIGN
San Francisco, California, USA

The pop art, cartoonlike visual character of this dialog box creates a dynamic and playful three-dimensional form for the containment of "Pop Justice," a logotype for one of England's most popular blogs. Vibrant, analogous colors and bold letterforms, sans their counters, further create visual impact without overpowering the logotype's spatial depth and volume.

FORM
London, United Kingdom

1983

Aluminum Alphabet Series
TAKENOBU IGARASHI
Tokyo, Japan

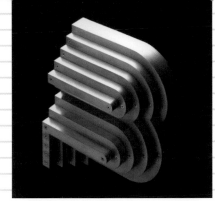

TAKENOBU IGARASHI (b. 1944) is a sculptor and designer who has continually explored the fusion of two-dimensional and three-dimensional form. His work is based on a language of basic elements—point, the purest element of design; line, which delineates locations and boundaries between planes; shape, realized flat or dimensional; texture, visual or tactile; and grid, whose horizontal and vertical axes provide order and logic to a composition.

While the majority of his work for the last thirty years has been in graphic identity, environmental graphics, and product design, his exploration and experimentation with letterform and isometric grids has brought him international attention and recognition. In the early 1980s, his two-dimensional, isometric alphabets, first conceived as a series of poster calendars for the Museum of Modern Art in New York City, quickly evolved into three-dimensional alphabetic structures that Igarashi called architectural alphabets.

The *Aluminum Alphabet Series*, the first to involve typographic sculptures, comprises twenty-six three-dimensional, aluminum letterforms. Each sculptural form consists of a series of aluminum plates of varying thickness joined together by flat-head aluminum fasteners. Here, Igarashi uses letterform to explore the potential of three-dimensional form. He says, "One of the charms of the Roman letter is its simple form. The wonderful thing is that it is created with the minimum number of elements; the standard structure is based on the circle, square, and triangle, which are the fundamentals of formation."

Letterforms are basically symbols or signs written on paper in a flat, two-dimensional world. Design of letterforms can be varied by extending their two-dimensional characteristics into a three-dimensional world. Letterforms can also be considered as simple graphic compositions of basic geometric elements—circles, squares, and triangles—and within these compositions are hidden possibilities for developing a greater set of shapes and forms.

Igarashi's approach for this series was to conceive letterforms as solid volumes divided into positive and negative spaces. A three-dimensional composition is realized when the form of the letter is extended in both its positive and negative directions; in other words, by generating spatial tensions in both directions. He states, "This is one example of my attempt to find a geometric solution between meaning and aesthetic form. Based on a 5-millimeter [1/4 inch] three-dimensional grid system, the twenty-six letters of the alphabet from A to Z were created by adding and subtracting on the x-, y-, and z-axes."

The *Aluminum Alphabet Series* is a unique, groundbreaking result of taking a conceptual, spatial, and mathematical view of letterforms and revealing some of the many possibilities of shape and form. It is the ultimate study in letterform, material, detailing, visual interpretation, and three-dimensional form.

Takenobu Igarashi and the *Aluminum Alphabet Series*

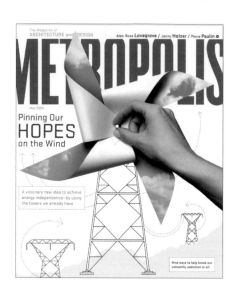

In this cover for *Metropolis* magazine, the juxtaposition of three-dimensional forms—a pinwheel and a person's hand—on a two-dimensional representation of the same form creates a visually dynamic, engaging, and memorable cover.

COLLINS
New York, New York, USA

Types of Forms

Forms can be real or illusory. Real, three-dimensional form contains actual volume or physical weight while illusory, two-dimensional form is perceptual. Real forms are three-dimensional such as objects, sculpture, architecture, and packaging. Illusory forms are illusions of three-dimensional shapes in two-dimensional spaces and can be realized three-dimensionally by using several graphic conventions to achieve illusory results.

Projections

Representing several surfaces or planes of a two-dimensional form all at once is one way to visually represent a three-dimensional form without it receding in space or in scale. The most common types of projections are as follows:

Isometric

An isometric projection is the easiest of projection methods where three visible surfaces of a form have equal emphasis. All axes are simultaneously rotated away from the picture plane and kept at the same angle of projection (30 degrees from the picture plane), all lines are equally foreshortened, and the angles between lines are always 120 degrees.

These three marks represent the breadth and spirit of the Smithsonian's Cooper-Hewitt National Design Week, an annual education initiative on design, by implying a three-dimensional volume or environment that contains iconic forms of furniture, lighting, and related functional objects. The figure-ground relationships evident in each of these marks further reinforce a dynamic, visual interplay between two-dimensional and three-dimensional forms.

WINK
Minneapolis, Minnesota, USA

Types of Projections

Isometric

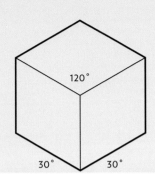

120°

30°   30°

Picture Plane

Plan Oblique (30°–60°)

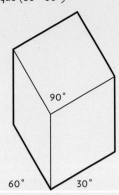

90°

60°   30°

Plan Oblique (45°–45°)

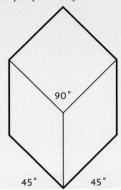

90°

45°   45°

Types of Perspective

One-Point

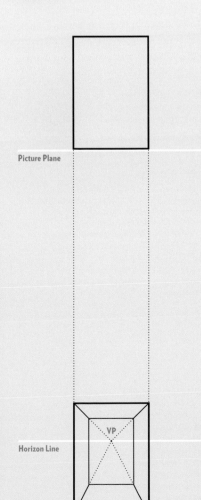

Picture Plane

VP

Horizon Line

Picture Plane

Two-Point

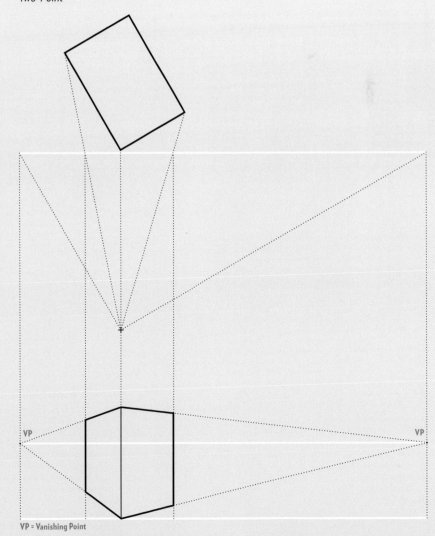

VP   VP

VP = Vanishing Point

This paper promotion for Neenah Paper uses a single ink color and laser die-cut shapes on a duplex cover to reveal custom display letterforms spelling out "1/2 the job." The layered cover provides depth, volume, and shadow to this typographic treatment, further strengthening these unique forms and ultimately the identity of the promotional message.

AND PARTNERS
New York, New York, USA

Axonometric (or Plan Oblique)
An axonometric, or plan oblique, projection is a parallel projection of a form viewed from a skewed direction to reveal more than one of its sides in the same picture plane.

In isometric and axonometric projections, all vertical lines remain vertical and all parallel lines remain parallel.

Spatial Depth

Three-dimensional space and depth can also be achieved when one surface of a form is overlapped and partially obscured by another form. One- and two-point perspective drawings exemplify creation of a form's spatial depth with two-dimensional shapes overlapping on a two-dimensional picture plane. (See diagrams on page 45.)

Tone and Shading

Form can also be visually indicated through tone, shade, and texture. The surfaces of a form curving or facing away from a directed light source appear darker than surfaces facing a directed light source. This effect suggests the rounding of a two-dimensional shape into a three-dimensional form.

This assignment requires the student to explore the visual relationships between typographic form and architectural form. This student based their photographic exploration and analysis on the angles and geometry found in Daniel Liebskind's Denver Art Museum and in the typeface, Futura.

CASSANDRA BARBOE,
Student
HENRIETTA CONDAK,
Instructor
School of Visual Arts
New York, New York, USA

This promotional poster series for the McGill School of Architecture uses form as a primary vehicle for communicating an emblematic element in architecture. Each lecturer's name is printed on a colored strip of paper and folded to evoke an architectural form. These paper strips were photographed together to announce the series and individually to announce each lecture. Each three-dimensional, photographic composition is unique, adding a strong visual dynamic to the series. An organizational grid for narrative, informational text is used consistently on all posters and is a contrasting juxtaposition to each free-form, three-dimensional photographic composition.

ATELIER PASTILLE ROSE
Montreal, Quebec, Canada

The primary visual element of this promotional poster celebrating the second anniversary of Casa da Musica, Portugal's world-renowned concert hall, relies upon its unique and unconventional symbol—a stylized, trapezoidal form derived from the building's architecture. This form is fragmented by facet and color, further implying a three-dimensional appearance as well as communicating the diversity of music performances scheduled during the anniversary season.

SAGMEISTER INC.
New York, New York, USA

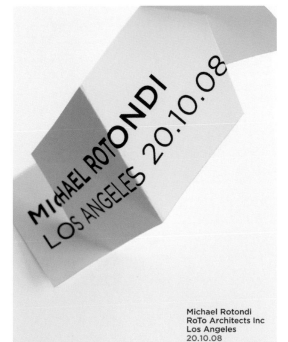

light \\'līt\\ *n*
1 a: something that makes vision possible

5

"Light is the ultimate messenger of the universe."
ANONYMOUS

Light is a constant source of kinetic energy, ever changing on the infinite continuum of day into night. It is also an essential design element in visual communication because it fundamentally allows us to "see" and visually experience our world as we know it. In visual communications, light

INTRODUÇÃO A FILOSOFIA

This dramatic book cover relies solely upon extreme contrast, subtle color, and intense light to bring a strong focal point to the eye in the photographic portrait of Martin Heidegger and his seminal book entitled *Introduction to Philosophy*.

CASA REX
São Paulo, Brazil

In each of these covers, X-ray photographic images of flowers accentuate the texture, linear structure, beauty, and illuminated brilliance of each cropped image, as well as the pure human emotions of each opera libretto. Pure, bright, saturated colors paired with asymmetrical placement of symmetrically composed labels containing serif type and decorative bordered line elements also reinforce the visual and narrative themes of each composition.

TAKAKO SAEGUSA, Student
MICHAEL IAN KAYE,
Instructor
School of Visual Arts
New York, New York, USA

is either used as a sensation of light, a source of light or illumination, a representation of it, or an awareness of it, on design elements in a graphic composition.

Technically, light is defined as an electromagnetic radiation of wavelengths that are visible to the human eye. It also refers to other wavelengths that are not detectable by the eye such as ultraviolet (UV) and infrared.

Historical References

In the fifth century, the Greeks recognized a direct link between the human eye and *(continued on page 52)*

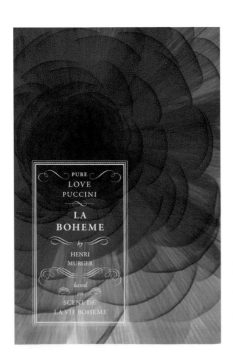

PURE
LOVE
PUCCINI

LA
BOHEME

by

HENRI
MURGER

*based
on*

SCENE DE
LA VIE BOHEME

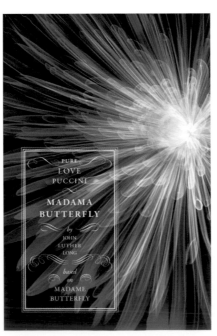

PURE
LOVE
PUCCINI

MADAMA
BUTTERFLY

by

JOHN
LUTHER
LONG

*based
on*

MADAME
BUTTERFLY

PURE
LOVE
PUCCINI

TOSCA

by

VICTORIA
SARDOU

*based
on*

LA
TOSCA

1928

bauhaus zeitschrift (*Bauhaus* magazine) Cover
HERBERT BAYER
Berlin, Germany

HERBERT BAYER (1900–1985), was a pioneering designer, typographer, architect, painter, photographer, and educator.

After completing his military service, he was an architect's apprentice working on commissions including interiors, furniture, and packaging.

In 1921, Bayer enrolled as a student at the Bauhaus in Weimar, where he studied under Wassily Kandinsky and later under Lazlo Moholy-Nagy. Following the closing of the Bauhaus, arrangements were made to transfer the school to Dessau, and in 1925 Bayer and five other former students including Marcel Breuer, Joost Schmidt, and Josef Albers were appointed teachers.

As an educator, he transformed the Bauhaus by eliminating the use of lithography and woodcuts and introducing movable type and mechanical presses to the Dessau workshops. The use of serif, black letter, and capital letterform ended; the use of sans serif, lowercase letterforms began. Typographic form was now asymmetric, simple, and direct.

During his years at Dessau, Bayer had been strongly influenced by Moholy-Nagy's enthusiasm for photography as a contemporary means of visual communication and started to experiment with various photographic techniques including collage, photomontage, and light.

Bayer's most original use of light (and shadow) was with his photomontage for the 1928 cover of the *bauhaus zeitschrift*. In this memorable composition, he uses light in a dramatic and striking manner. Additionally, Bayer makes use of a cube, ball, and cone (solidifications of Kandinsky's iconic square, circle, and triangle) along with sharpened pencil and transparent triangle juxtaposed over the surface of the magazine's cover. This image, classically simple and evocative, was one of the most widely produced examples of Bayer's graphic design. It not only identified the publication in a provocative manner, but it fully communicated the essence and philosophy of the Bauhaus and its avant-garde educational programs.

Bayer left the Bauhaus in 1928 and relocated to Berlin. In 1938, like many artists and designers in Germany at the time, he fled the Nazis and immigrated to the United States, where he became a self-appointed spokesperson for the Bauhaus movement.

Herbert Bayer and *bauhaus zeitschrift*

Both informational-based posters reveal and illuminate the beauty hidden within complex data. Each poster diagrammatically charts twenty-four hours of light and dark for each day of the year and is scientifically accurate and visually engaging.

ACCEPT & PROCEED
London, United Kingdom

how we see objects. Earlier thinking was that there was a visual "fire" or glow emanating from the human eye that allowed us to see. In the fourth century BC, Aristotle rejected this premise by concluding "if vision were produced by means of a fire emitted by the eye, like the light emitted by a lantern, why then are we not able to see in the dark?"

In the history of fine arts, the visual representation of light has inspired generations of artists and designers. One needs to consider only the paintings of Leonardo da Vinci, Rembrandt, Claude Monet, and Georges Seurat to understand how these visionaries captured and used light subtly, effectively, and meaningfully. In contemporary work, the photography of Ansel Adams and Robert Mapplethorpe provides the same insightful lessons and insights.

Properties and Characteristics

A graphic designer can determine how light ultimately influences and affects two-dimensional design elements in any composition. For example, light can be illusory by overlapping a shape or form with color, shade, tone, and texture, creating a sense of transparency or opacity. This graphic effect creates the appearance that light is coming through each

Light is represented in this theatrical production poster for *Finian's Rainbow* by a full spectrum of saturated color—cut paper with just a few strips within this pure graphic pattern breaking away from their strong, rigid vertical axis to create the start of a rainbow. Cut-out letterforms and landscape forms appear three-dimensional and in bas-relief due to light and shadow projected onto each of these compositional elements, further reinforcing light, depth, volume, and three-dimensional space.

SPOTCO
New York, New York, USA

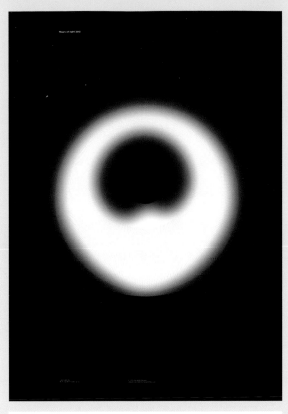

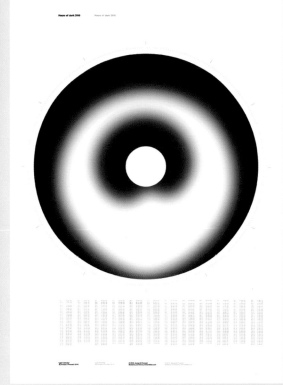

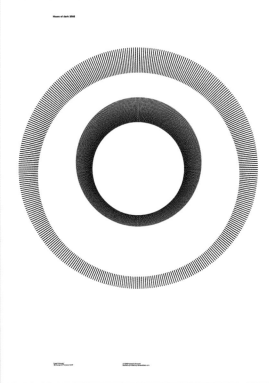

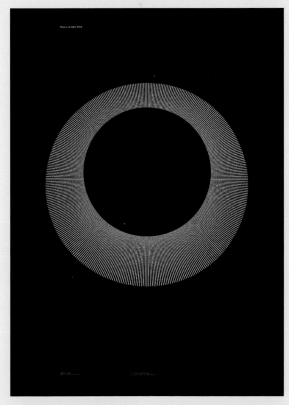

This assignment requires the student to explore the visual relationships between typographic and architectural form. This student based her photographic exploration and analysis on the monolithic proportions and use of light and transparency found in Pierre Chareau's modernist masterpiece building, La Maison de Verre, and the typeface, Futura Condensed.

MEAGHAN TIRONDOLA,
Student
HENRIETTA CONDAK,
Instructor
School of Visual Arts
New York, New York, USA

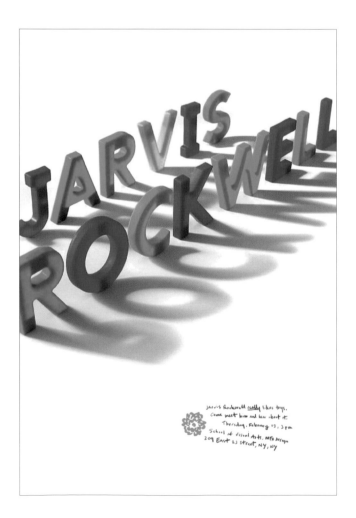

of these elements, or it can be completely impermeable and prevent light from appearing through another shape or form.

Light can also create the illusion of a third dimension on a two-dimensional surface through the use of shadow. This can be achieved by carefully determining where a light source is located above, below, behind, or beside compositional elements.

Light also assists with another design principle—contrast, allowing our eyes to perceive a broad range of colors and tones from light to dark. In addition to creating the illusion of three-dimensionality, light is critical for creating the illusion of depth on

In this promotional poster for a lecture given by the toy designer Jarvis Rockwell, light is projected through childlike, translucent, primary-colored plastic letters, creating colored shadows that are projected onto the poster's white background. The effect is iconic, playful, and immediately identified with a child's point of view.

ROGERS ECKERSLEY
DESIGN
New York, New York, USA

a two-dimensional plane. And it is also an essential element in any three-dimensional space where there is a need to emphasize objects and forms, such as in a retail display or museum exhibition.

Light is also a critical and essential element, property, and dimension of color, defined as a reflection and how we perceive the brightness of any color within the spectrum of colors. The amount of light in a color has a direct connection to its amplitude, strength, and visual impact. Other visual effects, such as shadow and contrast, are also visually perceived as varied light levels on a scale from light to dark.

This logotype for an independent boutique hair salon, is based on a clear-cut, powerful idea that relies upon the Miller & Green initials and the essential hairdressers' tool—a pair of scissors. The vibrant color combination of a bright lime green and dark brown reflects the salon's elegant yet vivacious character and was implemented across various applications including business stationery, promotional materials, and environmental graphics.

LANDOR
Paris, France

ROGERS ECKERSLEY DESIGN
New York, New York, USA

Simple, dramatic black-and-white photography and a bold figure–ground give this theatrical poster a strong yet subtle visual metaphor for the theme of the play *The Starry Messenger*. The texture of a starlit sky set against the stark white, background further reinforces the character-driven reference in the play's title.

The element of light is directly connected to other visual characteristics such as brilliance, chiaroscuro, fluorescence, gradient, luminosity, pearlescence, reflection, refraction, value, shade, tint, and tone.

Light provides graphic designers with the essential means to understand other visual elements, principles, and techniques such as color, shape, form, movement, texture, perspective, shading, motion, visual acuity, and depth perception. It is a critical element of visual communications for obvious reasons. Without it, the phenomena of visual perception and understanding would not exist.

The fundamental element of light can be conveyed through shadow and depth, as shown in this book cover. Light is directed upward from the bottom of the image, lengthening projected shadows vertically above each red element as well as giving them a more pronounced, three-dimensional appearance. The twenty unique and subtly distinct red dotlike elements represent the twenty love poems written by the Chilean poet Pablo Neruda. This visually distinctive cover is further strengthened by the symmetrical placement of these elements in contrast with an asymmetrical placement of the cover's typography.

KATYA MEZHIBOVSKAYA
New York, New York, USA

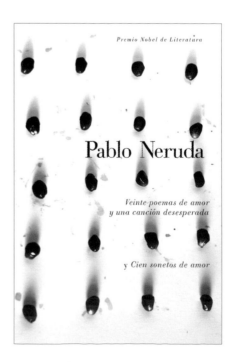

The use of a subtle color palette with the varied scaled decorative patterns for this branding and identity program for a San Francisco-based home furnishings company creates light, transparency, and depth on a two dimensional surface.

VOLUME
San Francisco, California, USA

A highly reflective material, contrasted with an over-scaled, large matte black dot, reinforces the message and meaning of this promotional poster for a light festival in Porec, Croatia. The poster's base material allows any light to be either absorbed or reflected, depending on where it is displayed.

STUDIO SONDA
Porec, Croatia

col·or \ˈkə-lər\ *n*
1 a: a phenomenon of light (as red, brown, pink, or gray) or visual perception that enables one to differentiate otherwise identical objects

6

"Color is the place where our brain and the universe meet."
PAUL KLEE (1879-1940), *Swiss, Author, Educator, Painter*

Color is one of the most powerful and communicative elements in a graphic designer's language. It affects all of us by providing visual energy and variety in what we see and experience on a daily basis. Color is used to attract attention, group disparate elements, reinforce meaning, and enhance

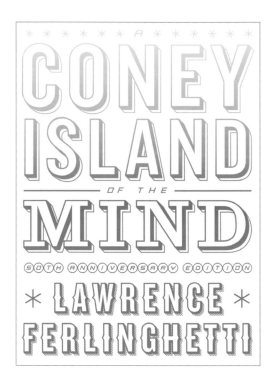

visual compositions. It can also immediately convey an attitude or an emotion, provoke a response, create emphasis and variety, communicate a specific message, and further strengthen an established hierarchy.

Color increases visual interest and can reinforce the meaning and organization of elements in any visual composition. As a primary visual element, color enhances the emotional and psychological nuances of any visual message. It assists in creating the mood you desire. For example, light colors produce pleasant responses whereas darker colors produce quieter effects.

(continued on page 62)

Vibrant, tertiary color combinations create a strong visual dynamic in these covers for Mohawk Papers' Via notebooks. Repeating horizontal patterns set in a variety of typographic treatments for "Via" further strengthens the diversity and broad applications of the paper line, as well as create a campaign that is fresh, bold, and vibrant.

ADAMSMORIOKA INC.
Beverly Hills, California, USA

A full-color gradient, from yellow to blue, is used on this book cover, *Coney Island of the Mind*, communicating the playful and festival-like spirit of the title and theme of the book. An intense color palette, as well as an eclectic set of typographic letter-forms, further expresses the central celebratory mood and emotional content of the book's poetry.

RODRIGO CORRAL DESIGN
New York, New York, USA

1984

1984 Los Angeles Summer Olympics
SUSSMAN/PREJZA & COMPANY
Los Angeles, California, USA

Since 1980, DEBORAH SUSSMAN (b. 1931) and her firm, Sussman/Prejza & Company, have advanced the field of environmental graphic design, creating urban sign programs for numerous cities in California as well as environmental graphics for Disney, Hasbro, and Apple Computer.

In the 1960s, Sussman worked with two pioneers of twentieth-century American design, Charles and Ray Eames, whose creative imprint revolutionized the look of postwar America. It was during this mentoring period that she became rooted in an Eamesian joy of color, pattern, cultural influences, and ethnic design.

Her environmental graphics program for the 1984 Summer Olympics literally changed the way we experience color in an urban environment. This comprehensive program guided an enormous international audience through a series of complex venues, while visually celebrating the games and the surrounding city on a grand scale and in a festival-like manner. Sussman's system of temporary structures, scaffolding, striped columns, large-scale graphics, and bright colors were inventive, functional, and extremely accessible.

The Olympic colors were unexpected, exciting, and distinct from the everyday visual fabric of an urban city. Magenta was the base color on which the color palette was built. Sports pictograms were white on magenta; freeway signs were magenta with aqua; the interaction of magenta against yellow, vermilion, and aqua was the most important interrelationship of the palette. The colors also had strong ties to locale—magenta and yellow are of the Pacific Rim, Mexico, and the Far East. Aqua is Mediterranean and a strong counterpoint to the warmer Pacific colors.

Colors were generally used in combinations of three or more, and the palette was divided to produce enormous visual variety. Each venue had its own palette that related to the character of its specific sport and to the ambient color and lighting of its surroundings. For example, gymnastics was represented by vermilion, yellow, and green; swimming by aqua and white. The colors worked very effectively in southern California light, appearing brilliant and vibrant at different times of the day.

Color made the 1984 Los Angeles Olympics a truly visual event. It transformed one of the largest cities in the world into an intimate, cohesive experience, as well as the manner in which visual communications would be approached for all future Olympics.

In considering color in her work, Sussman says, "My work with color is informed by content. It has roots in contextual sources and is inspired by geography, cultural history, user's needs, architecture, urban characteristics, and available materials. I work intuitively when selecting the actual palettes, often relating them to musical iconography. Ray Eames and Alexander (Sandro) Girard were my mentors. Wassily Kandinsky said, 'In general, color is a medium that has a direct impact on the soul.' This has been my experience and remains my belief."

Deborah Sussman and the 1984 Summer Olympics

Colors also inherently contain subjective meanings that communicate immediately without words or images. For example, red is associated with fire, blood, and sex; blue is associated with ice, sea, and sky.

Numerous classification systems have been developed to identify and categorize color for a variety of visual applications. These include systems and theories developed by Sir Isaac Newton (1701), Johann Wolfgang von Goethe (1810), Albert Munsell (1915), Johannes Itten (1961), and Josef Albers (1975).

Fundamental Properties
There are three fundamental visual properties of color:

Hue
Color in its purest form, or hue, is the identification given to each color such as yellow, red, or blue. This identification is the result of how we "see" light being reflected from an object at a specific frequency. Of these three fundamental properties, hue is the most absolute—we may "see" a color as yellow, red, or blue, but it is identifiable only when it is adjacent to another color with which it can be compared. A color with no visible hue, such as gray, is a neutral color.

Value
The lightness or darkness of a color is identified as its value. This property is also referred to as a color's luminance, brightness, or tone. It is fully dependent on a color's hue and intensity. Adding white to a color creates a lighter value, or tint; adding black creates a darker value, or shade of a color.

Value can be used to exaggerate the meaning of any visual message. When elements have changing color value, a viewer's eye is guided in, around, and through a visual composition. The degrees of contrast and relative amounts of value also provide movement to the composition. Because distant objects appear lighter in nature, value can also create the illusion of space and depth.

Saturation (also chroma)
Intensity or saturation is the brightness or dullness of a color, or its level of saturation. It is the measure of a color's purity, brightness, or grayness. A saturated color is vibrant and intense, as opposed to a desaturated color that is restrained and somber. Saturation is

the amount of gray in a color. As it increases, the amount of gray decreases. Brightness is the amount of white in a color. As it increases, the amount of white increases. A color with little or no saturation contains a large amount of white.

Saturated colors attract the viewer's attention. Use desaturated colors when function and efficiency are the priority. Desaturated, light colors are seen as friendly; desaturated, dark colors are seen as formal; saturated colors are seen as exciting and dynamic. Exercise caution when combining saturated colors, as they can visually interfere with one another and increase eye fatigue.

Emblem, an international group of branding specialists, relies solely upon bright, vibrant colors on their website for reinforcing the visual immediacy of their identity, as well as the site's navigational tools.

BLANK MOSSERI
New York, New York, USA

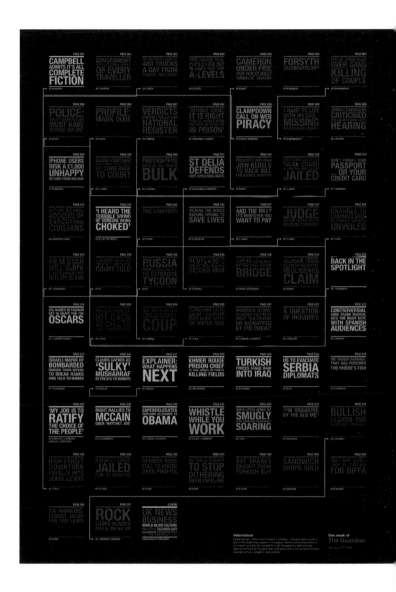

Color is used as a primary organizational and wayfinding tool in this information-based poster titled *One Week of the Guardian*. Based on the periodic table of elements, information is organized by category of interest and popularity. Relying upon a color key at the bottom of the poster, the viewer can interact with content in an easy and accessible manner by immediately identifying a specific topic with a limited number of colors—in this case, ten different color variables for categories such as News, Business, Culture, and Media.

DESIGNING THE NEWS
London, United Kingdom

A sophisticated color palette of vibrant and muted colors in a range of values and saturations is the primary element in the rebranding of Sprint's new retail experience. These diverse colors, combined with product- and user-based imagery, create a visual system that is clean and contemporary for the brand, as well as appealing to a younger audience.

MIRIELLO GRAFICO
San Diego, California, USA

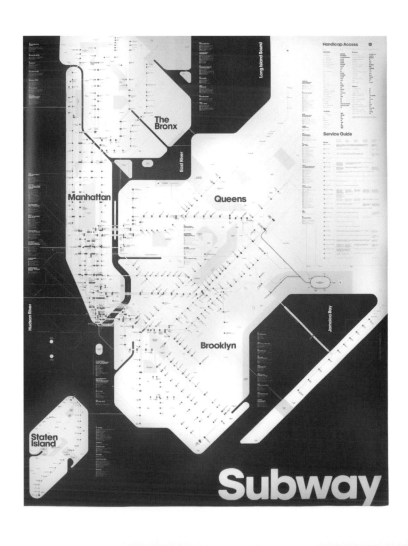

This rethinking of the iconographic New York City subway map in fluorescent red strips away the familiar color-coding of the circa-1970s version while still maintaining a level of hierarchy and functionality. The fluorescent red color becomes an unpredictable variable, as legibility changes completely under different lighting conditions.

The neon effect is intense and uncomfortable in some lighting conditions, while washed out and unreadable in other environments. Color is the primary element used in the extreme simplification of this visually complex information diagram.

TRIBORO DESIGN SOLUTIONS
Brooklyn, New York, USA

This standards manual is part of a student's senior thesis project for the rebranding and repositioning of Microsoft Corporation. In the overall program, as well as throughout the manual itself, color is used as a symbolic, functional communication device. For example, a palette of three secondary colors—orange, green, and purple—is used for the containment border of the MS logotype, reinforcing the diversity of the company's products and services. A subdued, muted color palette is used to organize, emphasize, and allow information to be clear and accessible without competing with the primary tricolors of the new logotype and symbol.

JOHN CLARK, Student
RICHARD POULIN, Instructor
School of Visual Arts
New York, New York, USA

Organizational Categories

Primary Colors
Yellow, red, and blue are primary colors. They are pure in composition and cannot be created from other colors. All other colors are created by combining primary colors.

Secondary Colors
Colors identified as secondary are created by combining two primary colors. Yellow and red create orange; red and blue create purple; and yellow and blue create green.

Tertiary Colors
Colors identified as tertiary are created by combining one primary color with one secondary color—red-orange, red-purple, purple-blue, blue-green, and yellow-green.

Complementary Colors
Colors, such as red and green, blue and orange, and yellow and purple, are complementary and are opposite one another on a color wheel. When mixed together, they desaturate or neutralize each other. However, when they are placed next to each other they increase in intensity.

Monochromatic Colors
Colors created with varying values of a single color are identified as monochromatic. This is achieved by adding white or black to a color. Monochromatic color schemes are perceived as homogenous and unified.

Analogous Colors
Colors created from adjacent colors on a color wheel and have minimal chromatic differences are identified as analogous colors. Analogous color schemes are also perceived as unified, but are more varied than monochromatic color schemes.

Triadic Colors
Colors created from colors equidistant from one another or located at the corners of an equilateral triangle juxtaposed on a color wheel are identified as triadic colors. Triadic color schemes are perceived as strong, dynamic, and vibrant.

Quadratic Colors
Colors created from colors located in the four corners of a square or rectangle juxtaposed on a color wheel are identified as quadratic colors.

In this poster, overlapping lines of intense colors are layered on a solid, black background, creating brighter hues, as well as an optical third dimension to the overall composition.

RYOTA IIZUKA, Student
SIMON JOHNSTON, Instructor
Art Center College of Design
Pasadena, California, USA

A subtle palette of rich, warm colors is evident throughout this admissions viewbook for Middlebury, a liberal arts school in Vermont. Each chapter begins with a typographically bold narrative followed by a series of diagrams, illustrations, and iconic duotone and four-color photographic imagery that gives the reader an understanding of the diversity and varied experiences of the multicultural student body at the school.

PHILOGRAPHICA
Brookline, Massachusetts, USA

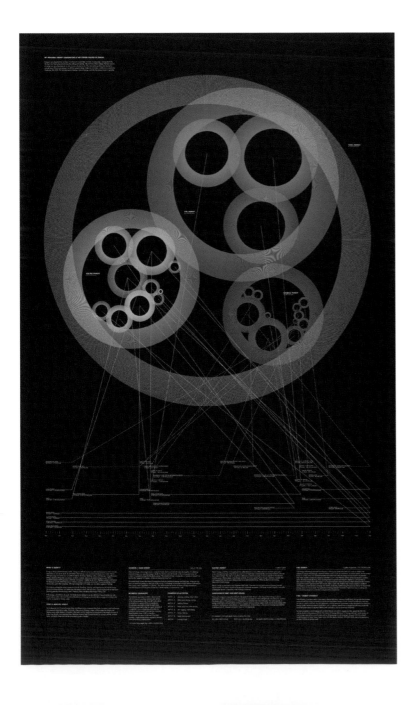

Comparative Relationships

All color relationships are relative. Colors can be identified as darker or lighter only when they are compared to other colors. Yellow is perceived as light; violet as dark. Yellow, for example, appears darker than white and has the lightest value of any color. A deep blue or violet appears bright against black and has the darkest value of any color (black being the absence of any reflected light).

Each color also has different levels of saturation. For example, red, blue, and yellow have different levels of intensity from bright to dull. Blue is not as bright as red or yellow; therefore, its intensity is not as high a level of brightness as found in the other two colors.

When complementary colors are juxtaposed with one another, each color appears brighter than the other. When analogous colors are juxtaposed, they tend to blend visually and therefore may be more difficult to distinguish from one another.

Color schemes, or color harmonies, have been developed to assist designers in choosing colors that work well together. The color wheel, a visual representation of the primary, secondary, and tertiary colors, forms the basis for color schemes.

Color Wheels

Color theorists have developed many different methods and systems for organizing and describing fundamental and comparative color relationships. In the late seventeenth century, Sir Isaac Newton (1643–1727) discovered that a prism separates light into a spectrum of seven colors—red, orange, yellow, green, blue, indigo, and violet. He also noticed that the colors at one end of the visible spectrum appear very similar to the colors at the other end of the spectrum. He then drew these two ends of the visible spectrum together, creating the first color wheel. This rudimentary model is very similar to color wheels used today to codify and organize all color relationships.

The structure of color is represented in a color wheel, which is organized in twelve units: three primary colors, three secondary colors, and six tertiary colors. A color wheel is a visual reference tool that illustrates comparative relationships between colors. Color wheels are two-dimensional diagrams of fundamental color relationships and only reference hues—the identification of colors, such as yellow, red, and blue. (see diagrams on page 68, 69)

By using a color wheel as a visual reference, designers can create meaningful relationships such as harmony or tension among color combinations.

A graduated color wheel contains a progressive series of values, or tints and shades, for each color. This visual reference also illustrates that a color's highest saturation point is not the same for each hue. For example, yellow is at its highest intensity toward the lighter end of the value scale, while blue is more intense at the darker end of the value scale. (See diagrams on page 183.)

A graduated color wheel is an effective reference tool for determining combinations of colors that are similar in value or saturation or determining contrast relationships.

Light and Temperature

Color is a property of light and can only be perceived when light is emitted or reflected by an object.

Additive color is created from a light source emitted from a video screen, computer monitor, or theatrical lighting. Additive primary colors are red, green, and blue with all other additive colors derived from them. *(continued on page 70)*

Vibrant and intense colors, are used in this magazine cover, *Latina*, to convey the spirit and culture of the Latin experience in Mexico. This message is further strengthened with the rich and varied color palette in the circular textile of the cover image as well as its juxtaposition with the intense yellow background color of the cover.

RODRIGO CORRAL DESIGN
New York, New York, USA

Color Wheels and Organizational Categories

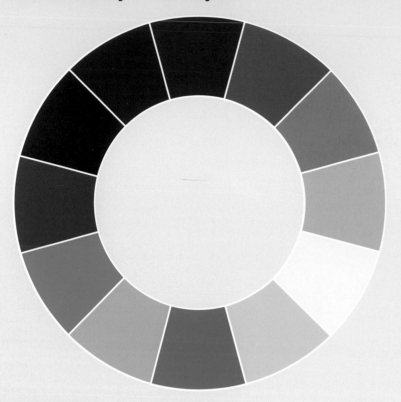

This color wheel illustrates the fundamental relationships among colors. The eight smaller color wheels shown here illustrate basic color relationships that can be applied to an infinite number of color palette combinations.

Primary Colors

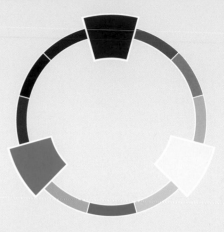

Secondary Colors

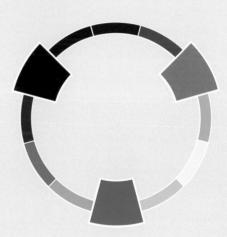

Tertiary Colors

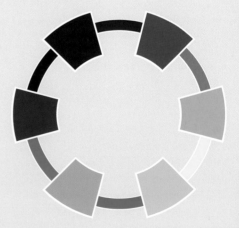

Complementary Colors

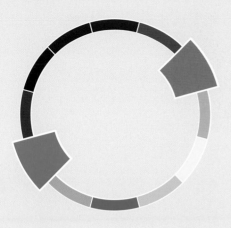

Triadic Colors

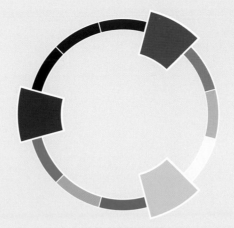

Monochromatic Colors

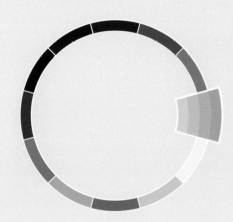

Quadratic Colors

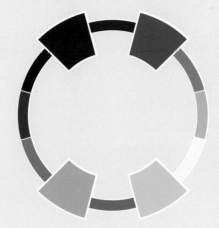

Analogous Colors

In this well-defined study of analogous colors used in an environmental graphics program for Cincinnati's Civic Center, color is also used as a metaphor for the Ohio River. It enhances the sense of movement in the river with analogous, saturated blues. These cool colors, although at times appearing alone as calming and meditative, in this context convey energy and a kinetic movement throughout the interior public spaces of the center. The main concourse, two city blocks long, and potentially a vacuous and impersonal public space, becomes transformed as a colored canvas on which the river unfolds in wall, ceiling, and floor treatments.

SUSSMAN/PREJZA
& COMPANY
Culver City, California, USA

THE BEST CREATIVE NONFICTION

VOL. 1

EDITED BY

LEE GUTKIND

creates additive secondary colors such as magenta from red and blue, cyan from blue and green, and yellow from red and green. Combining all three additive primary colors creates white, such as when spotlights of red, green, and blue are focused on the same area or subject to create a white spotlight. The absence of all additive primary colors—in other words, no light—creates black. RGB (red, green, and black) is an additive color system used for designing on screen.

Subtractive color is created from light reflected off a colored or pigmented surface. Subtractive primary colors are red, yellow, and blue. Combining two subtractive primary colors creates subtractive secondary colors: orange from red and yellow, green from yellow and blue, and purple from blue and red. Combining all three subtractive primary colors creates black. The absence of all subtractive primary colors—in other words, no pigment—results in white. CMYK (cyan, magenta, yellow, and black) is a subtractive color system used in offset printing.

Temperature of a color is also another subjective quality and relates to our visual experience. Colors considered "warm," such as red, orange, and yellow, remind us of heat

Value and saturation are both critical color considerations in the success of this cover, *The Best Creative Nonfiction*, Volume 1, for a collection of nonfiction writing. Four distinct colors, three warm and one cool, attract the reader's attention by communicating a bold visual for the nonfiction theme of this book, as well as frame the restrained, small-scale serif typography.

bideawee™

bideawee™

and communicate a feeling of warmth. Cool colors such as blue and green remind us of water and nature and communicate a feeling of coolness. Warm colors are brighter and more energetic; cool colors are calmer and more relaxed.

In addition to typography, color is one of the most valuable and influential elements in a graphic designer's vocabulary. It is a profoundly useful tool and has the power to communicate a wide range of emotions, codify diverse information, and establish an immediate connection with the viewer.

The bold, simple use of one bright, intense color—magenta—in this brand identity program for Bideawee, a New York City-based animal adoption center, conveys a message of friendliness, accessibility, and warmth without being literal. Vibrancy and visibility are further strengthened with a warm black background set against the intense value of the prominent magenta color. Lowercase, sans serif letterforms and simple line pictograms further convey a friendly and accessible message. The color also functions as a visual indicator to correctly pronounce this unusual name.

CARBONE SMOLAN AGENCY
New York, New York, USA

tex·ture \ˈteks-chər\ *n*
3 b: the visual or tactile surface characteristics and appearance of something

7

"One touch of nature makes the whole world kin."
WILLIAM SHAKESPEARE (1564-1616), *English, Author, Playwright, Poet*

Texture is defined as the look and feel of any surface. It is the surface quality of an object, be it smooth, rough, soft, or hard, and essentially a visual effect that adds richness and dimension to any visual composition. It can be seen and experienced by human touch or interpreted tactilely

A diverse set of compositional elements, such as large and small-scale typography, borders, frames, diagrams, and colors are used in this page spread to further enhance the textural qualities of the page and ultimately the reader's experience.

160OVER90
New York, New York, USA

by visual means. Textures can be described as flat, shiny, glossy, glittery, velvety, wet, feathery, gooey, furry, sandy, leathery, furry, cracked, prickly, abrasive, puffy, bumpy, corrugated, rusty, slimy, and so on.

Texture, along with other elements in a composition, can communicate a variety of different emotions and messages. Rough textures are visually active and kinetic, while smooth textures are passive and calm.

Primary Characteristics
Texture has characteristics similar to color. Like color, texture cannot function inde-

pendently without being integrated to other design elements such as line and form. It is used primarily to enhance other elements relying on shape and space to exist.

In visual communications, texture is the surface character of an object. It can be either two-dimensional or three-dimensional and distinguished by visual and physical properties such as rough or smooth and shiny or dull. A tactile texture such as sandpaper can be actually felt by touch; however, visual texture can only be suggested, interpreted, and understood by the human eye.

(continued on page 77)

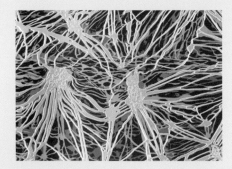

This capabilities showroom for W. L. Gore—maker of fluoropolymer Gore-tex products, presents the company's technical superiority in making ingredient products for a wide range of industries—from medical, to military, to leisure. Large-scale photographic images of material textures are used as emblematic and engaging visual backdrops for the presentation of complex data and scientific information in a compelling and accessible manner for a wide audience.

CARBONE SMOLAN
AGENCY
New York, New York, USA

1959

Goodbye, Columbus and 5 Short Stories Book Cover
PAUL RAND
New York, New York, USA

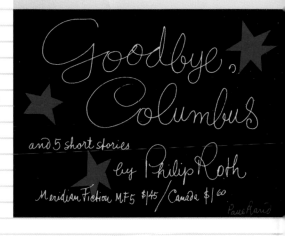

PAUL RAND (1914–1996) was a designer, author, and educator who shaped and influenced the course of twentieth-century graphic design. For forty years, he also devoted himself to teaching graphic design at Cooper Union, Pratt Institute, and Yale University. Through his work, writings, and teaching, he has educated and inspired generations of graphic designers worldwide.

Rand was educated at Pratt Institute, Parsons School of Design, and the Art Students League under George Grosz. In 1937, at the age of twenty-three, he became art director of both *Esquire* and *Apparel Arts* magazines, for which he created a series of now classic covers.

In 1941, he left the publishing world to become an art director for the William H. Weintraub Advertising Agency, where he created a series of innovative campaigns for Coronet Brandy, Dubonnet Aperitif, El Producto Cigars, and Orbach's.

With his early work for American publishers such as Meridian, Knopf, and Vintage, Rand proved that modernism did not have to be serious, cold, and clinical. Rand gave modernism "heart and soul." His whimsical approach, as well as his use of unconventional methods and familiar elements to communicate a variety of different emotions and messages, proved to be a new and groundbreaking interpretation of the European modernist movement in American graphic design.

His 1959 cover for Philip Roth's *Goodbye, Columbus* is a pivotal prototype for the use of familiar, humanistic, textural elements—irregular, cut-out shapes, the designer's own handwriting, and the powerful use of a graphic "kiss." The slightly parted lips, rendered in a bright, red lipstick on a stark, white field, are another example of visual texture that reinforced a real sense of physicality. This provocative image immediately and memorably communicates the sexually obsessive theme of the author's text, as well as the hands-on approach of the designer's process. Here, the textured image is a visual metaphor not only for the book's theme but also for the designer's creative, interactive response.

Rand continued to explore a broad range of possibilities with texture and abstraction in his publishing work—pure color fields, organic and ragged cut-out shapes, splatters of ink and paint, as well as the use of his distinctive handwriting. He approached book covers as if they were small canvases or sculptures where the artist or, in this case, the graphic designer, could express his individuality, intuition, and most importantly, creativity.

In American book publishing during the 1950s and 1960s, Rand influenced numerous graphic designers such as Alvin Lustig, Leo Lionni, Ivan Chermayeff, Tom Geismar, and Paul Bacon, who continued to pursue their beliefs that design in book publishing was an act of creative expression and invention.

Rand's "play" instinct transformed the written word through book-cover designs with wit, humor, and a timelessness unmatched in the history of graphic design.

**Paul Rand
and Goodbye, Columbus**

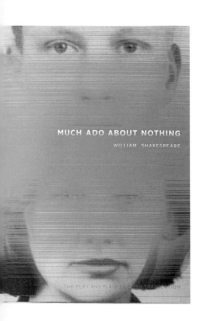

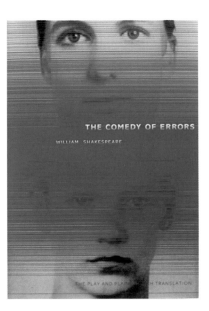

SOULPEPPER THEATRE 10TH ANNIVERSARY SEASON **FEB 27 — APR 19**

08 AS YOU LIKE IT
WILLIAM SHAKESPEARE

416.866.8666
soulpepper.ca

The character-based figurative illustrations in this series of posters for Soulpepper Theatre's 2008 season of plays have a visual textural quality that captures and strengthens each of the play's diverse themes while still communicating the essence of each of the main characters. In this context, texture is used as a common visual element, represented as line, pattern, tone, modeled color, and varied scale typography in each composition.

EDEL RODRIQUEZ
Mt. Tabor, New Jersey, USA

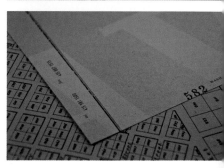

Types of Texture

There are three types or classifications of texture in visual communications:

Physical or Literal
Tactile texture, also defined as physical or literal texture, is an actual tactile variation on an object's surface. For example, wood, grain, sand, fur, glass, leather, canvas, and metal are all physical textures. This type of texture differentiates itself from visual texture by having a physical quality that can only be felt by human touch. One of the most obvious ways to evoke a response to texture is by using physical or literal textures—materials that already have noticeable and familiar textures. The specific use of this type of physical or literal texture in a visual communication can provide further emphasis, rhythm, movement, tension, pattern, and contrast, ultimately having a direct effect on its message and meaning.

Light is also important when considering physical or literal texture in a composition since it can influence how a surface is viewed and understood. Intense light on a smooth surface can obscure the immediacy and readability of an image, while the same effect can create a strong, visible contrast on a textured surface like wood or canvas.

The book covers for these three plays, Shakespeare's *Much Ado about Nothing*, *As You Like It*, and *The Comedy of Errors*, use a subtle and consistent visual metaphor to support each play's character-driven themes of identity. The primary visual element of each book cover uses a linear texture as a symbolic theatrical scrim or veil that partially hides or reveals photographic portraits or the identities of the each of the play's main character(s).

TAKASHI KUSUI, Student
JI LEE, Instructor
School of Visual Arts
New York, New York, USA

Inspired by the ancient Roman taverns it was named for, Aventine's identity and branding program has a strong textural appearance derived from the inline letterforms paired with smaller serif and sans serif typography. These contrasting typographic forms are further enhanced with line drawings, frames, and maps, as well as debossing and letterpress, which further enhances the textural identity, richness, and warmth of this program.

MARKATOS MOORE
San Francisco, California, USA

Kanuhura, a luxury resort located on a remote atoll in the Maldives, celebrates its authentic and remote locale with a wide range of textured brand elements—a hand-woven *K* monogram based on a repeating line pattern device; a custom typeface made of palm leaves; and a color palette evocative of white sand contrasted by aqua sea, sunsets, and local spices. This textural theme continues with hand-stitched "recycled" leather holders for information, wood stationery, and driftwood signs made in the island's craft workshops.

 PENTAGRAM
London, United Kingdom

Visual

The illusion of a physical texture on an object's surface is identified as visual texture. These illusory effects can be achieved through the use of design elements such as point, line, shape, form, light, tone, contrast, and pattern.

Every material and structure has its own inherent texture and needs to be taken into account when creating a composition. Materials such as canvas and watercolor paper are considerably rougher than bristol board or laser paper and may not be the most suitable for creating a flat, smooth surface.

Implied

An implied texture is a visual texture that has no basis in everyday reality. It is most often utilized in works of abstraction.

Creating Texture

Textures can be created through a variety of design elements and techniques such as repetition, typography, collage, assemblage, impasto, rubbings, transfers, moirés, erasures, and computer-generated effects.

Visual textures can be created by reproducing the color, tone, and pattern of actual textures; darks and lights can be used to suggest the grooves and irregular surface of the bark of a tree or the three-dimensionality of an irregular stone surface.

Lines of typographic text, painted surfaces, applications of dry media such as pencil or charcoal, or actual surfaces photographed or digitally scanned replicate actual texture but function as visual texture.

Texture provides any graphic design element with visual surface and feel. This can be achieved with line, shape, or even photographic images of specific surfaces.

This poster, titled the *Real Show* for the Art Directors Club of Metropolitan Washington, DC, combines different sizes and weights of sans serif typography with fluid, scriptlike hand lettering to enhance the visual texture of the poster's promotional message. Additionally, the textured border of the composition, as well as the extreme color contrasts between black and red and red and white, further enhances the textural characteristics of the poster's two-dimensional surface.

FUSZION
Alexandria, Virginia, USA

Continuous typographic line treatments are used as visual backdrops for the branding and identity of this Charles Shaw wine label series. These textural background treatments describe the taste, flavor, and character of each wine—Valdiguié, Shiraz, and Merlot—and are further enhanced by their subtle monochromatic color palettes, which provide maxi- mum contrast for identifying the wine name, year, vintage, and vineyard.

ANDREW LIM, Student
MICHAEL IAN KAYE, Instructor
School of Visual Arts
New York, New York, USA

The Everything Italian postcard series for Fox River Paper is composed of a set of eight themed postcards—all letterpressed to celebrate the textural surface qualities and properties of a new line of paper to add to its popular ESSE collection. All postcards use a diverse sampling of typography, patterns, and line drawings, all unified with the same color palette.

MIRIELLO GRAFICO
San Diego, California, USA

This dual front-and-back book jacket for *Miss Lonelyhearts* and *The Day of the Locust* uses texture as the primary element to communicate the essence of both novels—*Miss Lonelyhearts* with a repetitive pattern of hearts organized in a series of free-form, horizontal lines and with *The Day of the Locust* treated in the same manner but as filmstrips.

Both communicate the essence of each narrative, create a thematic connection with the reader, and ultimately convey a cohesive and unified message.

RODRIGO CORRAL DESIGN
New York, New York, USA

Built-up media, such as oil or acrylic paint, can produce rough textures from brushstrokes or palette knives. Type can also be used to create a visual texture that ultimately has more importance in a composition than the legibility of the letters themselves. In traditional printing with letterpress or metal type, each letterform or number to be printed consists of a raised image—an actual texture—on a flat background.

Texture gives a "tonal" quality to the surface of any design element such as a line, shape, or form, enhancing its visual presence as well as the viewer's emotional response. In this case, textural characteristics and qualities can be defined as descriptive adjectives in visual communications. Appropriate and meaningful texture can give the simplest visual element resonance and a spark of life. Effective use of texture can communicate a variety of emotions and messages.

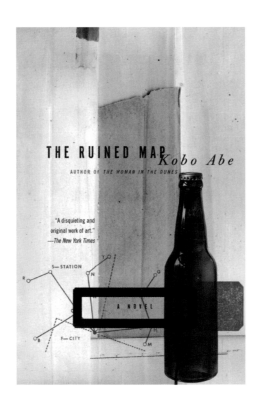

In this book cover for Kobo Abe's *The Ruined Map*, the visual characteristics of collage, assemblage, and photomontage of paper, board, object, line, image, and typography are used in various sizes and styles to enrich the overall textural power of the composition. Light and shadow, as well as a diverse range of tones coupled with a monochromatic color palette, add to the surface character and visual power of this active and kinetic book cover.

JOHN GALL
New York, New York, USA

Freehand line drawings, collage, and hand lettering add enhanced visual impact, strength, and texture to this poster series for the National Theatre School of Canada. The sole structured element evident in each composition is the framed typographic information at the top of each poster identifying the times, dates, and locations for each production.

LAURENT PINABEL
Montreal, Quebec, Canada

OCTOBER
21-25
2008
::: 7:30 P.M.

::: HYDRO-QUÉBEC STUDIO MONUMENT-NATIONAL
1182 ST-LAURENT BLVD.

PUBLIC PERFORMANCE
OF THE 2009 GRADUATING CLASS

$9
514 871-2224
ent-nts.ca

National Theatre School
of Canada

THE IMPORTANCE
OF BEING
EARNEST
by OSCAR
WILDE
directed by
BRENDAN
HEALY
(directing 2005)

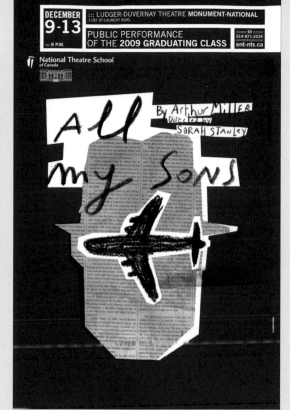

DECEMBER
9-13
::: 8 P.M.

::: LUDGER-DUVERNAY THEATRE MONUMENT-NATIONAL
1182 ST-LAURENT BLVD.

PUBLIC PERFORMANCE
OF THE 2009 GRADUATING CLASS

$9
514 871-2224
ent-nts.ca

National Theatre School
of Canada

By Arthur MILLER
Directed by
Sarah Stanley

All my sons

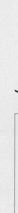

10–14
MARS
2009
20 H 30

::: STUDIO HYDRO-QUÉBEC MONUMENT-NATIONAL
1182, BOUL. SAINT-LAURENT

EXERCICE PUBLIC
DE LA PROMOTION 2009

9 $
514 871-2224
ent-nts.ca

École nationale de théâtre
du Canada

LE BRAS
CANADIEN
ET AUTRES
VANITÉS
de JEAN-PHILIPPE LEHOUX
(écriture dramatique 2008)
MISE EN SCÈNE GILL CHAMPAGNE

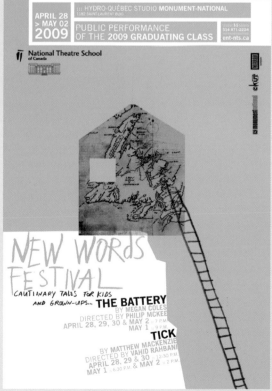

APRIL 28
> MAY 02
2009

::: HYDRO-QUÉBEC STUDIO MONUMENT-NATIONAL
1182 SAINT-LAURENT BLVD.

PUBLIC PERFORMANCE
OF THE 2009 GRADUATING CLASS

$5
514 871-2224
ent-nts.ca

National Theatre School
of Canada

NEW WORDS
FESTIVAL
CAUTIONARY TALES FOR KIDS
AND GROWN-UPS... THE BATTERY
BY MEGAN COLES
DIRECTED BY PHILIP MCKEE
APRIL 28, 29, 30 & MAY 2 ::: 7 P.M.
MAY 1 ::: 8 P.M.

TICK
BY MATTHEW MACKENZIE
DIRECTED BY VAHID RAHBANI
APRIL 28, 29 & 30 ::: 12:30 P.M.
MAY 1 ::: 6:30 P.M. & MAY 2 ::: 2 P.M.

scale \\'skāl\ *n*
5 b: a distinctive relative size, extent, or degree

"If you don't scale the mountain, you can't view the plain."
CHINESE PROVERB

The visual principle of scale is defined as a relative, progressive classification of proportion or a degree of size, amount, importance, and rank in a composition. Proportion and scale are related design principles in visual communications. Proportion refers to the size relationships of design

The primary communication element of this branding and identity program for Evolutiva, a firm specializing in leadership coaching, is a typographic poster composed of narrative content in varying scales and sizes that reflects the firm's values and explains key concepts of the firm's metaphor-based training programs. Words and statements are cropped, flipped, and fragmented in a variety of different configurations to further engage and provoke the viewer. Staff business cards were also cut from this same poster to emphasize both the element of surprise and the strategic thinking that highlights different leadership concepts.

BLOK DESIGN
Mexico City, Mexico

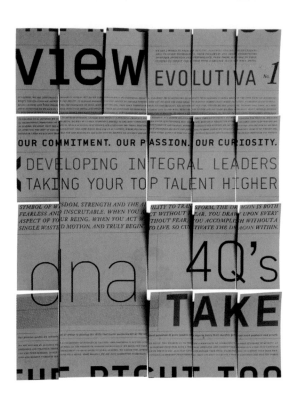

The inaugural issue of the McGill School of Architecture alumni newsletter uses extreme typographic scale as an eye-catching, attention-getting device. Small-scale, narrative-based typography is printed on newsprint in a single color—blue (evoking architectural blueprints)—with a vibrant, fluorescent orange overprint highlighting important information on select pages. To emphasize the school's many alumni, the names of all living alumni (approximately 3,000 names) were listed on the front cover with "I was here" overprinted in orange. The visual impact of this oversized typographic message juxtaposed with the diminuitive columnar text of the newsletter creates a bold, engaging invitation for the reader, as well as making it extremely personal for the reader to engage with and ultimately explore.

ATELIER PASTILLE ROSE
Montreal, Quebec, Canada

elements relative to the space they occupy in an overall composition. Scale refers to the size comparisons of the design elements in a composition, or a size relationship when comparing one design element to another.

On a day-to-day basis, we all make scale comparisons relating to size, distance, and weight.

These types of visual comparisons are usually based on known and familiar experiences that constantly provide us with a visual reference or orientation. For example, a skyscraper or snow-capped mountain on the horizon may be difficult to judge in terms of size. However, when we juxtapose either of these with a familiar scale reference such as a person, car, or even a book, it is easier for us to immediately quantify and understand.

Types of Scale

The visual principle of scale can be categorized as either objective or subjective.

Objective

This type of scale is the literal, or objective, definition of scale and is the actual dimensions of a physical object or a literal correla-*(continued on page 86)*

1935

Normandie Poster
ADOLPHE JEAN-MARIE MOURON (A. M. CASSANDRE)
Paris, France

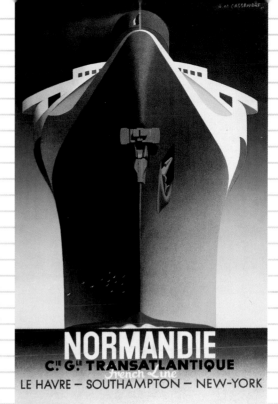

ADOLPHE JEAN-MARIE MOURON, also known as A. M. Cassandre (1901–1968), was one of the most influential poster designers of the twentieth century. Born in Khrakov, Ukraine, in 1901, Cassandre spent most of his life in Paris following his family's emigration to France during the Russian Revolution of 1917. As a young man, he studied drawing and painting at the Ecole des Beaux-Arts and at the Academie Julian.

Cassandre was a man of many talents and, like most creative individuals, he experimented throughout his life and career with a wide variety of techniques and styles. From 1922 to 1940, he devoted himself to the art of the poster. In the latter part of his life, he returned to his first love, painting, as well as teaching graphic design at the Ecole des Arts Decoratifs and then at the Ecole d'Art Graphique.

In 1936 his work was exhibited at the Museum of Modern Art in New York City, which led to numerous cover commissions from *Harper's Bazaar*.

At the age of 24, he furthered his growing reputation with works such as *Bucheron* (*Woodcutter*), a poster created for a French cabinetmaker that won first prize at the 1925 Exposition Internationale des Arts Decoratifs et Industriels Modernes. Additionally, his innovative approach for the Dubonnet wine company was among the first posters and advertisements designed to be seen and read by passengers in moving vehicles.

His love of fine art, combined with his typographic sensitivity and natural ability to combine these two distinct disciplines into coherent and visually dynamic design solutions, enabled Cassandre to become one of the earliest and most successful commercial artists and poster designers in the world. Inspired by surrealism and cubism, his posters are memorable for their innovative graphic solutions and their frequent references to twentieth-century avant-garde painters such as Max Ernst and Pablo Picasso.

Normandie, an iconic poster that afforded him international fame and recognition, is a primary example of how Cassandre used scale as a dynamic compositional element in all of his work.

The poster's frontal view is completely symmetrical with an extreme upward angle that emphasizes the ship's monumental scale and art deco lines. It is composed in a manner that draws our eyes irresistibly upward to the sky. The immense scale of the ship's prow is further emphasized by the French flag at the prow's apex as well as a group of tiny gulls and sea foam close to the horizon line where ship meets sea. This reductive, erect composition towers over the monolithic text NORMANDIE that also functions as a stable, typographic pedestal for the image of the ship.

The majority of Cassandre's posters were based on a true sense of proportion and scale, which governed their overall structure, rhythm, and final composition. His primary objective was always to make the object the center of a poster's attention. Through exaggerated scale, he was able to celebrate the geometry of form as well as use this fundamental principle as a memorable, storytelling device.

A. M. Cassandre and the Art of the Modern Poster

Large-scale letterforms and numbers such as *W* for whole wheat, *2* for 2% fat content, *L* for large eggs, and *4* for four sticks of butter are primary communication elements in Archer Farms food packaging. This unorthodox typographic treatment creates an impactful and informative visual hierarchy of scale that clearly identifies product, type, and amounts for the shopper.

WERNER DESIGN WERKS
St. Paul, Minnesota, USA

tion between an actual object and its graphic representation. An example of objective or literal scale is a "scale" drawing of a chair that is realized on a sheet of 8 1/2 X 11-inch (21.6 X 28 cm) paper; however, the actual chair in "real" scale is of a size to accommodate the human figure.

This type of scale is also used in maps, architectural plans, and models. It is a scale ratio defined numerically as two quantities separated by a colon (:). For example, a scale noted as 1:50 is one unit of measurement, such as inches or meters, and represents fifty of the same units at full size.

Subjective

This type of scale refers to a person's impression of an actual object. For example, a car or a house may be described as having an immense or intimate scale due to how it relates to our physical selves, as well as our knowledge and familiarity with cars and houses. Subjective scale is relative only to our own personal experiences and is, therefore, subjective in nature.

Effective Use of Scale

Scale can be used as an effective design principle to create variety, emphasis, and

This identity and packaging for a new product line of disposable and biodegradable wooden cutlery made by Aspenware, named **WUN** (wooden utensils naturally), elevates the product above the "natural food" niche. Sans serif typography in large-scale caps contrasted with small-scale numbers and lowercase identifiers on the front of the packaging further reflects the restraint and eco-conscious nature of the brand.

BLOK DESIGN
Mexico City, Mexico

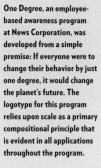

One Degree, an employee-based awareness program at News Corporation, was developed from a simple premise: If everyone were to change their behavior by just one degree, it would change the planet's future. The logotype for this program relies upon scale as a primary compositional principle that is evident in all applications throughout the program.

LANDOR
Paris, France

visual hierarchy in any visual communication. A proper use of scale contributes to the stability, visual comfort, and memorable aspects of any composition, while an incorrect scale will create discomfort, dysfunction, and a cramped awareness in a composition.

An element within a composition can appear larger or smaller depending on the size, placement, color, texture, and visual weight of the elements around it. Additionally, contrast in size can create visual emphasis, hierarchy, depth, movement, and tension within any composition.

When compositional elements are all the same size and equal in visual scale, the composition will appear flat and one-dimensional. It will lack contrast, tension, rhythm, and movement. It's as if we were listening to a musical composition and heard only one, continuous, monotonous note—always the same, never fluctuating in tone or resonance. All of the previous design elements referenced, when used in an effective, appropriate, and meaningful manner, can create a sense of depth and movement in any visual composition. Scale is also an essential design element and critical consideration in achieving this end result.

Scale can be used to direct a viewer's attention through a singular design element, such as an image or typography, as well as a composition of multiple visual elements.

A graphic designer also needs to consider scale in practical and functional ways. Professional work today requires graphic designers to consider a variety of different media and vehicles for conveying their work. From the traditional realms of printed matter, to the small-scale requirements of the digital world of websites and electronic interfaces, and the large-scale requirements of environmental graphics and exhibitions, scale is an important and constant consideration.

Context

The visual principle of scale is also fully dependent on context. In visual communications, familiar comparisons are less intuitive; therefore, the graphic designer relies upon scale to communicate those comparisons in an immediate and understandable way.

We all have experienced the jarring visual phenomenon of first printing out a sheet of paper with work we have been designing on screen, and to our surprise, something is amiss. We have methodically

This information-based poster, titled *World's Proven Oil Reserves*, uses various scales and sizes of transparent color circles to create a visually dynamic composition that communicates which major countries around the world have the largest oil reserves. Overlapping circles also create distinct color combinations that further convey another layer of information on the relationship of oil dependency from one country to another. The poster's asymmetrical composition expands beyond its edges, which further reinforces the extreme scale changes from one country to another.

BRYAN FAREVAAG, Student
GENEVIEVE WILLIAMS, Instructor
School of Visual Arts
New York, New York, USA

evaluated and resolved a visual composition in one scale (on screen) and now expect the same spatial and visual relationships to be achieved and maintained at a completely different scale when they are printed out on an 8 1/2 X 11-inch (21.6 X 28 cm) sheet of paper. This consistently happens often among most designers today.

We automatically make comparisons every time we receive sensory information. Objects are "too hot" or "safe to touch" because we immediately compare them to our previous experiences. Additionally, as human beings we tend to make size comparisons based on our own relationships to human scale. For example, our perception of scale in the adult world is completely different from our perception as small children.

Optical Effects and Scale

Scale is a fundamental design principle that also helps the viewer perceive spatial illusion, such as the size of objects and their relative scale in a composition. Small elements recede, larger ones come forward. Compositional elements that are closer to us appear larger than objects of the same size that are located farther away.

Restraint in typographic scale and an effective use of a monochromatic color palette provides a unique visual identity for this brand of hair care products—Frizz. The unusual shape and small scale of the packaging further reinforce the distinct qualities of this product line.

WOLFF OLINS
New York, New York, USA

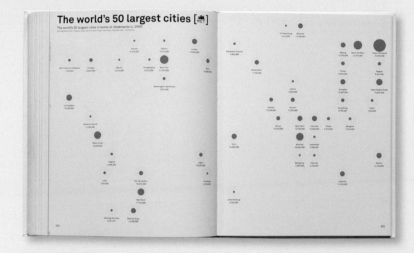

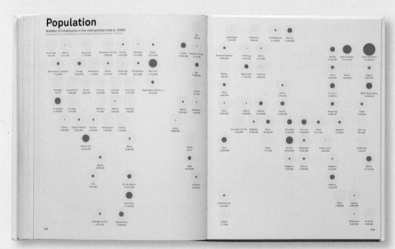

A system of varied-scale orange dots is used as a primary
communication device in
this atlas and accompanies
the reader through the
analysis and comparison
of 101 capital cities around
the world. These functional
dots, sized according to
comparative data on each
city, communicate specific
statistical information and
data such as population,
area, and crime. A strict page
grid develops into a type of
three-dimensional chart, as
successive pages of circles are
stacked, allowing a quick flip
through the book to reveal
changes in pollution, density,
public transport, and other
statistics.

JOOST GROOTENS
Amsterdam, The Netherlands

The following compositonal treatments
can be used to achieve optical and spatial
illusions in a visual composition:

Overlapping and Position
An optical device that can automatically
interpret scale and depth, as well as evoke
either realistic or unusual spatial effects,
is overlapping. A compositional element
partially hidden by another appears to be
located behind it in space and therefore
will appear smaller in scale. Each element
obscuring part of another helps the viewer
make spatial sense of the composition.

In addition to overlapping, the position
of elements relative to the overall picture
plane helps the viewer organize them in a
composition. The area at the bottom of the
picture plane is often seen as foreground—
the portion of a visual composition that is
closest to the viewer. The area at the center
of the picture plane is often interpreted as
middle ground—the portion of a visual composition of varying depth that is at midpoint
distance to the viewer. The upper area of a
visual composition is often seen as background (with the exception of landscapes in
which the sky seems to project forward from

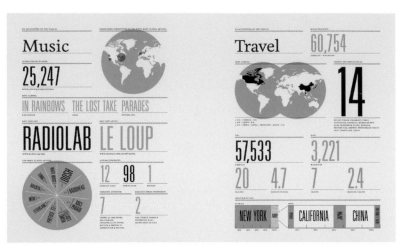

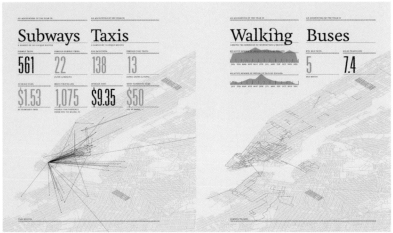

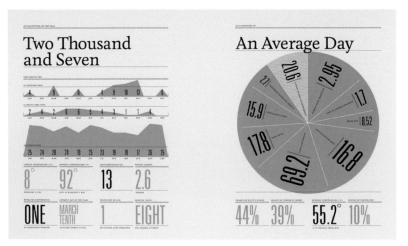

In the third edition of this annual, ongoing project, the designer investigates ways to analyze, capture, depict, and ultimately encapsulate a year of personal activity graphically. Bar charts, area charts, maps, and pie charts illustrate the textures and experiences of a complex and diverse life in New York City over a period of 365 days. In this context, scale plays a critical role in helping the reader engage with a variety of dense and detailed statistical data and narrative information in an accessible and intuitive manner.

NICHOLAS FELTON
New York, New York, USA

the background over the head of the viewer). In Western culture, we tend to interpret the lower portion of a composition as closer than the upper portion because representational paintings in art history have been composed in this manner.

Atmospheric Perspective
In addition to overlapping and position in a composition, graphic designers can rely on atmospheric perspective to further indicate scale and spatial depth. This effect can be used when there is need for a specific element or area to appear more distant than the other elements in the composition. This can be achieved by using softer edges, less value or contrast, and less detail in these elements so that they appear farther back in the compositional space.

When compositional elements are extremely close to the viewer, they may be seen in reverse atmospheric perspective: The closest elements are blurred or brought out of focus, with the sharpest edges and strongest value contrast in the elements that are a bit farther away.

No matter what size a designer's work will be when finally realized, it must have its own true sense of scale.

Scale is used as an effective communication tool in the permanent exhibition areas of the California Academy of Sciences. Here, scale provides an immediate visual hierarchy to exhibition content, whether it is object or artifact, large photographic imagery, or small narrative and interpretive information-based panels allowing the visitor to get an immediate overview of the exhibition's themes or an in-depth presentation of detailed information on a specific exhibition theme.

VOLUME INC.
San Francisco, California, USA

This promotional poster announcing exhibitions, performances, workshops, and lectures at the Pump House Gallery in London uses extreme scale changes in typography and imagery to further capture the viewer's attention as well as create a visually dynamic and memorable composition.

FRASER MUGGERIDGE
London, United Kingdom

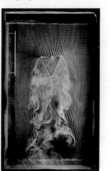

pump house
gallery

Frederic Remington, *The Smoke Signal* (detail), 1905; featured on USA postage stamp, 1961. Private collection.

SMOKE

an exhibition with performances, talks and workshops on the theme of smoke, curated by *Implicasphere*

5 October – 14 December 2008

Launch event Sunday 5 October, 2–5pm
with Simon Patterson's *Landskip* at 2pm

Étienne-Jules Marey, 'Smoke Machine study: prism presenting one of its bases to the air stream', 1901. Courtesy Collection Cinémathèque Française, Paris.

Free admission

move·ment \ˈmüv-mənt\ *n*

5 a: the suggestion or illusion of motion in a painting, sculpture, or design

9

"**Everything in the universe has rhythm. Everything dances.**"
MAYA ANGELOU (B. 1928), *American, Actor, Author, Civil Rights Activist, Poet*

Movement is defined as the act or process of moving or a change of place, position, or effort. It can be actual or implied. In a painting or photograph, for instance, movement refers to a representation or suggestion of motion. In sculpture, movement refers to implied motion, with the exception

This symbol for the Darien Library is derived from the simple movement seen when flipping the pages of a book, and in this identity interpreted through a progression of transparent, overlapping color tints. The symbol also refers to an ocean wave or the wing of a bird, all suggesting movement and ascent.

C+G PARTNERS LLC
New York, New York, USA

of mobiles and kinetic sculptures that have actual motion, such as found in the work of Alexander Calder.

In visual communications, movement apparent in a drawing, painting, photograph, book cover, or even magazine spread forces our eyes to move constantly and attend to one or more elements within the composition. Our eye may be brought to the center of the composition because there is a bright color there and then to another location that contains typography functioning as a headline in a bold typeface. Here, the responsibility of the graphic designer is to direct the viewer's attention through a specific sequence of visual experiences, as opposed to letting the eye randomly go from one element to another in a composition.

The primary function of movement in visual communications is to guide the eye of the viewer through and around any visual message. In a three-dimensional composition or space, a graphic designer needs to consider not only movement realized with light and color, but also with the physical movement of the viewer through, in, and around the total environment.

(continued on page 96)

This assignment requires sophomore students to consider fundamental design principles—in this case, movement—found in their environment and in everyday objects. With photography, they explore their surroundings and document examples of "movement" found in surprising and intriguing situations. The final images are cropped to a 3 X 3-inch (7.6 X 7.6 cm) square and then composed in a 3 X 3 nine-square composition further communicating the student's examination of interrelationships in form, color, texture, scale, tension, contrast, and pattern between the various photographic images. This visual exercise helps students increase their understanding of fundamental design elements; increase their awareness of the natural and built environment; become more comfortable with a camera and with composing compelling and communicative photographic images; crop photographic images to create interesting, dynamic and impactful compositions; find visual relationships between seemingly disparate images; and become familiar with digital image software such as Adobe Photoshop, Adobe Bridge and Camera Raw.

JONATHAN SIKOV CASTELLANO, Student
ANNABELLE GOULD, Instructor
University of Washington
Seattle, Washington, USA

Gran Premio dell'Autodromo di Monza (Monza Grand Prix) Poster
MAX HUBER
Milan, Italy

MAX HUBER (1919–1992) was one of the most significant graphic designers of the twentieth century and an influential figure in the history of modern graphic design.

He studied at the Kunstgewerbeschule in Zurich and worked as an art director before moving to Milan in 1940, where he became art director of Studio Boggeri. Huber was also a member of the distinguished association of Swiss modernists called the Allianz—a group whose members included Hans Arp, Max Bill, Le Corbusier, Paul Klee, Leo Leuppi, and Richard Paul Lohse.

In his early career, Huber was greatly influenced by the teachings of modernist masters such as Max Bill and Lazlo Moholy-Nagy and therefore among the first designers in Italy to apply avant-garde principles and aesthetics to commercial graphic design such as posters, jazz record album covers, and book covers. Some of Huber's most memorable achievements were on a completely different scale and remain in the minds of generations of Italians, such as his identity programs for the department store chain La Rinascente, the supermarket chain Esselingsa, and for media giant RAI.

One celebrated example of this modernist approach is Huber's memorable posters for the Monza races. Starting in 1928, Huber designed promotional posters and flyers for the Monza car races in Italy, mainly for the Grand Prix and the Lottery Race. This poster series illustrates how he brought the visual element of movement to two-dimensional compositions.

Huber's 1948 poster for the motor races at Monza incorporated illusions of visual perspective that reinforced a great sense of movement and speed—letterforms are disappearing in the distance and are in counterpoint to the arrows moving forward. Additionally, varied typographic sizes and vibrant transparent colors laid over one another provide exaggerated depth, rhythm, and movement to the poster's overall composition. For example, the red and blue arrows give direction to the street. The type identifying the event, *Gran premio dell' Autodromo*, rushes across the field of the poster with visual speed as if it transformed itself into one of the cars racing at that very moment.

This innovative poster illustrates Ettore Sottsass's dictum of 1947: "One can state that the people of Greece would never have existed without the sea, and that the sea is their great story. I believe our great story, by contrast, is speed (velocita)."

It is also important to note here that the dramatic and distorted visual effects Huber created with typography were highly readable and impactful without the assistance of contemporary methods of photocomposition, digital composition, and computerized image manipulation software.

Huber relied upon the basic tenets of perspective to convey distance, depth, and motion in a unique and memorable way. This poster is a classic visual representation that is simultaneously suggestive and powerful on the theme of movement.

The Monza posters and flyers embody a joyfulness conveyed by combining vibrant colors, balanced lines, and oblique angles, all lending rhythm and spatial harmony to the composition. It is a choreographed composition of visually moving dynamics.

Max Huber and the Monza Grand Prix

Elements and Techniques

Movement in any visual composition is realized and fully dependent upon combining the basic elements of visual communications, such as line, shape, form, and texture to produce the look and feel of motion. These design variables can create a collective sense of movement that causes the viewer's eye to move through an overall composition or focus specifically on an isolated group of elements within a composition.

Visual techniques, such as repetition and rhythm, can also enhance the characteristics of movement in a two-dimensional or (three-dimensional) composition. In many

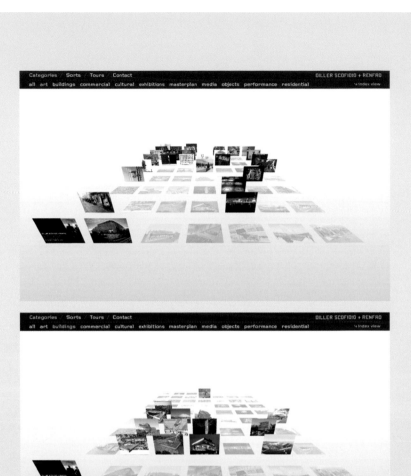

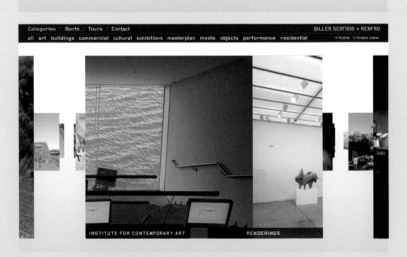

The primary project section of this website for Diller Scofidio + Refro, an architectural design firm, as well as its interface navigation from section to section, provides a series of extremely kinetic movements that immediately engage and hold the viewer's interest. With each inquiry, a new and dynamic composition is achieved through one-point perspective and the dimensionalization of flat photographic images into three-dimensional planes located in space. Additionally, as the cursor moves off the common one-point perspective left or right of that common point, so does the composition. It is fluid, organic, and immediate.

PENTAGRAM
New York, New York, USA

ways, these two techniques can be thought of as visual "music" since they relate directly to creating the "tempo" of any composition.

With the repetition of line, shape, form, and color, a visual sequence can also guide the eye of the viewer along a specific visual path or defined sequence of events. A repetitive visual sequence in a composition can be regular, irregular, gradual, or exaggerated in its visual character.

Rhythm

Rhythm is most often thought of in terms of sound and music, defined as alternating occurrences of sound and silence. In visual

The branding and identity program for Media Trust, an organization that works in partnership with the media industries throughout the United Kingdom in building effective communications for charities and nonprofit organizations, uses movement as a fundamental visual element in all levels of its branding system. The company's brand architecture relies upon a one-color, contemporary logotype for the parent brand, a series of subbrand logotypes defined for all of its service organizations, and a "box fan" symbol that adds visual interest to related print collateral material.

FORM
London, United Kingdom

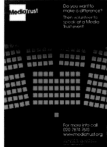

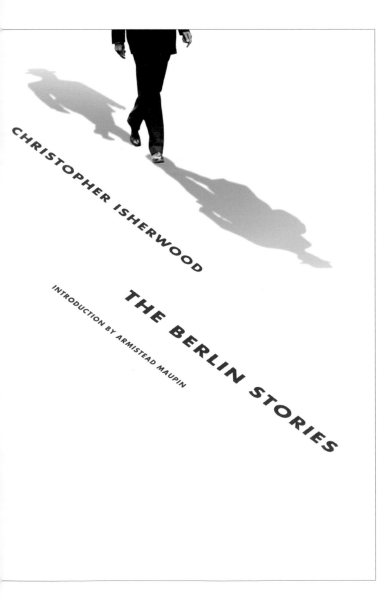

CHRISTOPHER ISHERWOOD

THE BERLIN STORIES

INTRODUCTION BY ARMISTEAD MAUPIN

This provocative book cover for Christopher Isherwood's *The Berlin Stories* symbolizes the dual presence of two paths or points of view in the book, comprising two short novellas—*Goodbye to Berlin* and *Mr. Norris Changes Trains*. Movement is articulated in dynamic and meaningful ways in this composition; from the cropping of the figure at the top of the cover, to the shadows projected in opposing directions, to the typography angled and aligned with the direction of the man walking.

MOTHER DESIGN
New York, New York, USA

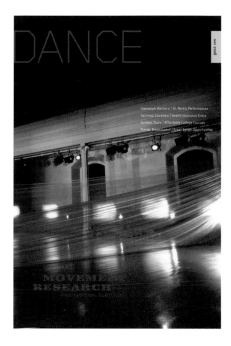  

communications, it can be described in the same way. Sound and silence are replaced with form and space—active and passive, primary and secondary. Creating rhythm with visual elements in a composition is similar to the role of choreography in dance. With visual form, choreography is the implied movement of compositional elements perceived by the eye of the viewer.

Rhythm can also be acheived with the repetition or alternation of compositional elements, often with defined intervals organized between them. It can create a sense of movement, as well as establish pattern and texture in any composition.

Types of visual rhythm are often defined with the following characteristics:

Regular
A regular visual rhythm occurs when the graphic intervals between the compositional elements, and often the actual elements themselves, are similar in size, length, weight, or visual character.

Flowing
A flowing visual rhythm can convey a sense of movement and is often perceived as a more organic and natural graphic form in its visual character.

With the redesign of *Dance* magazine, this student effectively redefined movement with unusual croppings of photographs to further celebrate the art of dance, as well as active and inactive zones for related information necessary for an effective magazine cover. Here the use of perimeter or edge, typographic variation on graphic form, texture, and composi-

tion, and scale collectively contribute to the strong dynamic movements of each of the cover compositions.

LAURA GRALNICK, Student
RICHARD POULIN, Instructor
School of Visual Arts
New York, New York, USA

"Film Project" was created by Blok Design and Toxico to support independent film-makers and videographers who face challenges in developing and completing their films. To avoid wasting limited resources, postcards, mailers, and stationery were created by recycling overruns from their own existing projects, along with old postcards and jackets from discarded vinyl LPs; the project's logotype was silk-screened as a layered overprint to this previously printed material. With these cost-savings methods, a kinetically dynamic visual program was developed that clearly expresses the essence of film, pacing, rhythm, and movement, as well as smart use of limited resources and creative risk.

BLOK DESIGN
Mexico City, Mexico

Progressive

A progressive rhythm is created with a sequence of compositional elements through a defined progression of steps.

Rhythm gives character to movement in a composition. Visual rhythms can be evenly paced and static or irregular and full of exaggerated gestures.

Other Considerations

Movement and rhythm are critical to the compositional aspects of any singular work of graphic design, as well as the construction and organization of multiple images, pages, and frames, such as books, magazines, motion graphics, and websites. In these examples, movement and rhythm enhance variation and change in content while providing a variety of scales, tonal values, and textural variations while maintaining a visual and structural cohesiveness.

In many ways, both movement and rhythm are transparent in visual communications. They exist only in an implied sense through the arrangement and organization of elements of varying size, shape, form, color, texture, and contrast in a composition.

A series of highly kinetic photographic images by Bill Beckley is used in a variety of scales, color palettes, pairings, and croppings throughout this monograph brochure to further celebrate the visual qualities and nuances of movement found in this photographer's work.

KATYA MEZHIBOVSKAYA
New York, New York, USA

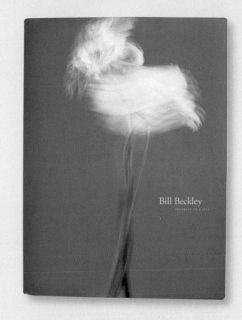

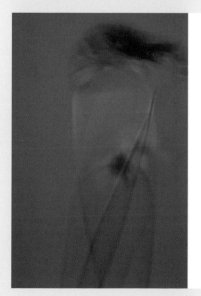

space \\'spās\ *n*

2 a: a limited extent in one, two, or three dimensions: distance, area, volume

4 a: a boundless three-dimensional extent in which objects and events occur and have relative position and direction

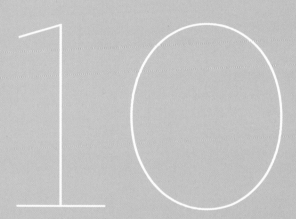

"I think that the ideal space must contain elements of magic, serenity, sorcery, and mystery."

LUIS BARRAGÁN (1902–1988), *Mexican, Architect*

Space is an essential design element in all visual communications. However, unlike other elements such as line, shape, form, color, and texture, space cannot be placed or located in a composition. Space refers to the distance or area between, around, above, below, or within other elements

The modulated page grid and the overall size of this brochure for Daycorp Property Development share the same proportional relationship that allows for the creation of related spatial compositions from page spread to page spread throughout the brochure. Additionally, the modulated structure of the brochure's custom letterforms, com- bined with regulated and consistent letterspacing and leading, creates uniform positive and negative spaces in each page composition.

VOICE
Adelaide, Australia

such as lines, shapes, forms, colors, textures, frames, and images in a composition. It can be two dimensional or three dimensional and described as flat, shallow, deep, open, closed, positive, negative, actual, ambiguous, or illusory.

The fundamental principle of space is an integral design element to be considered in any two-dimensional composition and can appear open, dense, compact, loose, empty, full, flat, or voluminous depending on how space is being used, organized, divided, or in other words—activated.

Describing Space

Space is usually identified as negative space or white space—terms that refer to the empty but often active areas of any visual composition that are void of the graphic elements. Space containing elements such as shapes, forms, images, and such is identi- fied as positive space. The varied degrees or amounts of negative or positive space in any composition can create an illusion of depth through the careful, established spatial rela- tionships of foreground and background or figure–ground relationships. When negative and positive space are equal, spatial depth is lacking and a more visually static composi- tion is created.

For example, think of compositional space as a room in your home. The room is a three-dimensional space containing your personal possessions—or compositional ele- ments. Is it cluttered or is there ample room to live, work, and relax? You design the room by filling it with objects on its walls, floors, and ceilings. The graphic designer does the same thing by creating a composition with shape, form, color, image, and type within a two-dimensional space.

(continued on page 106)

1939

Boy and Girl on a Fence,
Rural Electrification Administration Series Two Poster
LESTER BEALL
New York, New York, USA

LESTER BEALL (1903–1969) was a twentieth-century American graphic designer notable as a leading proponent of modernist graphic design in the United States.

He was born in Kansas City, Missouri, and later moved to Chicago, where he studied at the University of Chicago and later at the Art Institute of Chicago. As a self-taught graphic designer, he initially designed exhibits and wall murals for the 1933 Chicago Century of Progress World's Fair. In 1935, he relocated to New York City and eventually opened his own design consultancy in Wilton, Connecticut.

Beall was deeply influenced by the European avant-garde and produced award-winning work in a minimalist, modernist style for clients such as the *Chicago Tribune,* Hiram Walker, *Collier's,* Abbott Laboratories, Time-Life, and International Paper. Throughout his work and career, he was known for utilizing angled elements, vibrant colors, iconic arrows, silhouetted photography, and dynamic shapes in an innovative and provocative manner.

Among his most recognized works are a series of public information posters that he designed for the U.S. government. The Rural Electrification Administration (REA) was one of the primary public improvement projects initiated by President Franklin Delano Roosevelt to revive a battered U.S. economy by building dams and hydroelectric power plants in rural areas of the country. The REA, a part of the U.S. Department of Agriculture, was responsible for promoting the use of electricity in rural areas throughout the United States. This now classic series of large-format posters received national and international attention. All three sets of six silk-screened posters for the REA were designed and produced over a four-year period. Their graphic simplicity and flat illustrative elements were appropriate for an audience with minimal reading skills and were reminiscent of the public posters designed by the Russian Constructivists twenty years earlier. Each poster is a thorough and thoughtful study in minimalist form and compositional space.

Boy and Girl on a Fence, a poster from Series Two, is considered one of the greatest American posters of all time. It features a young boy and girl smiling and looking to the future as they lean against a wood fence bordering their farm. Beall used flat, vibrant color, photomontage, and a juxtaposition of angled and orthogonal bands to further enhance an implied and active space in the poster's composition. It also conveys the strong, humanistic, and patriotic spirit of rural America. This poster series is also an early example of graphic design put to work for the public good.

In 1937, Lester Beall was the first American graphic designer to be honored with a one-man solo exhibition at the Museum of Modern Art in New York City.

Lester Beall and the REA Posters

This symbol for a real estate developer, LargaVista Companies, uses pictorial space to convey a three-dimensional volume or environment through an isometric projection of form contained within a six-sided trapezoid.

HINTERLAND
New York, New York, USA

Types of Space

In addition to the formal considerations of space as a compositional element, graphic designers can create specific types of compositional space to further enhance and strengthen any visual message:

Actual Space
The area that a visual composition physically occupies is identified as actual space.

Pictorial Space
The manipulation of flat surfaces to create a perception of depth, movement, or direction is called pictorial space. It relies on illusion to deceive the mind and eye of the viewer.

Psychological Space
A visual composition that influences the mind and eye of the viewer is called psychological space.

Physical Space
In this type of compositional space, the elemental, aesthetic, and functional requirements of space are critical physical considerations for any graphic designer, since they require an interface with the built environment. A wayfinding sign program for an airport, an exhibition of art and artifacts in a museum, or a large-scale display for an urban retailer are all representative examples of physical compositional space.

Characteristics and Techniques

Historically, artists and designers have created a number of methods to interpret and perceive spatial depth in a composition.

Compositional space in visual communications is essentially flat. It has height and width but not depth. However, the illusion of spatial depth and three-dimensional space in

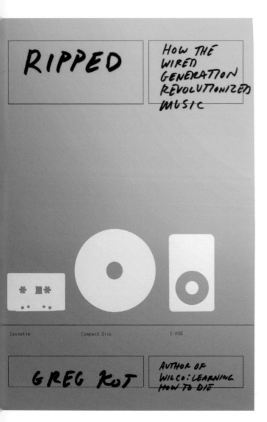

The open compositional space of this book cover for *Ripped: How the Wired Generation Revolutionized Music*, guides the reader's eye in immediately focusing on the three relevant music devices iconographically represented—tape cassette, CD, and iPod.

THE OFFICE OF
PAUL SAHRE
New York, New York, USA

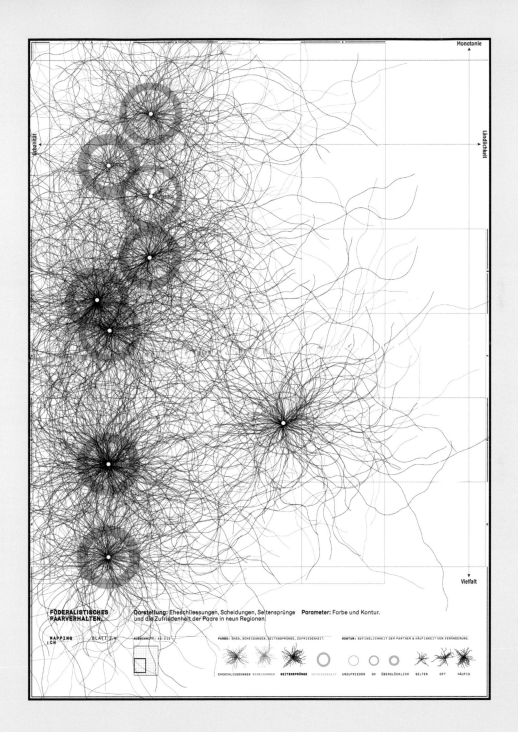

These information-based posters use both positive and negative white space to create imaginary visual landscapes for the intersection and interplay of statistical data formulated in this study on people living in selected cities. Key cities are ranked according to their diversity and the degree to which they are rural or urban. Circles and spheres illustrate relationships between values and emotions—fidelity and infidelity, happiness and sadness. The different densities of colors suggest arbitrary ranking and proximity, implying that there is no simple explanation for this data.

LORENZO GEIGER
Bern, Switzerland

The choreographic process, which begins with dancers improvising off Shen's conceptual framework, "was a rigorous assessment of the human body's capabilities."

An effective use of compositional space is illustrated in these page spreads for *Dance* **magazine. Reliance on extreme scale variations with compositional elements, such as photographic imagery, typographic blocks of text, repetitive patterns of images, and bands of flat color, further reinforces movement across the active and inactive spaces of each page.**

LAURA GRALNICK, Student
RICHARD POULIN, Instructor
School of Visual Arts
New York, New York, USA

compositions can be achieved in the mind, as well as the eye, of the viewer through specific visual characteristics and techniques.

Relative size in spatial relationships is one of the easiest visual characteristics to create the illusion of space in a two-dimensional composition. A larger element will always appear closer in a composition than a smaller one.

Overlapping in spatial relationships is another way to suggest depth in a two-dimensional composition. When compositional elements overlap one another, they are perceived as if one is covering parts of the other so that one appears in the foreground and the other appears covered and in the background of the composition.

Location in spatial relationships refers to where an element is found vertically in a two-dimensional composition. The bottom of the composition is perceived as the foreground; the area nearest to the viewer and the top of the composition is perceived as its background—the area farthest from the viewer. The higher an element is placed in a composition, the further back in the composition it is perceived.

Types of Perspective

There are three types of perspective techniques that a graphic designer can rely upon to further enhance spatial depth:

Atmospheric Perspective

This type of perspective in spatial relationships is another visual effect that relies on elements such as color, tone, and contrast to create the illusion of space in a two-dimensional composition. When elements appear in the distance and farther away from the viewer, atmospheric haze can obscure their visibility. This effect can be achieved

This book cover for *The Language of Things* immediately focuses the reader's attention on the pristine white space that dominates the cover's overall composition. Small-scale, iconic-color halftone images and a black dialog box containing the title and author of the book are relegated to a secondary position and are set against this stark white space.

MOTHER DESIGN
New York, New York, USA

by changing or modifying the visual characteristics of the composition's elements—by lightening their value, lowering their contrast, softening their edges, minimizing their detail, or muting their color. For example, increasing the blue tone of an element also creates a sense of depth in a composition because cool colors appear to recede whereas warm colors appear to come forward.

Linear, or One-Point, Perspective
Parallel lines converging toward a single vanishing point located on a horizon line is called linear, or one-point, perspective. Perspective lines above a horizon line are drawn diagonally down toward the vanishing point; lines below this line are drawn diagonally up toward it. Vertical lines indicate height and horizontal lines indicate width; in both orientations the lines remain parallel. (see diagram on page 45)

This page spread utilizes effective and meaningful white space to create a visual immediacy with the free-form silhouette of the large-scale image as well as with the common intense red color found in each photograph.

MERCER CREATIVE GROUP
Vancouver, BC, Canada

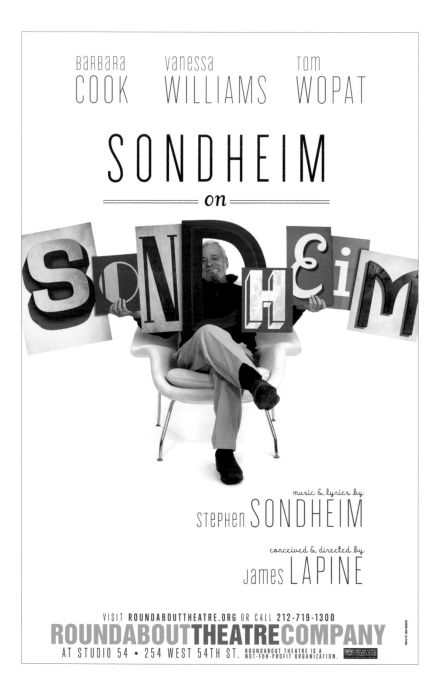

For example, if you see for miles along a straight road, the sides of the road in reality are parallel to one another; however they appear to draw closer and closer to one another and finally disappear at a vanishing point far off in the distance. It is one of the most common visual techniques to create spatial depth in two-dimensional compositions. This technique was first developed and used by Renaissance artists; they initially plotted perspective lines as a base to their compositions, using them to create realistic illusions of depth in drawings and paintings of architectural scenes.

Planar, or Two-Point, Perspective
In this type of perspective, the two visible sides of an element stretch away toward two vanishing points in the distance located on a horizon line. Vertical lines within the composition remain parallel to one another. The remaining lines that in reality appear parallel in the composition also appear to diminish diagonally toward one of the two vanishing points to either side of the horizon line. (See diagram on page 45.)

Using these visual characteristics and techniques, singularly or in combination with each other, will strengthen the illusions of depth and space in any visual composition.

While ample white space provides a visual anchor for its primary photographic image, typographic scale and weight variations used in this promotional poster for the theatrical production *Sondheim on Sondheim* **create atmospheric perspective, which further reinforces an illusion of spatial depth in an otherwise flat, two-dimensional composition.**

SPOTCO
New York, New York, USA

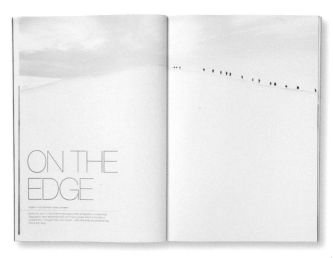

The effective use of ample pictorial or "white" space is apparent in these page spreads for Akzo Nobel's *A Magazine* and further shows how depth, movement, and direction can create dynamic and active compositions.

PENTAGRAM
London, United Kingdom

This brochure cover for Merce Cunningham's *Green World* effectively illustrates how location is a critical consideration in spatial relationships when wanting to achieve depth and perspective in a visual composition. In this example, the smaller die-cut circles located at the top of the composition appear farther away, or in the background, as opposed to the circles located toward the bottom, which appear closer to the reader's eye, or in the cover's foreground.

PENTAGRAM
New York, New York, USA

bal·ance \ˈba-lən(t)s\ *n*
6 a: an aesthetically pleasing
integration of elements or harmonious
or satisfying arrangement
or proportion of parts or elements,
as in a visual composition

11

"What I dream of is an art of balance."
HENRI MATISSE (1869-1954), *French, Painter, Printmaker, Sculptor*

Balance occurs when visual elements within a composition are equally distributed and arranged to communicate a feeling of stability and harmony. This visual principle can be described as formal and symmetrical, dynamic and asymmetrical, or radial. Our response to balance is intuitively

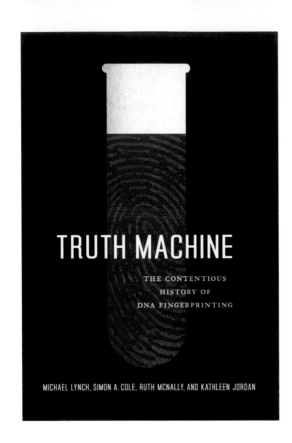

TRUTH MACHINE

THE CONTENTIOUS
HISTORY OF
DNA FINGERPRINTING

MICHAEL LYNCH, SIMON A. COLE, RUTH MCNALLY, AND KATHLEEN JORDAN

This book cover for *Truth Machine* reflects a well-resolved combination of symmetry and asymmetry that creates a unified balance to the overall composition. The large-scale compositional elements of image and typography are symmetrically, or formally, balanced, while the secondary title of the book is symmetrically composed but integrated to the overall cover, reflecting an asymmetrical or dynamic balance to the cover composition.

ISAAC TOBIN
Chicago, Illinois, USA

linked to taking our first steps as human beings. It is that essential need to stand, walk, and run that also relates to our fundamental, primal need to prefer balance in our lives, as well as in any composition.

Balance is achieved in a composition by arranging dissimilar elements with different visual characteristics.

Types of Balance

There are three types of visual balance:

Formal Balance

Symmetry, or formal balance, is the easiest type of balance to achieve in any visual composition. It is used extensively in architecture because it inherently conveys permanence and stability, as well as automatically provides a singular focus to whatever is placed in the center of a composition. It is also based on a mirror image. For example, if you draw a line down the center of a drawing of a gothic cathedral, elements on either side will appear as a mirror image.

Formal balance occurs when elements are arranged equally in a compositon, appear stable or static, and are identical and reflect one another.

(continued on page 117)

ARCTIC

ESTD 1917

CLUB HOTEL

The logotype for Arctic Club Hotel, combined with a single spot-line illustration, creates a symmetrically, or formally, balanced typographic composition. This compositional balance is further maintained when this logotype is framed, contained, and applied to the hotel's advertisments, website, stationery, press kit folder, and guest collateral print materials.

URBAN INFLUENCE
DESIGN STUDIO
Seattle, Washington, USA

Charles Ross: Light Placed Poster
JACQUELINE CASEY
Cambridge, Massachusetts, USA

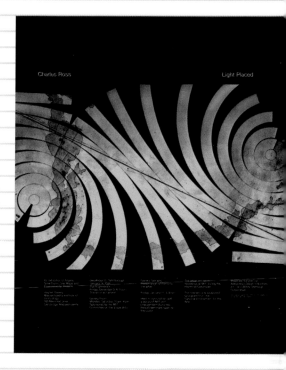

In 1955, JACQUELINE CASEY (1927–1991) started her professional career as a graphic designer when she joined the Office of Publications (Design Services Office) at the Massachusetts Institute of Technology (MIT) in Cambridge under the design direction of fellow classmate Muriel Cooper. When Cooper joined MIT's faculty in 1972, Casey took over as director, where she created a series of iconic promotional posters to publicize MIT events and exhibitions.

For over three decades, she was a woman working in a man's world, not only in the MIT Office of Publications but also in the environs of the entire MIT community that served as her sole client.

Born in Quincy, Massachusetts, she received a certificate of fashion design and illustration and a bachelor of fine arts degree from the Massachusetts College of Art in 1949. Following graduation, she worked in fashion illustration, advertising, interior design, and trade publications prior to her position at MIT.

Casey worked at MIT for over thirty years, during which time she developed a unique design philosophy, a memorable body of work, and a thought-provoking visual brand for the Institute.

In F. H. K. Henrion's 1983 book *Top Graphic Design*, Casey said, "Being a graphic designer at MIT continues to be a fascinating experience for me. My job is a constant learning experience. While MIT has its roots in tradition, the University represents all that is experimental, exciting, and future-oriented."

Her work was influenced by the modernist movement, the International Style, and by designers such as Karl Gertsner, Armin Hofmann, and Josef Müller-Brockmann. She developed a visual language that was purely her own but strongly connected to proportion, grid, and European san serif typography.

Balance also played a fundamental role in all of Casey's posters. They are humanistic visual metaphors—precise, clean, imaginative, engaging, and personal in tone and message.

Each of her posters contains a singular focal point or primary visual element that immediately attracts the viewer. In each case, a critical balance between visual and narrative form occurs, allowing the viewer to engage not only with his or her own imagination, but with their understanding of the poster's subject matter.

Casey's work engaged the intellect and curiosity of her academic audience because it was a seamless, balanced integration of type and image, as well as a memorable and powerful vehicle for storytelling.

Jacqueline Casey at MIT

This poster, titled *Rhythm Textures*, examines a series of selected quotes from Jack Kerouac's *On the Road* and uses formal balance to afford the reader ease and organization when accessing its dense and diverse content. The basic structure and tenor of each sentence or quote is graphically documented or mapped to further illustrate the writer's use of narrative rhythms and textures in the text, such as italicized words, commas, semicolons, dashes, colons, and question marks. Color classifies characters and themes within the text, such as blue for Dean Moriarity (protagonist), purple for travel, and brown for parties, drinking, and drugs. Each notation for each quotation is numerically coded for further reference with a specific number for part, chapter, paragraph, and sentence. All twenty quotes are listed at the bottom of the poster and cross-referenced with this numerical codification.

STEFANIE POSAVEC
London, United Kingdom

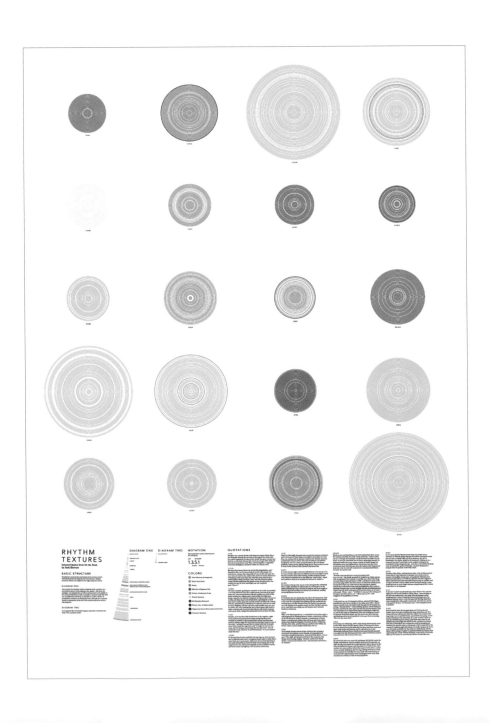

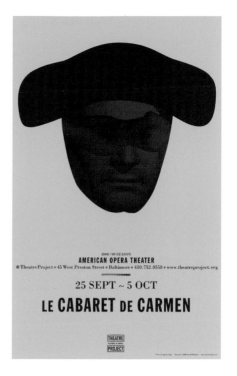

Dynamic Balance
Asymmetry or dynamic balance is more interesting and more difficult to achieve. It occurs when elements are arranged deliberately unequally in a composition and appear random and dynamic. Here, the composition lacks balance and appears off-kilter. Although it has a more casual appearance, it requires careful planning to ensure that it always appears visually balanced.

Radial Balance
This type of balance is based on a circle and occurs when visual elements in a composition radiate out from a central, common point in

a circular direction and their visual weight is equally distributed. Radial balance creates a strong focal point, always leading the eye to the center of the composition. Stars, watch faces, spokes of a wheel, and sunflowers are all prime examples of radial balance.

Degrees of Balance
Graphic designers can rely upon color, direction, location, shape, texture, value, and weight to emphasize a visual element to achieve a state of balance. Varied degrees of balance can be created in a composition through a combination of the following related design elements and principles:

Color
Our eyes are more drawn to color than to a neutral image. Small elements of vibrant color can offset larger elements of neutral color in a composition. Additionally, complementary colors visually weigh more than analogous colors.

Direction
Our eyes can be directed to a specific location in any visual composition based on its arrangement and composition of design ele-

ments. If elements are oriented in a specific direction, our eyes will also be led in that same direction.

Location
A smaller element located farther away from the center of a composition will always balance a larger element located closer to its center. Additionally, larger elements located on one side of a composition can be balanced by smaller elements located at the far end or on the other side of a composition. This is also the basis for asymmetry or informal balance.

Shape
Small, intricate shapes can balance larger, simpler shapes. Similarly, large uncluttered areas within a composition that have little or no detail can be balanced with small, irregular shapes, because the eye is usually drawn to the more intricate shapes.

Texture
Smaller areas containing textures, such as variegated, irregular, or random linear fluctuations, can balance larger areas with smoother, innocuous textures.

This promotional poster series for Baltimore's Theatre Project illustrates an effective use of formal compositional balance. Formal balance, or symmetry, is used to organize each typographic grouping consistently from poster to poster, while still achieving harmony and balance with the varied illustrations and photographic images used to ultimately **communicate the theme, character, and message of each play.**

SPUR DESIGN
Baltimore, Maryland, USA

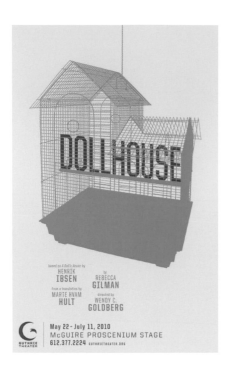

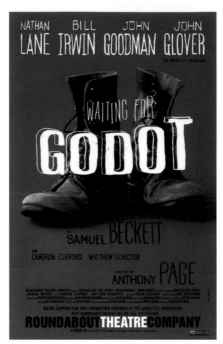

Compositional balance of elements that are diverse in scale and visual character can create active and powerful asymmetrical, or informal, compositions, as shown in these promotional posters for the Guthrie Theater, Chicago, and the Roundabout Theatre Company, New York City.

SPOTCO
New York, New York, USA

Value

Value refers to the lightness or darkness of elements. Black against white has a much stronger contrast or visual weight than gray against white; therefore, small elements of high contrast can be used to balance larger elements of low contrast.

Weight

The perceived physical weight of an element in any composition contributes to its visual interest. For example, a visually heavier element has more visual interest than a visually lighter element of the same size.

This set of covers for various municipal publications is part of an overall branding and identity program for the city of Melbourne. In these examples, the diversity of visual content used in each of these covers—such as line art, illustration, photography, and typographic styles—still allows a visual unity and cohesiveness due to reliance on asymmetry or an informal balance to each and every cover composition within the overall program.

LANDOR
Paris, France

This eye-catching poster is part of an public awareness program that reintroduces classic literature to junior high school students. Its reliance on compositional balance through formal symmetry, as well as its use of iconic imagery, creates a provocative visual metaphor that is universal and appealing to a young audience.

MIKEY BURTON
Philadelphia, Pennsylvania, USA

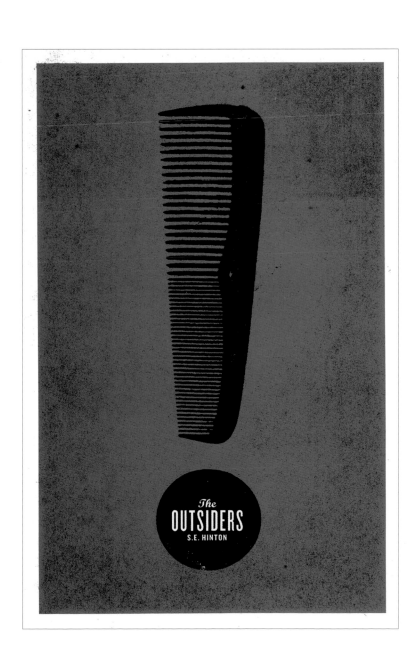

Asymmetrical, or informal, balance is clearly evident in this promotional poster for a film screening of *Man on Wire* at the Cathedral Church of Saint John the Divine in New York City. This type of compositional balance combined with the simplicity of the photographic image and blacklettering creates a visual invitation that is both eye-catching and memorable.

PENTAGRAM
New York, New York, USA

Visual balance can be affected not only by the size of compositional elements but also by their intrinsic value such as lightness or darkness. This is also described as an element's visual weight. When compositional elements are of equal visual weight, they are in balance.

Visual balance is an essential requirement in all visual communications. Just as balance is a state of physical equilibrium where everything comes to a standstill, it is also a state of visual harmony in which all characteristics of a composition are mutually interconnected and interrelated.

Join Phillippe Petit
for a screening of *Man on Wire*
April 15, 2009 at 7pm

The Cathedral
Church of **Saint John**
the Divine

Based on traditional Islamic arabesque patterning, this symbol for the Dubai Waterfront Canal District represents the entire city, as well as its eight distinct districts. Formal or symmetrical balance is used here as a primary compositional principle to integrate line, texture, color, and pattern in a cohesive, unified manner.

POULIN + MORRIS INC.
New York, New York, USA

In this atlas, formal and directional balance are used as primary organizational and compositional principles, helping the reader to access the analysis and comparison of 101 capital cities around the world. Dense information, organized in a series of horizontal bands of varied heights and containing different statistical data, shares a common leading system that unifies these variables from column to column, page to page, and spread to spread.

JOOST GROOTENS
Amsterdam, The Netherlands

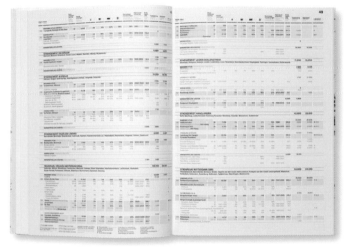

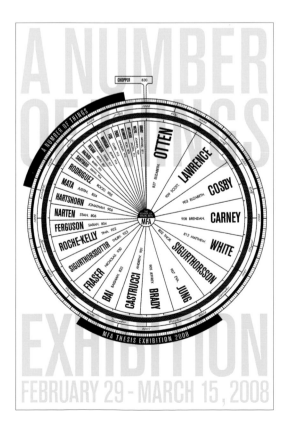

The balanced composition of this promotional poster for a student thesis exhibition at the School of Visual Arts relies solely upon one shared and common center point for the circular diagram and the justified, large-scale sans serif typography framing the upper and lower portions of the poster.

BRYAN FAREVAAG, Student
GENEVIEVE WILLIAMS, Instructor
School of Visual Arts
New York, New York, USA

sym·me·try \ˈsi-mə-trē\ *n*
1: balanced proportions;
also: beauty of form arising from
balanced proportions

12

"Symmetry is static—that is to say quiet; that is to say inconspicuous."

WILLIAM ADDISON DWIGGINS (1880-1956), *American, Book Designer, Calligrapher, Typographer*

Symmetry is a fundamental and timeless principle of visual perception. In visual communications, symmetry conveys balance, stability, and harmony. When visual elements are completely balanced or centered, they are in a state of equilibrium where all elements have equal weight. The result

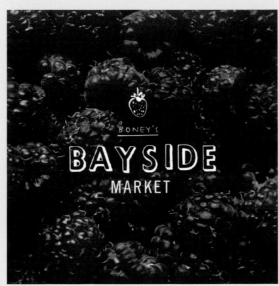

L

LEO INGWER
EST. 1939

The visual integration of an uppercase *L* and *I* illustrate a strong symmetry, or balance, with this logotype for Leo Ingwer Jewelers, even if the combined letterforms are not truly symmetrical in graphic form. Additionally, the scale and typographic treatment of the company's name and year established further strengthens the symmetry of this typographic composition.

AND PARTNERS
New York, New York, USA

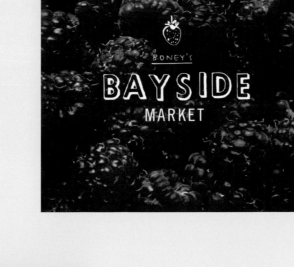

is a state of visual balance and is identified as symmetry. It is a compositional state where design elements are organized on the central axis of a composition (either its horizontal or vertical axis). A similar compositional state can be achieved when design elements are organized in relation to each other's central axes. A symmetrical composition is static, stationary, and balanced, with the negative spaces around its elements or the contours of its elements located around its central axis all appearing the same or of equal weight.

(continued on page 126)

The branding and identity program for Boney's Bayside Market, from packaging and advertisements to environmental graphics and shopping bags, uses symmetry combined with casual sans serif typography, hand-drawn letterforms, textural food photography, and quirky line illustrations to further communicate the feel, ambiance, and ultimate experience of shopping at a family-owned, neighborhood gourmet food market.

MIRIELLO GRAFICO
San Diego, California, USA

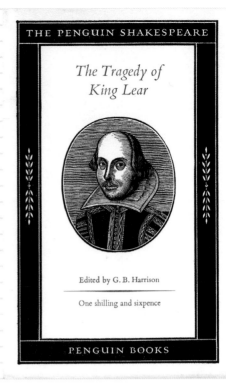

In 1947, JAN TSCHICHOLD (1902–1974) emigrated from Switzerland to Great Britain to accept a position at Penguin Books as its new design director. Founded in 1935, Penguin Books was one of the most commercially successful book publishers in Great Britain.

Prior to Tschichold's arrival in London, Penguin paperbacks were not produced with any specific design standards or production criteria. Their existing standards, dated and limited, were generic and inappropriate in comparison with the publisher's reputation and offerings. Tschichold quickly realized that a new and unique set of compositional rules and standards were needed at the publishing house.

Tschichold's redesign of Penguin books in the late 1940s not only revolutionized typographic conventions but also reintroduced compositional standards that had long been labeled out-of-date.

Tschichold developed a pragmatic look for Penguin Books that was extremely appropriate for a large number of book titles, while increasing a level of balance, consistency, and readability throughout their catalog. In his view, adherence to the tenets of classical typography—symmetry, legibility, a balance of type styles, wide margins, contrast, simplicity, and integrated rules and ornaments—were all integral to a book's timeless function.

Tschichold had begun to reject the rules of *Die Neue Typographie* (*The New Typography*) and functional Bauhaus principles while designing books in Switzerland between 1933 and 1946. He realized then that symmetrical and asymmetrical typographic treatments could equally accomplish the requirements and goals of successful book design.

While at Penguin, he established a new set of general design principles based on his broad vision of good design. These guidelines were documented in a four-page essay titled "Penguin Composition Rules," demanding that all Penguin designers follow these standardized rules for all aspects of book design and composition.

Tschichold also designed many book covers himself, including the Penguin edition of Shakespeare's *The Tragedy of King Lear*, released in 1949. While conventional in design, it is a clear and well-balanced composition that is immediately legible to the reader. Its solid black border is reinforced by inset hairline rules that provide a strong frame for the symmetrical typography set in Monotype's Perpetua. During his tenure, Tschichold standardized the design for Penguin's extensive book series, and *The Tragedy of King Lear* is a prime example of the basic compositional principles he devised for Penguin Classics, making them instantly recognizable to the consumer.

By raising the aesthetic level of a mass-market publisher of paperback books, Tschichold brought to life the timeless principle of symmetry that graphic designers still rely upon today. Tschichold later wrote, "We do not need pretentious books for the wealthy, we need more really well-made ordinary books."

Jan Tschichold and the Penguin Classics

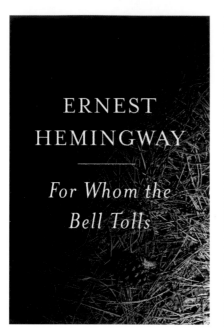

ERNEST
HEMINGWAY
——
*For Whom the
Bell Tolls*

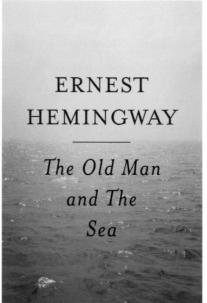

ERNEST
HEMINGWAY
——
*The Old Man
and The
Sea*

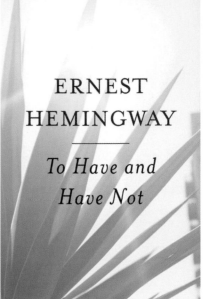

ERNEST
HEMINGWAY
——
*To Have and
Have Not*

**In this monogram for Tiffany
& Co., the designer uses
ligature, as well as in-depth
knowledge of and intimacy
with letterform, to create
a unified, balanced symmetry
for an already simple idea.**

LOUISE FILI LTD.
New York, New York, USA

Symmetrical, or formal, balance is also known as bilateral symmetry. It is achieved by repeating the reverse of an image on the opposite side of a vertical axis; each side becomes the mirror image of the other side. Symmetrical balance is considered formal, ordered, stable, and quiet.

The compositional principle of symmetry has also long been associated with physical beauty, natural or man-made. Symmetry can be found in virtually all forms of the natural world, including the human body, animals, and plants. Classical architecture also combines symmetrical types, creating unified, dynamic, and memorable forms. Prime examples found in the man-made environment are Notre Dame Cathedral, the Eiffel Tower, and the U.S. Capitol.

Types of Symmetry
There are three types of basic symmetry:

Reflective
Horizontal and vertical symmetry are identified as reflective symmetry. This type of symmetry is created by mirroring equivalent elements around a central axis or mirror line. Reflective symmetry can be achieved in any

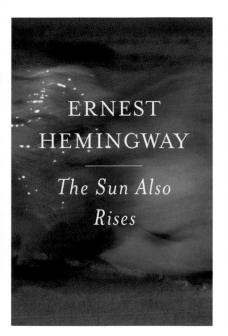

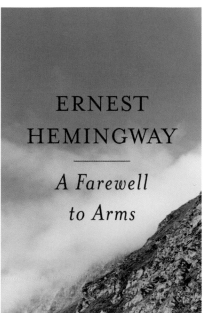

ERNEST HEMINGWAY

The Sun Also Rises

ERNEST HEMINGWAY

A Farewell to Arms

This series of book covers for five Ernest Hemingway novels relies upon traditional symmetry combined with serif typography to celebrate these classic, seminal books. The use of textural images as visual metaphors allows the reader's imagination to further connect with the familiar themes of these iconic novels.

THE OFFICE OF
PAUL SAHRE
New York, New York, USA

orientation as long as its elements are the same on both sides of the mirror line. Forms found in nature, such as a monarch butterfly, exhibit reflective symmetry.

Horizontal symmetry is created with an imaginary horizon or a left-to-right line functioning as the divider of the composition, with the top and bottom sections mirroring one another. A landscape reflected in a still pond is an example of horizontal symmetry.

Vertical symmetry is created with an imaginary vertical or a top-to-bottom line functioning as the divider of the composition, with the left and right sections mirroring one another. A Rorschach inkblot is an prime example of vertical symmetry.

Each of the fourteen contained and framed blocks of typographic text in this cover for *Los Angeles* magazine is composed in a symmetrical manner, and collectively composed as one overall symmetrical composition, further illustrating the diversity and power of this guiding compositional design principle.

TIMOTHY GOODMAN
San Francisco, California, USA

THOMAS MANN

Three Quandaries

DAVID LUKE
Translation & Introduction

Symmetry functions as the compositional guide for the typographic and line elements of this slipcase cover for a set of three novels by Thomas Mann—*Tristan*, *Death in Venice*, and *Gladius Dei*. While the trees are not truly symmetrical in the photographic composition, they are visually balanced and add a powerful metaphor to the title of this book set.

JOHN SURACE, Student
ANITA ZEPPETELLI,
Instructor
School of Visual Arts
New York, New York, USA

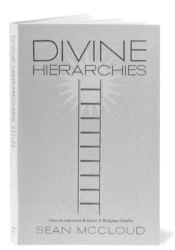

DIVINE
HIERARCHIES

Class in American Religion & Religious Studies
SEAN MCCLOUD

This book cover for Sean McCloud's *Divine Hierarchies* illustrates how symmetry can create a state of visual equilibrium and balance through the effective and meaningful use of centered compositional elements, appropriate scale, color, value, and typographic style.

ROGERS ECKERSLEY
DESIGN
New York, New York, USA

TO HELP SEE
POSSIBILITIES
VISIT WWW.SVA.EDU

School of VISUAL ARTS

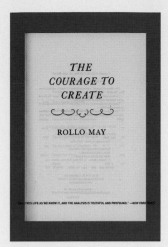

The typographic compositions for Rollo May's *The Courage to Create* and *Man's Search for Himself* both use symmetry as a guiding compositional principle, combined with vibrant colored frames and reviewer's pull quotes to further reinforce the dynamic, relational balance between these two book covers.

MOTHER DESIGN
New York, New York, USA

Rotative
Rotating equivalent elements in an outward direction from a common center point while drawing attention inward is identified as rotative symmetry. This can occur at any angle or frequency as long as its elements share a common center point. Arabesque and mandala patterns are examples of man-made rotative symmetry. A sunflower is an example of rotative symmetry found in nature.

Translative
This type of symmetry is created by locating equivalent elements in different areas of a composition. Translative symmetry can occur in any direction and over any distance as long as the basic orientation of its design elements is maintained. Continuous patterns found in architectural surfaces such as façades, friezes, and pediments are primary examples of translative symmetry.

Aside from its aesthetic properties, symmetry has other characteristics that are potentially beneficial to graphic designers. Symmetrical forms are seen as figure elements rather than ground elements in any visual composition. They traditionally receive more attention and are more memorable than any other compositional organiza-tions. Symmetrical forms are also simpler than asymmetrical forms, which makes them more immediate and recognizable in a visual composition to the reader's eye.

This promotional poster for the School of Visual Arts is based on a common eye test chart as well as the compositional design principle of symmetry and was designed to catch the attention of prospective students as they traveled the New York City subway system.

MIRKO ILIĆ
New York, New York, USA

Bilateral symmetry is an integral compositional principle used on this brightly colored, triangular background pattern as well as with the decorative typographic and line elements contained within the larger triangular frame used on these wine labels for Tratturi Primitivo.

LOUISE FILI LTD.
New York, New York, USA

asym·me·try \\(ˌ)ā-ˈsi-mə-trē\\ *n*
1: lack of balance or symmetry

"Asymmetry is the rhythmic expression of functional design."
JAN TSCHICHOLD (1902-1974), *German-Swiss, Author, Book Designer, Educator, Typographer*

Asymmetry is the opposite of symmetry. Asymmetrical balance, also called informal balance, means without symmetry. This definition by itself has nothing to do with balance. It means only that images within a composition do not mirror one another. The term, however, is usually used to

The symbol for Overture, a web search engine, is composed of a series of concentric *O*'s organized in an asymmetrical perspective that further conveys balance and movement, as well as referencing a target, informational hierarchy, and unlimited reach. This asymmetrical symbol also takes on an added visual dynamic when used as a greeting in reflected neon, cropped top and bottom, and interpreted as an environmental graphic wall mural.

C+G PARTNERS LLC
New York, New York, USA

describe a kind of balance that does not rely upon the principle of symmetry. With asymmetry, one dominant form or compositional element is often offset by smaller forms or compositional elements. In general, asymmetrical compositions tend to have a greater sense of visual tension than symmetrically balanced compositions.

References in Nature
Asymmetry in nature is uncommon and is a skill development trait identified as "handedness," a property of an object (such *(continued on page 134)*

J. Christopher Capital's business stationery is identified with a centered monogramlike logotype and organized within asymmetrical compositions for its letterhead, envelope, and business card.

HINTERLAND
New York, New York, USA

1937

Konstruktivisten Poster
JAN TSCHICHOLD
Basel, Switzerland

JAN TSCHICHOLD (1902–1974) was born in Leipzig, Germany, the eldest son of a sign painter and calligrapher. He studied calligraphy, engraving, typography, and book arts at Leipzig's Academy for Graphic Arts and Book Production. Soon after establishing himself as a graphic designer, he became aware of the need for a new approach to typography.

At the time, typography was based on the principle of centered type or symmetry, using frame, border, and ornament to provide further texture, distinction, and individuality to each composition. Tschichold identified this approach as the "box block style" of typography, an approach that was predictable, uninteresting, and outdated.

In August 1923, he attended the first Bauhaus exhibition in Weimar and quickly started to assimilate this new design philosophy. Influenced and informed by the work of modern avant-garde artists and designers such as Herbert Bayer, Paul Klee, El Lissitzky, and Piet Zwart, Tschichold wanted to liberate visual form from its restrictive rules and provide designers with greater freedom and flexibility.

He believed that typographic information had to be purely functional and composed in a clear and precise manner, or else it would be ignored. Starting in 1925, he began writing a series of articles and publications proposing a revolutionary approach to a "new" typography—an approach strongly influenced by both the Bauhaus and the Russian Constructivists.

The major tenets of the New Typography were asymmetric compositions of elements based on their relative importance, the preference for sans serif type, and the creative use of white space. These tenets were ultimately summarized in Tschichold's treatise titled *Die Neue Typographie* (*The New Typography*, 1928) and in *Typographische Gestaltung* (*Asymmetric Typography*, 1935).

In 1926, he was appointed by Paul Renner to teach typography and lettering at the Munich Meisterschule fur Deutschlands Buchdrucker, and he continued to lecture there until 1933.

In 1933, Tschichold was arrested and accused by the Nazis of being a "cultural Bolshevik," creating "un-German" typography. Soon after his release, he and his family immigrated to Basel, Switzerland. In the later part of his life, Tschichold ultimately embraced principles of both symmetry and asymmetry, as well as the use of serif and sans serif typography in his work.

Jan Tschichold and *Die Neue Typographie*

Kho Liang Ie, *Garden Chair*, 1960
inv. no. 2003020; version with armrests
inv. no. 20070018
Steel tube, black enamelled; plastic
42.5 × 80 × 57 × 58 cm; ø 22 mm
CAR, Katwijk
Lit.: I. van Ginneke, *Kho Liang Ie*, Rotterdam 1986,
pp. 49, 92; P. Vöge & B. Westerveld, *Stoelen;
Nederlandse ontwerpen 1945–1985*, Amsterdam
1986, pp. 57, 110

This garden chair has a frame of curved and welded, black-lacquered steel tubing. The seat and backrest are made of self-supporting, orange-red synthetic strips that are attached to the frame by means of clamps of the same material. These synthetic strips are all identical and have been manufactured using the injection moulding technique. The legs end in rubber studs. The frame of the model with armrests is lacquered grey, the strips are identical. The orange-red synthetic caps on the armrests are blind-riveted to the tubular metal supports.

CAR was a company that was primarily engaged in producing practical and budget-oriented furniture. The firm manufactured tubular constructions for canteen chairs and tables, terrace furniture, office furniture, and hall chairs. Almost all the furniture that Kho Liang Ie designed for the CAR company was quite simple, and the accent lay on its suitability for industrial production and modular construction. The designs for models 305/315 and 309 were reasonably successful. A variation in seats and backrests, in either wood or synthetic material and upholstered if required, could be mounted on the subframes. In the 309 series, the subframe had two steel tubular extremities to which a plastic seat could easily be attached. The plastic components were ordered in the Far East and assembled in the factory in Katwijk. (see inv. nos. 20070009, 20070014).

In the more adventurous design for the strip chairs, technology could not cope with the designer's ideas. In terms of form, this chair was far ahead of its time: the red plastic strips gave the chair an extremely futuristic appearance. Unfortunately, it turned out that the design was also far ahead of developments in the synthetics industry. Under the influence of sunlight, the material rapidly declined in quality, becoming fragile and brittle. The attachment of the strips by means of synthetic caps also proved to be impractical and vulnerable. After a few months, the decision was taken to halt production. If the chair had been developed a few years later, these problems would probably not have arisen and the chair would undoubtedly have become a classic.

102

---

as a living organism) that is not identical with its mirror image. This is fully evident in a person's tendency to use one hand rather than the other.

Other examples of handedness and left-right asymmetries in nature are the left dolphin lung that is smaller than the right to make room for its asymmetrical heart; a fiddler crab's different-size large and small claws; the narwhal's left incisor tusk, which can grow up to 10 feet (3 m) long and form a left-handed helix; the eyes of a flatfish, located on one side of its head so it swims with one side upward; and several species of owls whose size and ear position assists them in locating their prey.

Compositional Characteristics

Asymmetry is achieved when one side of a visual composition does not reflect the other side. Asymmetrical balance is a type of visual balance in which compositional elements are organized so that one side differs from the other without impacting the composition's overall harmony. Consequently, when an asymmetrical composition is disturbingly off balance, the result is jarring and disorienting.

As a compositional principle of visual communications, asymmetrical balance is more complex and more difficult to achieve than symmetrical balance. It involves organizing compositional elements in a way that will allow elements of varying visual weight

The asymmetrical balance of this page spread is achieved simply with the effective use of scale, proportion, and grid. Reliance on extreme large- and small-scale photographic images, a dynamic layout of typographic columnar text, and activation of a flexible page grid all add to the visual impact and kinetic qualities that can be achieved with an asymmetrical composition.

JOOST GROOTENS
Amsterdam, The Netherlands

This poster for promoting developing artists' films and videos throughout the United Kingdom relies upon the immediacy and power of pure typography and is organized in an asymmetrical composition to gain and hold the viewer's attention. An obvious hierarchy of typographic sizes and colors, as well as the use of horizontal, linear rules to highlight, group, and separate information, makes this poster easily and readily accessible to the reader.

FRASER MUGGERIDGE
London, United Kingdom

PICTURE THIS

WWW.PICTURE-THIS.ORG.UK

Developing artists' film and video through commissions, exhibitions and research

DOWN AT THE BAMBOO CLUB: FILM, PARTICIPATION AND RE-ENACTMENT
VICTOR ALIMPIEV   BARBY ASANTE
DAVID MALJKOVIĆ   MANDY MCINTOSH
IAIN FORSYTH   MARK WILSHER
& JANE POLLARD

BRISTOL MEAN TIME RESIDENCY
RACHEL REUPKE

VISUAL ARTISTS IRELAND RESIDENCY
LINDA QUINLAN

PRAYER PROJECT
DAPHNE WRIGHT

SLOW ACTION
BEN RIVERS

INTERNATIONAL FAUNA (A RELATIONAL COMMISSION FOR ANTI-BODIES)
MELANIE JACKSON

DIEGO GARCIA
AIKATERINI GEGISIAN

WAY OF THE GOAT
VARSITY OF MANEUVERS

THE NIGHT-TIME ROOM
RONNIE CLOSE

ASSOCIATE DANCE ARTIST
LISA MAY THOMAS

and a forthcoming project by
HITO STEYERL

Picture This   ARTS COUNCIL ENGLAND

This 74-foot-high (22.6 m) sandblasted limestone tablet engraved with the forty-five words of the First Amendment is traditionally composed with serif all-cap letterforms in an asymmetrical organization, and located on the modernist, all-glass façade of the Newseum building, also in an asymmetrical manner. This treatment accentuates the large-scale typography as a bas-relief and permanently displays the first amendment as a timeless element set in a modern context.

POULIN + MORRIS INC.
New York, New York, USA

to balance one another around an axis or pivot point. This can be best visualized as a literal balance scale that represents visual weights in a two-dimensional composition. For example, it is possible to balance a heavy weight with a group of lighter weights on equal sides of a pivot point. In a visual composition, this might be a cluster of small elements balanced by a larger one. It is also possible to imagine compositional elements of equal weight but different mass (such as a large mass of feathers versus a small mass of stones), on equal sides of a pivot point. Unequal visual weights can also be balanced by shifting the pivot on this imaginary scale.

Maison Theatre's playful and childlike symbol is composed of two triangular, transparent color shapes layered on top of one another to create a third unique triangular shape. An all-cap treatment of the theater's name functions as a typographic base for this asymmetrically balanced symbol. To further appeal to a youthful audience, the symbol is applied to a variety of print collateral materials with bright saturated colors, hand-drawn letterforms and script lettering, and triangular patterning—all active and dynamic asymmetrical compositions, reinforcing the unique, visual character of the theatre's overall message and brand.

LG2BOUTIQUE
Montreal, Quebec, Canada

MONNET DESIGN
Toronto, Ontario, Canada

13

Asymmetrical balance is informal and generally more active and dynamic than symmetrical balance. While symmetrical balance is achieved through repetition, asymmetrical balance is completely dependent upon contrast and counterpoint in a composition. It results from combining contrasting design elements, such as point, line, shape, form, and color, evenly distributed along an axis of a composition.

Asymmetry is also a compositional state where elements are organized in a nonsystematic and organic manner to achieve visual balance. This type of visual balance relies upon the critical interaction and integrity of

The book cover for *The Good Men Project: Real Stories from the Front Lines of Modern Manhood* uses asymmetry to create visual tension, balance, and eye-catching recognition for the buyer and reader. These characteristics are further strengthened with the effective use of an iconic photographic image, bold typography, vibrant color, and distinctive proportions.

POULIN + MORRIS INC.
New York, New York, USA

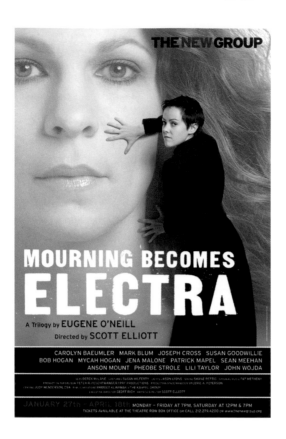

The varying visual weight of the photographic and typographic elements in this promotional poster for **The New Group Theater** creates an asymmetrical composition that is fully balanced due to contrasts and counterpoints evident in the scale, color, and tone of the poster's compositional elements.

ROGERS ECKERSLEY
DESIGN
New York, New York, USA

compositional elements and negative space, as well as their location and proximity to one another, to create tension, balance, and meaning in any visual communication.

These types of balanced compositions are inherently active and kinetic, and communicate the same to the viewer.

Asymmetrical compositions require a more disciplined and analytical eye due to their unique and ever-changing spatial requirements. Here the graphic designer has to constantly and consistently evaluate and assess potential compositional solutions based on spatial relationships varying from element to element and size to size, whether positive or negative, figure or ground.

In visual communications, the graphic designer's reliance on the principle of asymmetry in creating asymmetrical compositions increases the viewer's ability to organize, differentiate, and interact with a broad range of visual content.

The overall asymmetrical composition of this brochure cover for the **Old Police Headquarters** building, a renovated, historic, mixed-use real estate development in downtown **San Diego**, is reinforced by smaller asymmetrical characteristics of the cover—the composition of its typographic elements and the cropping of its photographic image as well as the cropping

and placement of the project symbol bleeding off the right-hand edge of the cover.

URBAN INFLUENCE
DESIGN STUDIO
Seattle, Washington, USA

Future Flight, a promotional poster for the Australian Graphic Design Association, functions as an announcement for a series of member programs and offerings. The immediacy and dynamic visual character of this poster is solely due to its asymmetrical composition. Additionally, the use of varied colors and scales of paper planes, as well as their illusive appearance of ascending and flying beyond the edges limitations of the poster, strengthens the asymmetry of this composition.

LANDOR
Paris, France

The asymmetrical composition and organization of this website's navigational elements for Mac Industries, a precision machining and fabrication company, allow the user to easily access various types of information, sections, and tools in a logical and easily understandable user-friendly sequence.

INFINITE SCALE DESIGN
Salt Lake City, Utah, USA

ten·sion \'ten(t)-shən\ *n*

3 c: a balance maintained in artistic work between opposing forces or elements

14

"Tension is the great integrity."
RICHARD BUCKMINSTER FULLER (1895-1983), *American, Architect, Author, Inventor*

The principle of tension in visual communications is critical to effective graphic design. Tension is primarily a visual, as well as psychological, attention-getting device. It is also a tenuous balance maintained between opposing formal elements, often causing anxiety, stress, angst, or excitement,

Color and compositional placement are two key factors in creating a visual tension with this identity program for **BPI**, a lighting design consultancy. The lowercase, tri-letter acronym is always located at the lower edge of any print collateral so that the descender of the *p* can touch and bleed off the bottom edge. This visual tension is also reinforced with a vibrant fluorescent yellow used consistently throughout this program, whether figure or ground.

POULIN + MORRIS INC.
New York, New York, USA

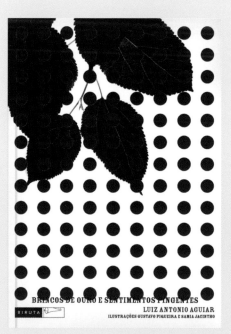

exuberance, and joy for the viewer. Tension and balance are interrelated principles in visual communications. Like balance, tension is an obvious and constant presence in our everyday lives. Unfortunately, we cannot experience one of them without the other. When something is out of balance in our life, we feel tense and anxious. For example, when we observe a daring feat, such as a high-wire act at a circus, it makes us feel uneasy and tense since there is always a potential for the performer to fall. The same experiences and emotions can be conveyed and ultimately felt in any visual message.

(continued on page 145)

This set of book covers for **Biruta**, a Brazilian publishing house, uses visual tension as an eye-catching device. Each cover layers a high-contrast black-and-white photographic image turned and cropped in an unusual and jarring orientation with an over-scaled dot pattern. The effect is bold, dynamic, and relevant to each book theme, and full of compositional imbalance.

CASA REX
São Paulo, Brazil

1923

Laga Company Advertisement
PIET ZWART
Amsterdam, The Netherlands

PIET ZWART (1885–1977), a Dutch craftsman, draftsman, and architect, was born in Zaandijk, an industrial area north of Amsterdam. From 1902 to 1907, he attended Amsterdam's School of Arts and Crafts, where he became interested in architecture. His early work involved designing textiles, furniture, and interiors in a style that showed his affinity for de Stijl.

Zwart was influenced by many of the modern, avant-garde movements of the early twentieth century, as well as Tschichold's *The New Typography*. He was one of the first modernist designers in Holland to apply the principles of de Stijl and Constructivism to commercial advertising during the 1920s.

From 1921 to 1927, Zwart worked for H. P. Berlage, the most influential Dutch architect of the era. While working in Berlage's office, he received his first typographic commission and designed the first of many advertisements for Laga Company, a Dutch flooring manufacturer.

These dynamic and arresting advertisements are early examples of Zwart's interest in typography, pure compositional form, and asymmetrical tension. Here, he mostly used found type and letterforms from various printers' cases. While photographs and photomontage were used sparingly, when he did rely on these forms, they were never used as embellishment or decoration. Every visual element, whether typographic or photographic, was used to collectively create a more meaningful and powerful message.

With this early work, Zwart rejected conventional symmetry and traditional typographic rules. He considered the design of a visual composition as a "field of tension" brought to life with a combination of asymmetrical balance, contrasts of size and weight of elements, and a dynamic interaction between positive and negative space.

Zwart synthesized two very distinct and contradictory points of view in his work—the Constructivist movement's visual playfulness and de Stijl's formal functionality. He ultimately created a unified language that has prevailed for the last eighty years and to this day strongly influences contemporary designers.

Piet Zwart and Laga Company

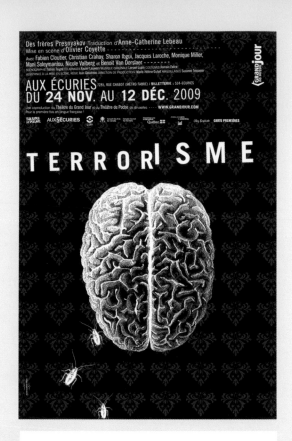

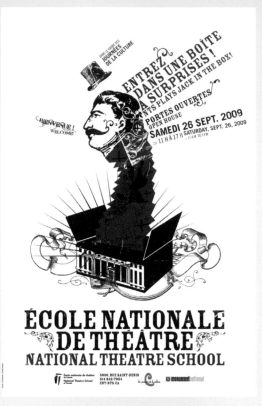

Visual tension is used as an eye-catching, riveting, attention-getting principle in these four posters for Montreal-based theater companies. Gestural hand-drawn letterforms, bold emotional line illustrations, and angular typographic compositions all add to the dynamic contrasts and imbalances evident in these theatrical posters.

LAURENT PINABEL
Montreal, Quebec, Canada

Characteristics and Effects

Tension is a critical compositional element that depends completely on opposing visual forces. In the related fields of applied and performing arts, such as architecture, music, and dance, the same holds true. In architecture, monumental structure is juxtaposed with curvilinear, natural form in the Eiffel Tower and the Guggenheim Museum. In music, loud sounds compete with soft tones in the compositions of Tchaikovsky and Philip Glass. In dance, movement appears harsh and irregular with fluid and gentle gestures in the choreography of Martha Graham and Merce Cunningham.

Tension can be realized through a wide range of contrasts and imbalances—between medium and message, form and content, pattern and texture, scale and proportion. It results from opposing forces and unresolved relationships, not only in visual form but also in narrative content.

It can also be achieved through the compositional element of space. Varied proximity of elements can result in visual tension that brings an apparent and dynamic interest to a composition. Equal and regular spacing creates visual static and uniformity.

A simple, asymmetrically placed graphic line not only creates a palatable, visual tension on this cover for *The Prisoner of Guantanamo*, it immediately communicates the emotional, firsthand experience of the novel. It also represents the political, emotional, conceptual, and relevant spirit of the book's narrative, as well as literally illustrating what it looks like to peer through the prison gates toward the beaches of Cuba.

JOHN GALL
New York, New York, USA

The John P. McNulty Prize, in association with Aspen Institute, supports extraordinary young leaders making creative, effective, and lasting contributions to their communities. The program's logotype is organized in three vertical bands anchored to the upper right-hand corner of any print collateral, creating a visual tension and excitement that is an essential character of the program. Color and typography are also used effectively and to further reinforce this compositional dynamic.

POULIN + MORRIS INC.
New York, New York, USA

For example, a space between two or more elements can affect not only their spatial relationship but also the perception of that relationship by the viewer. As these two or more elements move together, a visual tension can result. When they touch, a new shape or hybrid shape is created, and at some point, as they move apart, they become disassociated with one another. The graphic designer can think of tension as a conversation in which compositional elements communicate with one another. This conversation can be quiet and understated, or it can be loud and chaotic. The resulting dialogue can be affected profoundly by the position and number of elements in a composition. Proximity groupings can create patterns, a sense of rhythm, or other visual relationships that can elicit a response from the viewer. However, the graphic designer needs to keep in mind that this visual conversation should always be in support of the message's content.

Tension can also be created by the imbalance of design elements in a composition. With asymmetrical compositions, visual tension is in response to gravity and its obvious effect on the individual elements.

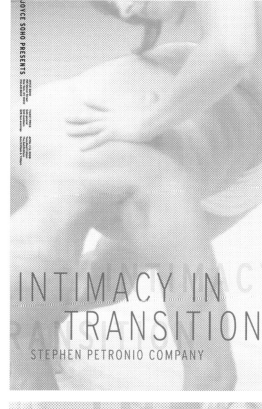

This poster series for the Stephen Petronio Company is a thorough study in spatial tension. Each composition is an integral representation of visual tension and balance, effectively using cropped photographic images contrasted with horizontal and vertical typographic elements, and varied layers of color and dot patterns— all collectively strengthening the tension between elements as well as the composition of each poster.

LAURA GRALNICK, Student
RICHARD POULIN, Instructor
School of Visual Arts
New York, New York, USA

The intersection of two extremely different-size lines of typography, combined with their alternating direction and orientation, adds to the visual tension and distinctive visual character of this graphic identity program for Pfau Long Architecture. Saturated and muted colors also contrast with one another, creating another level of visual tension.

PUBLIC INC.
San Francisco, California, USA

It can create varied degrees and levels of excitement and visual tension depending on the degree of asymmetry.

Our lives are filled with opposites— happy, sad, angry, calm, crying, laughing. Effective visual communications echo these opposites in our lives, making us connect and engage with them in a much more immediate and meaningful way. This language of opposites is a language of tension, and it helps us understand so many things and experiences.

Visual tension speaks to the good and the bad, the easy and the difficult—in life, as well as in graphic design. Effective visual communications is often filled with tension.

A single vertical rule placed between the words *support* and *resist* in the title of this book creates a visual tension in a powerful and immediate way. This graphic rule also symbolizes the essence of the book's content, which celebrates design innovation in structural engineering.

THINK STUDIO
New York, New York, USA

These page spreads from the School of Visual Arts' *Senior Library* show how disparate, unrelated visual images can be cropped and paired to create a balanced, visual tension that ultimately provides unity and cohesiveness to the totality of each page spread, as well as to the overall book.

POULIN + MORRIS INC.
New York, New York, USA

clo·sure \ˈklō-zhər\ *n*
1: the process or ability to fill in missing parts of a visual stimulus; a Gestalt principle of visual organization holding that there is an innate tendency to perceive incomplete objects as complete

15

"**Imagination is the beginning of creation. You imagine what you desire, you will what you imagine and at last you create what you will.**"

GEORGE BERNARD SHAW (1856-1950), *Irish, Playwright*

In visual communications, closure can basically be described as a visual illusion. Closure literally means the act of closing or the condition of being closed. It is also a definitive finish or conclusion. As human beings, we have an innate need to make sense of what we see; therefore, if we anticipate

In the identity, stationery, and website for the Max Protetch Gallery, the appearance of the *x* in the logotype is only partially closed and incomplete, bringing an additional visual nuance to the overall program. This form of closure provides an interactive engagement with the viewer, allowing them to fill in the blanks and ultimately create a visual conclusion.

LAURA GRALNICK, Student
RICHARD POULIN, Instructor
School of Visual Arts
New York, New York, USA

maxprotetch

maxprotetch

STUART KRIMKO

511 West 22nd Street New York, NY 10011
T 212.633.6999 stuart@maxprotetch.com

511 WEST 22ND STREET NEW YORK, NY 10011
T 212.633.6999 F 212.691.4342 INFO@MAXPROTETCH.COM

a form we will always complete it. In human nature, we are constantly searching for resolution in everything we see and do. We have been taught to strive for the perfect balance in our lives. Even when we experience something incomplete or imperfect, we continually look for closure or a better-balanced sense of resolution.

In personal relationships we always expect a happy ending. When this doesn't occur, we feel unrest and disappointment. This is a example of our basic human need for resolution. In visual communications, closure is an equivalent visual resolution.

Historical References

A classic representation of closure in art history is in Michelangelo's *The Creation of Man* on the ceiling of the Vatican's Sistine Chapel. Here, God is reaching his pointed finger outward toward the finger of Adam's hand. In our minds, the fingers appear to touch, symbolically representing creation and birth. The fingers do not touch, yet they are perfectly positioned to imply such. If they were any farther apart, or conversely, if they were touching, the quality of this critical compositional relationship, as well as the visual perception of closure, would be lost.

Visual Characteristics

Closure is completely dependent upon spatial relationships in a composition. It is used to create visual interest for viewers because it engages them to complete the composition in their own mind's eye.

It is also dependent on the distance from one object or shape to another. When related objects are too far apart from one another, they have no immediate and apparent visual relationship. When related objects are composed in close relationship to one (continued on page 154)

Precision and accuracy are the essential visual metaphors for this symbol identifying O'Shaughnessy Asset Management, a financial investment firm. A circular *O* letterform is pierced and interrupted by an arrowlike apostrophe pointing to its center. The viewer can immediately complete the full circular profile of the letterform; however, interrupting the letterform in this manner not only creates visual interest but also adds meaning to its overall message.

C+G PARTNERS LLC
New York, New York, USA

1955

Theaterbau von der Antike bis zur Moderne
(Theater Construction in Antiquity and Modernity)
Exhibition Poster
ARMIN HOFMANN
Zurich, Switzerland

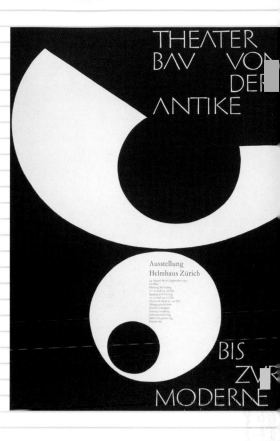

For over forty years, ARMIN HOFMANN (b. 1920) has devoted his life to teaching art, design, and the principles of visual perception and communications. His students' works are benchmarks of visual excellence, as well as the envy of students and teachers of graphic design worldwide.

In 1937, he studied foundation art at the Kunstgewerbeschule in Zurich; he also worked as a draftsman and lithography apprentice in Winterthur and as a lithographer and designer in various studios in Basel, Switzerland.

Hofmann began his career as an influential educator at the Allgemeine Gewerbeschule Basel School of Art and Crafts (later known as Schule fur Gestaltung or AGS) at the early age of 26. He followed Emil Ruder as the head of its graphic design department and was instrumental in developing the graphic design style known as the International Typographic Style or Swiss School.

His teaching methods and maxims were unorthodox and broad based, setting new standards that became widely known in design education institutions throughout the world. His independent insights as an educator, married with his rich and innovative powers of visual expression, created a body of work enormously varied—books, exhibitions, stage sets, logotypes, symbols, typography, sign systems, and most memorably, posters.

His exhibition poster titled *Theaterbau von der Antike bis zur Moderne* for the Austellung Helmhaus in Zurich is a simple, compositional study in black and white, figure–ground, and closure engaging the viewer with the compositional elements and principles of asymmetry, tension, contrast, and scale.

His posters are widely recognized for their contrasts in simplicity and complexity, representation and abstraction. They have a direct and immediate connection to the viewer's eye—engaging, challenging, and communicative. They pique interest and convey a clean and understandable message. Hofmann's posters are pure and symbolic visual statements. He has written that "a poster does more than simply supply information on the goods it advertises; it also reveals a society's state of mind."

Paul Rand, a close friend and longtime colleague of Armin Hofmann, has described Hofmann's contributions to the graphic design profession: "Few of us have sacrificed so much time, money and comfort for the sake of their profession as has Armin Hofmann. He is one of the few exceptions to Shaw's dictum, 'He who can, does; he who cannot, teaches.' His goals, though pragmatic, are never pecuniary. His influence has been as strong beyond the classroom as within it. Even those who are his critics are as eager about his ideas as those who sit at his feet. As a human being, he is simple and unassuming. As a teacher, he has few equals. As practitioner, he ranks among the best."

Armin Hofmann and the Austellung Helmhaus

The visual identity system for an exhibition titled *Graphic Design in China* relies solely on fluorescent light installations evident in each exhibition venue that spell out the names of each designer and disciplines represented in the exhibition. Custom letterform installations were photographed and used as primary visual elements in a series of pro-motional posters for the exhibition. These illuminated, stencil-like letterforms are another visual representation of the design principle of closure in graphic design.

SENSE TEAM
Shenzhen, China

another, they become meaningful and therefore related. They also become complements to one another, creating tension and engaging the viewer in a more immediate manner.

Closure is most successful when visual elements in a composition are simple and singular, recognizable patterns, such as geometric shapes. When shapes and patterns are not easily understood, they become unfamiliar; therefore, closure will not occur in the mind of the viewer.

Compositional Forms

The principle of closure refers to the condition of being closed. A form that is closed is fully described or complete. However, a form that is interrupted, partially closed, or incomplete can still be understood.

Closure is the recognition of meaning in an unclear or incomplete composition because the viewer has been able to draw on previous experiences to discover sufficient similarity between it and their own individual memories. It allows the viewer to bring something to an ultimate, visual conclusion.

By providing this opportunity in a composition, the graphic designer also creates an interactive experience for the viewer. They

Elements of this branding program for Bergen Street Studio, an architecture, planning, and interior design firm, rely upon the principle of closure to further engage the viewer. For example, the announcement card shows *bergenst* anchored to the right side of the card as if it continues off the page. On its reverse side, the word continues as *reet* as well as the full name of the firm. This compositional device is considered a form of visual closure, allowing the viewer to fill in the blank.

POULIN + MORRIS INC.
New York, New York, USA

scrap house

Stencil-like, typographic "scraps" or fragments give an unusual, hybrid appearance to these letterforms. The visually inconsistent characteristics of this logotype for Scrap House, a temporary demonstration home blitz-built using scrap and salvaged materials, provides visual interest and engages the viewer to complete this puzzlelike image.

MENDE DESIGN
San Francisco, California, USA

become engaged with the visual communication and therefore become more intimately involved with the visual process of assimilation, understanding, and memory.

Closure also provides us with balance and harmony. Visual closure gives the graphic designer the same results. Even if the goal of the designer is to create tension in a composition, closure is still part of the compositional equation.

This design principle enables graphic designers to reduce complexity and increase visual interest in a composition by relying upon simple and recognizable elements to communicate information. For example, a logotype composed of recognizable elements such as multiple, repetitive lines does not need to complete many or all of its lines and contours to be meaningful and effective. Reducing the number of lines in the logotype not only reduces the visual complexity of the logotype, it also makes it more engaging for the viewer to complete in their own mind.

Forms of Perception

Closure is a principle of visual perception where the eye tends to perceive a set of individual elements as a single, recognizable

Acquire New York, a licensed real estate brokerage firm, caters to affluent residential real estate buyers. Its logotype relies upon traditional serif typography, graphic patterning evocative of engraved currency and stock certificates, rich saturated colors, and fragmented linear brackets framing all of these elements into one cohesive unit. While a fully closed frame is not needed, it is implied through the visual principle of closure.

POULIN + MORRIS INC.
New York, New York, USA

whole as opposed to separate elements. It is also one of the principles of visual communication referred to as a "gestalt principle of perception," which means that we tend to perceive a single pattern so strongly that we will close gaps and fill in missing information to complete the pattern if necessary.

For example, when individual line segments are positioned along a circular path, they are first perceived holistically as a circle, and then as multiple, independent line segments. Our tendency to perceive information in this way is automatic and subconscious; it is most likely a function of an innate preference for simplicity over complexity, and pattern over randomness.

Many forms of visual storytelling rely upon closure in a similar way. For example, in film and in comic books, singular and discrete scenes are presented to the viewer, who in turn supplies what occurs in between each scene. Essential information is provided by the storyteller, and the remaining information is provided by the viewer.

By using this design principle effectively and creatively, a designer can enhance immediacy, interest, and understanding in any visual communication.

Coral Technologies is a systems software provider that bases their entire business on continuous communication and connection with their clients. Their symbol uses simple, stylized imagery to communicate this essential need for continuity with two separate and divorced icons. The viewer, however, perceives these icons immediately as a holistic whole before acknowledging that they are literally and visually distinct and separate.

TRIBORO DESIGN SOLUTIONS
Brooklyn, New York, USA

This acronym-based logotype for **BLT Architects**, a full-service architectural design firm, comprises a series of san serif monumental letterforms in two distinct weights and framed with two linear corner brackets. These two line elements imply a fully resolved, continuous, and articulated square frame; however, by using only partial fragments of the square, an illusion allows the viewer to close the frame in their own mind's eye.

POULIN + MORRIS INC.
New York, New York, USA

The large-scale, sans serif letterforms used in this poster for *La Radio dans le Noir* are of ample scale and familiarity to withstand the overlay of geometric forms that block and fragment their identity and reading. The viewer ultimately resolves each of these individual letterforms in their own mind, therefore retaining their identity and meaning as well as the overall visual impact and meaning of this powerful typographic composition.

CATHERINE ZASK
Paris, France

ex·pres·sion \ik-'spre-shən\ *n*
2 a: a mode, means, or use of significant representation or symbolism; *esp:* felicitous or vivid indication or depiction of mood or sentiment

16

"All that is good in art is the expression of one soul talking to another; and is precious according to the greatness of the soul that utters it."

JOHN RUSKIN (1819-1900), *English, Art Critic, Artist, Poet*

Expression is a design principle fully dependent on the graphic designer's individual ideas, personal moods, sole emotional outlook on the world, and place within it. It is perceived visually, as well as psychologically, in any visual message. It is also a completely subjective principle and reflects

The central image of this promotional poster for the School of Visual Arts combines visual metaphor and narrative form with the graphic designer's personal point of view, interpretation, and ultimate expression of creativity defined here as an organic, evolving process requiring nourishment and constant care.

GAIL ANDERSON
New York, New York, USA

directly on the time and experiences in which the designer has lived. Expression cannot be taught; it is learned by each and every graphic designer. It is also a reflection of the designer's inner thoughts, dreams, fears, and passions. As a result, an inherent bias completely depends upon our separate experiences or realities. Dreams, fantasies, and imagination also influence a designer's creative process and choices.

In everyday occurrences and interactions, we hear someone say that they have "expressed their opinion." However, visual expression is something more concrete, more specific, and more intentional. Meaningful and memorable visual expression occurs when the fundamental elements and principles of graphic design are used selectively and collectively by a graphic designer to create a "visual experience" for the viewer.

Since the beginning of human development, we have had the desire, as well as the basic need, to express ourselves. While graphic design as a discipline has had a relatively short history, with the name *graphic design* first coined by William Addison Dwiggins in 1922, visual communication and visual expression has always been an integral (continued on page 164)

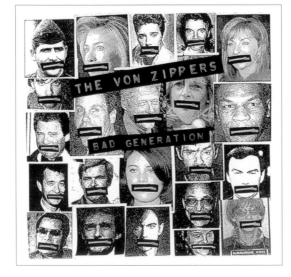

Utilitarian processes and found objects such as a photocopier, zippers, and a Dymo lettering machine are the designer's palette, so to speak, in expressing their point of view and interpretation of a "bad generation" for this CD cover.

ART CHANTRY DESIGN CO.
Tacoma, Washington, USA

1989

Les Noces Poster
BRUNO MONGUZZI
Lugano, Italy

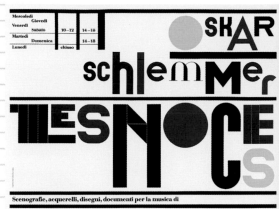

BRUNO MONGUZZI (b. 1941) was born in the small town of Ticino in the southern lake district of Switzerland. He studied graphic design at the Ecole des Arts Decoratifs in Geneva, and then in London.

During this time, he was influenced by the work of modernist designers such as Carlo Vivarelli, Josef Müller-Brockmann, Herbert Bayer, Jan Tschichold, and Piet Zwart. Monguzzi began his career in 1961 as a designer with Antonio Boggeri at Studio Boggeri in Milan, Italy, and remained there until its closing in the early 1980s.

Now residing in the secluded town of Meride, in northern Italy, Monguzzi is also a renowned teacher of graphic design, first in Lugano and later throughout the world. In 1981, Monguzzi was the sole curator and designer of the Studio Boggeri retrospective at the Milan Trienalle. In 1983, in collaboration with Jean Widmer's Visuel Design studio, he won the international competition for Paris's Musee d'Orsay's identity and sign system.

Monguzzi is known as a thoughtful and thought-provoking designer and educator. His professional work, as well as his teaching, has always focused on the enrichment and betterment of the human experience through visual expression in graphic design. He has consistently created modern and timeless work that is as visually rich as it is diverse in design, content, and ultimate meaning. It is also devoid of any specific style.

Monguzzi's work and has been admired by many of his colleagues and described as "street communication at its most impressive. Informational, elegant, bombastic, and magnetic. Always a great light on any city thoroughfare. . . . It takes hold of your eye with an initial onslaught of beauty, then sense, then he hands you the gift of intellectual communication."

From 1987 to 2004, he was the sole designer for Museo Cantonale d'Arte in Lugano. His poster titled *Les Noces* for the Museo is an emblematic example of how he has realized visual form as a true form of expression—enlivening, enriching, and enlightening. It is clear from this work that he has a passion for form, craft, and function as well as for history, which allows him to integrate the past with the present.

For example, in this poster Monguzzi uses thirty-six letterforms—twenty-two letters are from Herbert Bayer's alphabets, which are mostly from his Bauhaus Universal type variations of 1925; one letter is from Theo van Doesburg's work, four letters are of his own assemblage, and three are from Schlemmer's *The Husband's Prayer*. All of these letterforms are in some manner or another historically and thematically connected to either Oskar Schlemmer or Igor Stravinsky. In this context he, has used expressive and historical-relevant typographic letterforms as a means to marry the past with the present.

He is a true poet of expressive form and function.

Bruno Monguzzi and Museo Cantonale d'Arte

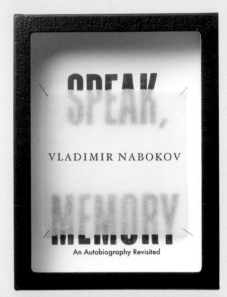

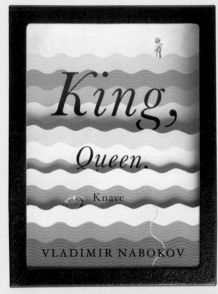

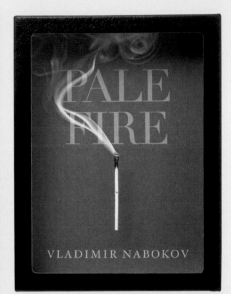

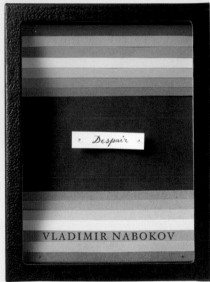

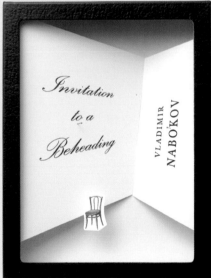

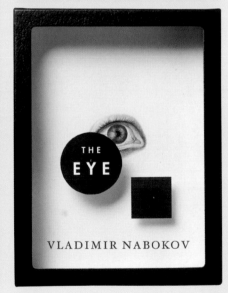

The redesign of a series of Vladimir Nabokov's book covers for Random House was a true exercise in collaboration and visual expression. Each cover was designed by a different graphic designer, whose sole requirement was to use the same black framed specimen box—the type used by collectors like Nabokov to display insects. Each box is then composed with paper, ephemera, insect pins, and the like, selected to evoke the book's content and theme. The designers represented here include Michael Bierut (*Speak Memory*), Peter Mendelsund (*King, Queen, Knave*), Stephen Doyle (*Pale Fire*), Barbara deWilde (*Stories*), Marian Bantjes (*Transparent Things*), Dave Eggers (*Laughter in the Dark*), Jason Fulford and Tamara Shopsin (*Despair*), Helen Yenthus and Jason Booher (*Invitation to a Beheading*), John Gall (*The Eye*), Chip Kidd (*Ada, or Ardor*) Carin Goldberg (*Pnin*), and Sam Potts (*The Real Life of Sebastian Knight*).

JOHN GALL
New York, New York, USA

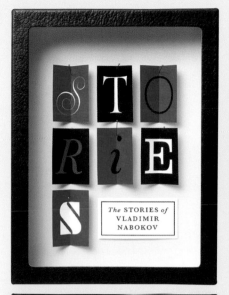

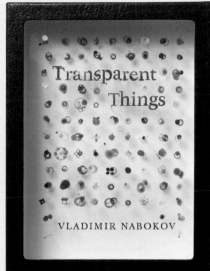

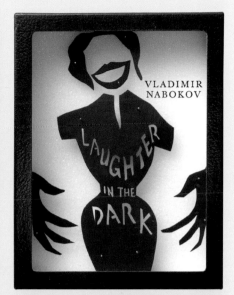

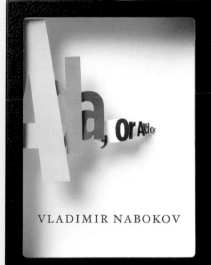

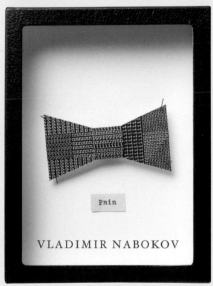

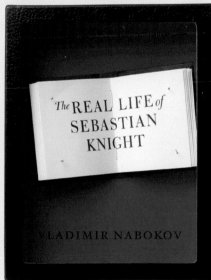

The duality of a playing card is the basis for this promotional poster celebrating "Amore y Arte" ("Love and Art") and the integral relationship between Frieda Kahlo and Diego Rivera, two of the most celebrated Mexican modernists of the 20th century.

CARBONE SMOLAN AGENCY
New York, New York, USA

part of our history. It is evident in the prehistoric cave paintings of northern Spain and southern France, in the Roman Forum's Trajan Column, in the illuminated medieval manuscripts of the Middle Ages, and in the mesmerizing neon signs of Times Square and Piccadilly Circus.

Expression is also a quality of inner experience or the emotions of the graphic designer communicated through other visual elements in a composition. Historically, this is evident in all forms of visual art, including painting and sculpture. The viewer cannot separate actual form and its integral expression when viewing memorable work such as Picasso's *Guernica*, the paintings of Jackson Pollock and Jean-Michel Basquiat, or the sculptures of Alexander Calder. Expression transcends all visual artists and graphic designers, as well as their own, individual personal experiences.

Visual communications provide a means for the graphic designer to "express" their imagination in ways that do not rely upon spoken or written language. Every element used in visual communications has the potential to express something. Although the explanation and ultimate use of design elements and principles may seem cut-and-dry,

МЕЂУ-
NARODNI
FESTIVAL
PROČITANIH
KNJIGA

Trg Marafor, Poreč

www.knjiznicaporec.hr

BOOKtiga 23.-25.IV.2009.
I. Međunarodni festival pročitanih knjiga 2008, Poreč, Trg Marafor

In keeping with the themes and goals of this festival of used books in which attendees buy, sell, and exchange books, the designers decided to add value to old and used goods by reusing the remaining posters from last year's festival. The new promotional posters were now more visually expressive due to the evidence of tattered edges, repainted fronts accentuating visible old text, and hand lettering used in lieu of digital typography. This concept and theme was also used throughout the rest of the visual campaign, including recycled and reprinted sponsor T-shirts and shopping bags.

STUDIO SONDA
Poreč, Croatia

Unusual, three-dimensional constructions representing de Stijl and Constructivism, a monochromatic "blanc" floral arrangement, animal fur, and kaleidoscopic colors all take on expressive meanings and messages when also representing the iconic black letter *T* of the *New York Times Style Magazine*.

JANET FROELICH
New York, New York, USA

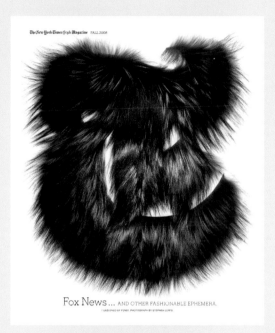

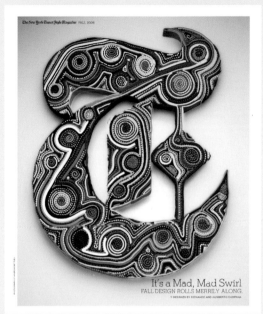

Une fête pour Boris

THOMAS BERNHARD / DENIS MARLEAU
du 24 au 27 FÉV. 2010

Théâtre Français
2009–2010
WAJDI MOUAWAD
DIRECTION ARTISTIQUE
VIDÉO + PHOTOS
CNA-NAC.CA/TF

AU STUDIO À 20 H
TEXTE DE **THOMAS BERNHARD** TRADUCTION DE CLAUDE PORCELL
MISE EN SCÈNE DE **DENIS MARLEAU**

AVEC SÉBASTIEN DODGE, CHRISTIANE PASQUIER ET GUY PION Conception, vidéo et scénographie : Stéphanie Jasmin et
Denis Marleau Montage et diffusion vidéo : Pierre Laniel Musiques : Nicolas Bernier et Jérôme Minière Design sonore : Nancy Tobin
Éclairages : Marc Parent Mannequins et poupées : Claude Rodrigue Costumes : Isabelle Larivière Maquillages et coiffures : Angelo Barsetti
UN SPECTACLE D'UBU COMPAGNIE DE CRÉATION · En coproduction avec le Festival d'Avignon, le Festival TransAmériques, l'Usine C, Le Manège
Mons, la Maison de la culture d'Amiens, l'Espace Jean Legendre Théâtre de Compiègne et Cankarjev Dom

CENTRE NATIONAL DES ARTS
NATIONAL ARTS CENTRE
BILLETTERIE DU CNA
lundi-samedi 10 h à 21 h
TARIFS DE GROUPE
613-947-7000 x384
BUZZ endirect
⏣ 90,7 ᶠᵐ PREMIÈRE CHAÎNE
ticketmaster.ca
613-755-1111

GEORG BÜCHNER /
BRIGITTE HAENTJENS

WOYZECK

du 9 au 13 FÉV. 2009

Théâtre Français
2009–2010
WAJDI MOUAWAD
DIRECTION ARTISTIQUE
VIDÉO + PHOTOS
CNA-NAC.CA/TF

AU THÉÂTRE À 19 H 30
TEXTE DE **GEORG BÜCHNER**
ADAPTATION POUR LA SCÈNE DE **BRIGITTE HAENTJENS**, AVEC LA COLLABORATION DE LOUIS BOUCHARD,
FANNY BRITT, STÉPHANE LÉPINE ET MARIE-ELISABETH MORF
MISE EN SCÈNE DE **BRIGITTE HAENTJENS**

AVEC PAUL AHMARANI, CATHERINE ALLARD, MARC BÉLAND, RAOUL FORTIER-MERCIER, PIERRE-ANTOINE LASNIER,
GAÉTAN NADEAU, SÉBASTIEN RICARD, ÉVELYNE ROMPRÉ ET PAUL SAVOIE Dramaturgie : Mélanie Dumont
Scénographie : Anick La Bissonnière Costumes : Yso Éclairages : Alexander MacSween Environnement sonore : Claude Cournoyer
Maquillages : Angelo Barsetti UN SPECTACLE DE SIBYLLINES

CENTRE NATIONAL DES ARTS
NATIONAL ARTS CENTRE
BILLETTERIE DU CNA
lundi-samedi 10 h à 21 h
TARIFS DE GROUPE
613-947-7000 x384
BUZZ endirect
⏣ 90,7 ᶠᵐ PREMIÈRE CHAÎNE
ticketmaster.ca
613-755-1111

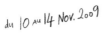

du 10 au 14 NOV. 2009

hedda gabler

HENRIK IBSEN
THOMAS OSTERMEIER

AU THÉÂTRE À 19 H30 — EXCLUSIVITÉ CANADIENNE
UN SPECTACLE DE LA SCHAUBÜHNE AM LEHNINER PLATZ (ALLEMAGNE) PRÉSENTÉ EN ALLEMAND AVEC SURTITRES FRANÇAIS ET ANGLAIS
TEXTE DE **HENRIK IBSEN**, TRADUCTION ALLEMANDE DE HINRICH SCHMIDT-HENKEL (ROWOHLT THEATER VERLAG, REINBEK)
MISE EN SCÈNE DE **THOMAS OSTERMEIER**

AVEC KAY BARTHOLOMÄUS SCHULZE, ANNEDORE BAUER, LARS EIDINGER, JORG HARTMANN, LORE STEFANEK
ET KATHARINA SCHÜTTLER Scénographie : Jan Pappelbaum Costumes : Nina Wetzel Éclairages : Erich Schneider
Musique : Malte Beckenbach Dramaturgie : Marius von Mayenburg Vidéo : Sébastien Dupouey

CENTRE NATIONAL DES ARTS
NATIONAL ARTS CENTRE
BILLETTERIE DU CNA
lundi-samedi 10 h à 21 h
TARIFS DE GROUPE
613-947-7000 x384
BUZZ endirect
⏣ 90,7 ᶠᵐ PREMIÈRE CHAÎNE
ticketmaster.ca
613-755-1111

Théâtre Français
2009–2010
WAJDI MOUAWAD
DIRECTION ARTISTIQUE
VIDÉO + PHOTOS
CNA-NAC.CA/TF

du 14 au 17 OCT. 2009

HIPPOCAMPE

PASCAL BRULLEMANS / ERIC JEAN

AU STUDIO À 20 H
TEXTE DE PASCAL BRULLEMANS, EN COLLABORATION AVEC ERIC JEAN ET LES ARTISTES
MISE EN SCÈNE D'ERIC JEAN

AVEC DOMINIC ANCTIL, MURIEL DUTIL, ANNE-SYLVIE GOSSELIN, DOMINIQUE QUESNEL, ISABELLE LAMONTAGNE,
GAÉTAN NADEAU ET SACHA SAMAR Scénographie : Magalie Amyot Costumes : Stéphanie Cloutier Éclairages : Étienne Boucher
Conception sonore : Jean-François Pednô Maquillages et coiffures : Angelo Barsetti UN SPECTACLE DU THÉÂTRE DE QUAT'SOUS

CENTRE NATIONAL DES ARTS
NATIONAL ARTS CENTRE
BILLETTERIE DU CNA
lundi-samedi 10 h à 21 h
TARIFS DE GROUPE
613-947-7000 x384
BUZZ endirect
⏣ 90,7 ᶠᵐ PREMIÈRE CHAÎNE
ticketmaster.ca
613-755-1111

Hand-drawn, black letter-forms and line illustrations, dynamically cropped and composed, are extremely expressive visual elements communicating the intense, emotional, and araw power of each of these theatrical productions—*Une Fête pour Boris*, *Hedda Gabler*, *Hippocampe*, and *Woyzeck*.

These unusual, unconventional, and highly expressive hand-built letterforms spell out the statement "Good Work" and are composed of drawing pencils—a clear and meaningful message for any designer who values the interconnection between the "medium and the message."

the quality of these elements and principles is perceived solely through the expression of the total message.

Imagery, such as photography and illustration, is the most powerful form of visual expression. When used in combination with typography, color, and other relevant design elements, it can create a distinct and memorable message that will always be associated with a specific human emotion. Understanding form, shape, line, space, and color is also essential to visual expression. With these tools, a graphic designer can fully embrace, as well as explore, new concepts, technologies, materials, and styles with confidence and assurance.

Unlike narrative form in which words are organized in a specific sequence to form sentences, visual expression provides a range of forms, symbols, and ideas with malleable meanings. It can help graphic designers achieve greater power and influence in their craft and discipline—a power to inform, educate, and/or persuade a single person or collective audience in a meaningful and memorable way.

A series of bold and expressive monochromatic textures are used as simple and unique visual metaphors for capturing the spirit and flavors of Mijovi and each of its products. Combined with bold sans serif lowercase typography and bright saturated colors, this packaging not only stands out among the overcrowded shelves of competing products but also communicates the essential brand message of this line of beverages. The imagery is metaphorically derived and symbolizes the spirit of individuality, energy, and ultimate self-expression.

ab·strac·tion \ab-'strak-shən, əb-\ *n*

1: considered apart from concrete existence

2: not applied or practical; theoretical

3: having intellectual and affective artistic content that depends solely on intrinsic form rather than on narrative content or pictorial representation

17

"A designer knows that he has achieved perfection not when there is nothing left to add, but when there is nothing left to take away."

ANTOINE DE SAINT-EXUPÉRY (1900-1944), *French, Author*

Abstraction is independent of our visual world. It is an illusion of our own visible reality and solely a sensory experience. In graphic design, abstraction provides us with alternative ways of communicating visual messages containing specific facts and experiences. It is a visual language that does

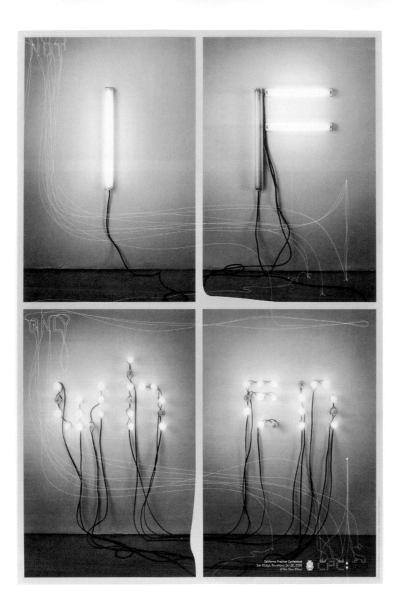

Simplification and distillation of letterforms using different light fixtures and bulbs is the primary visual metaphor for this promotional poster announcing an American Institute of Architects San Diego-sponsored conference. The conference title, "If Not, Then When?" spelled out in an abstract manner further conveys the theme of the conference, which explores how the practice of architecture is being transformed in the twenty-first century.

MENDE DESIGN
San Francisco, California, USA

not rely upon the literal nature of things— familiar and identifiable to us in our own world. Relying on an abstract visual language can reshape the familiar into the expressive. It is free from objective content, context, and meaning. It can be symbolic, interpretive, imaginary, impressionistic, nonrepresentational, nonobjective, or nonfigurative.

Historical References

Abstraction is not a twentieth-century phenomenon. It has been a part of our visual language since early mankind. From naïve *(continued on page 173)*

The abstract outline of a heart in this symbol suggests a human-centered approach to healthcare, beyond the traditional realms of science, chemistry, and manufacturing for the pharmaceutical company Kyorin. Continuing this human viusal metaphor, the center of the symbol is an "inner smile."

C+G PARTNERS LLC
New York, New York, USA

Nightwood Book Cover
ALVIN LUSTIG
New York, New York, USA

NIGHTWOOD

djuna barnes

One of the most prolific collaborations between a graphic designer and client in twentieth-century American design was the one shared by ALVIN LUSTIG (1915–1955) and the progressive publisher New Directions Books in the 1940s and 1950s. During this time period, Lustig designed dozens of groundbreaking book covers and jackets for the Modern Reader and New Classics book series for New Directions.

A designer, writer, and educator in Los Angeles and New York City, Lustig was one of the first designers to approach his craft and profession in a nonspecialized manner. He believed that all design was a matter of form and content and that the role of the designer was that of a synthesizer, not of a style maker. His diverse work included books, book jackets, advertisements, magazines, trademarks, letterheads, catalogs, record albums, sign systems, furniture, textile design, interior design, product design, and architecture.

Lustig's first New Directions book covers began as an experiment with geometric patterns, but soon he was adapting forms familiar to him from his knowledge of modern painting. Within a few years, Lustig was incorporating biomorphic glyphs or what he called symbolic "marks" that recalled the work of abstract modernist painters such as Paul Klee, Joan Miró, Clifford Still, and Mark Rothko. His most striking and memorable book jackets combined modern typography with complex fields of line, shape, form, color, texture, and image.

He explained, "The primary intention in designing the book jackets of the New Directions series was to establish for each book a quickly grasped, abstract symbol of its contents that would be sheer force of form and color, attract and inform the eye.

Such a symbol is a matter of distillation, a reduction of the book to its simplest terms of mood or idea. The spirit of the book cannot be expressed by naturalistic representation of episodes or by any preconceived formal approach, but can only develop naturally from its own nature."

The reliance on modernist visual form was a means of communicating the book publisher's commitment to an intellectual literary tradition distinct from the mainstream—a new and sophisticated visual language that at once created and affirmed New Directions' place within a highly competitive and overcrowded market.

Lustig's visionary "distillation" of form and image developed into a complex, abstract, efficient, and resolutely modern visual language, simplified yet never simplistic, unique yet never forgettable.

Alvin Lustig and New Directions

This book cover series for a set of **Irvine Welsh** novels uses abstracted illustrations to further enhance the graphic design of each cover as well as convey the raw, emotional themes of each book. Saturated colors, bold sans serif, all cap letterforms, and textures collectively add power and impact to the expressive qualities of these cover compositions.

JAMUS MARQUETTE,
Student
KEVIN BRAINARD, Instructor
School of Visual Arts
New York, New York, USA

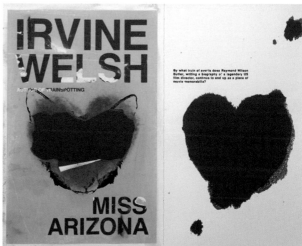

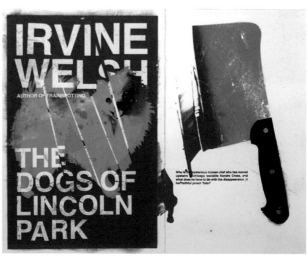

graphic gestures found in prehistoric cave paintings and stylized hieroglyphs in Egyptian funereal tombs to graphic emblems used in medieval science, heraldry, and religious rituals, abstraction is an integral design principle in all of these visual forms.

Levels of Abstraction

Abstract visual language is created by simplifying and distilling form and content. It depends solely upon its own intrinsic form rather than on narrative content or pictorial representation. A graphic designer who relies upon abstraction as a means to communicate a visual message also requires the viewer to connect immediately, intuitively, and emotionally with that same message.

There are different degrees or levels of abstraction in visual communications, from the least abstract to the most abstract.

For example, a photographic image (closer to a true representation than any other image type, such as illustration) has the lowest level of abstraction, since it only replicates the actual content or meaning of the actual image. Exact duplication of the reality represented in a photographic image is not possible because that reality is distorted as soon as the photographer takes

The cracked slab of limestone used in this poster is an abstract visual metaphor representing the legendary city of Bam and its citadel located in southern Iran, which was among the world's most famous architectural landmarks. In 2003, an earthquake destroyed the city and caused the death of more than 40,000 people. For the first anniversary of this earthquake, this promotional poster announced an exhibition and conference on the potential renovation of the city.

DID GRAPHICS INC.
Tehran, Iran

ALFALFA STUDIO LLC
New York, New York, USA

The mission of Amphibian Stage Productions, a theatrical production company, is to produce "innovative and engaging" theatrical works that challenge the way people see the world around them. This brand identity draws from abstract amphibian forms and patterns used to create a visual vocabulary appealing to all theatergoers —young and old.

the photo, as well as in the viewer's visual perception and interpretation of that photographic image.

The next level of abstraction is not based on reality or any recognizable form, but is represented by signs or something else to communicate a visual message. Letterforms, numbers, punctuation, and words are all signs—representations or visual expressions of written and verbal language.

The highest level of abstraction is evident in glyphs, pictograms, and symbols. These graphic forms are more abstract than signs because their meaning can be *(continued on page 177)*

The typography in this theatrical poster for a production of Shakespeare's *Macbeth* has been abstracted to a certain degree to imply a towering castlelike wall enclosing an environment that will have to be breached and broken down, but it still maintains an immediate identity for the title of the play. Color, typographic form, exaggerated scale, contrast, and proportion all add to the overwhelmingly dark and serious tone of this message.

CATHERINE ZASK
Paris, France

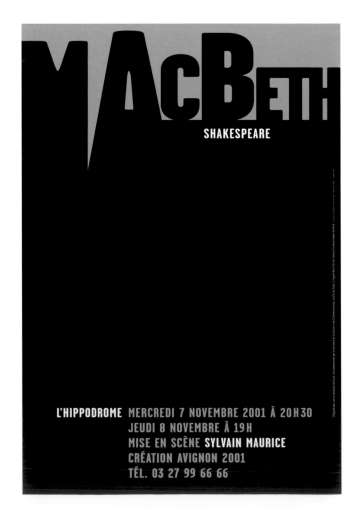

Meet Girls:

Approaching women is easy. Confidently walk up and say hi.

There's no need to be anxious or nervous, just be yourself and let
your bravado shine. Humor is always a great way to break the ice.

You Will Mingle:

Mingling at any party is easy and fun. You'll be pleasantly surprised

how interested others will be in you and what you have to say.

Just relax and go with the flow. Everyone is there to have a good time

and not to be judgemental.

Both of these posters, titled *You Will Mingle* **and** *Meet Girls***, use expressive abstractions of a person's eye and head to communicate the potential intensity and anxiety one can feel when considering these two natural yet uncomfortable social situations. Supporting typography functions as a narrative counterpoint to each visual representation.**

JASON LYNCH, Student
WILLIAM MORRISEY,
Instructor
School of Visual Arts
New York, New York, USA

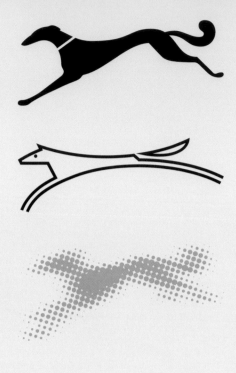

This series of stylized graphic variations for Alfred A. Knopf Publishers' classic Borzoi dog symbol uses visual simplification, interpretation, and levels of abstraction as a means to update and provide alternative graphic choices when incorporating the symbol on various book titles and spines.

TRIBORO DESIGN SOLUTIONS
Brooklyn, New York, USA

An abstract human form made from found objects— threads and a button—and represented in a manner that is both lyrical and dancelike becomes a powerful and memorable figurative icon for this poster announcing a spring dance concert. Custom-drawn, lowercase letterforms identifying "open source" are also abstracted, evoking visual qualities similar to the reductive human form directly below this titling.

CHEMI MONTES DESIGN
Arlington, Virginia, USA

interpreted by the viewer on many levels. Symbols are not realistic in graphic form but represent concepts and ideas, which may be reflected spiritually, socially, politically, sexually, or culturally. For example, a triangle can represent inspiration, the gay-rights movement, or oppression in Nazi Germany during World War II.

Total abstraction bears no trace of any visual reference to anything recognizable. For example, color is completely free of objective representation and is a fully abstract visual form.

Using abstraction in visual communications provides the graphic designer with a broad palette of graphic form that has no concrete meaning yet can evoke powerful, memorable, and meaningful visual messages and responses.

Théâtre/Public

Théâtre Oracle un cahier orchestré par Henri Meschonnic

© Catherine Zask 2008

In this promotional poster for an "orchestrated performance" by Henri Meschonnic, a French essayist, poet, and theorist of language, the primary image is of a man reduced and abstracted to a soft and illusive visual gesture. It appears figurative and, at the same time, not figurative. It is unfamiliar, yet engaging. Sans serif typography oriented on a vertical axis also acts as a strong counterpoint and frame for this image, giving it added strength and presence on the page.

CATHERINE ZASK
Paris, France

tone \ˈtōn\ *n*

7 a 1: color quality or value

7 a 2: tint or shade of color **b:** the color that appreciably modifies a hue or white or black

18

"Every moment of light and dark is a miracle."
WALT WHITMAN (1819-1892), *American, Essayist, Journalist, Poet*

In visual communications, tone (also identified as value or shade) means the degree of lightness or darkness apparent on the surface of an object. Tone is also the relative degree of a color's lightness or darkness—its content of black or white. It can be characterized by the degree of light that

Muted tones of color, pattern, and typography are used as visual, figurative textures to further enhance the identity program for Ödün, a Mexico City restaurant featuring cuisines from China, Thailand, Japan, Vietnam, and other Asian countries. The overall identity, as well as its broad palette of tones, colors, and patterns, was inspired by a diversity of flavors, scents, and spirits found throughout Asian cultures.

BLOK DESIGN
Mexico City, Mexico

falls on an object and how it is then reflected, and ultimately perceived. It is also one of the most important principles in visual communication because it helps define an object's size, form, and position relative to orientation and composition.

Because the majority of our perceptible world is defined by color, it is critical that we understand its characteristics and effects.

Characteristics

Tone gives a composition unique characteristics that cannot be achieved with flat color. These visual characteristics are spatial depth, texture, and movement. Tone can also increase visual impact in a powerful and immediate way or create extreme visual restraint and nuance that is still obvious and palatable to the eye of the viewer.

Color is an absolute presence in our visual world; therefore, it is extremely difficult to extract the characteristic of chroma or hue from all of its other qualities.

Value

A tone (or shade) is a color to which black or another dark color or hue has been added to make it darker, thereby tending to make (continued on page 182)

Experimenta typographica
WILLEM SANDBERG
Amsterdam, Holland

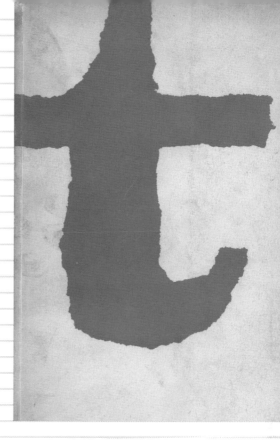

WILLEM SANDBERG (1897–1984) was a Dutch typographer and graphic designer, as well as a unique presence in the Dutch cultural world during the 1940s and 1950s.

He was born in Amersfoot, Holland, and studied art at the State Academy of Art in Amsterdam. As a young man, he served as a printer's apprentice in Herrliberg, Switzerland. In 1927, he studied in Vienna and then at the Bauhaus in Dessau. Following his return to Amsterdam, he worked as a graphic designer until he was appointed deputy director of the Stedelijk Museum in Amsterdam in 1938.

His main sources of inspiration were Hendrik Werman and Piet Zwart, both groundbreaking Dutch typographers whose pioneering work abandoned the tenets of conventional symmetry. Sandberg also initially agreed with the "neue typographie" of Jan Tschichold and began to incorporate lowercase typographic characters and unjustified text in the majority of his work.

During World War II, Sandberg became a wartime hero as the only surviving member of a Dutch resistance group that in 1943 burned down Amsterdam's Municipal Office of Records in protest against the administration of the Nazi government.

After Europe's liberation in 1945, Sandberg became the director of the Stedelijk Museum. It was at the Stedelijk that he personally designed hundreds of its catalogs and posters, providing the museum with a unique brand and identity. As a designer, he produced innovative work characterized by the use of bold type, vivid colors, textured papers, and signature torn-paper forms.

From 1943 to 1945, while hiding from the Germans and working for the underground resistance, Sandberg produced the basis for *Experimenta typographica*, a series of print experiments in form, space, and tone presented in eighteen short, mostly handmade, books that were finally published in the 1950s and subsequently inspired his later work. These experiments included unjustified text settings and sentence fragments composed freely, with varying type weights and styles for visual interest or emphasis. They are void of symmetry and use bright colors, strong contrasts, and subtle tones for rhythm and pacing. Crisp sans serif typography is combined with large-scale, torn-paper, collaged letterforms with rough, irregular edges.

These sensitive explorations of compositional tone and space became enormously influential among a generation of graphic designers, as well as becoming the basis for many of Sandberg's later Stedelijk Museum catalogs, which were seen and then imitated around the world.

His body of work was a provocative marriage of the "neue typographie" combined with the expressive freedom of surrealism and the inevitable compromises of a wartime Europe.

Willem Sandberg and Experimenta typographica

In this series of brochures and posters for a regional theater and arts center, titled *Lux*, lighter, intense tints of color are used as tonal textures and patterns that provide a visually rich and animated series of background layers for the typographic information running throughout these collateral print promotions.

HELMO
Montreuil, France

it more neutral in color. For example, black added to green creates a darker shade of green. Value changes in pure colors or hues are called shades and tints. This can be more clearly understood by viewing these variables on a color wheel.

Toning (or shading) shows changes from light to dark or dark to light in a composition by darkening areas that would be shadowed and by leaving other areas light. The blending of one value into another is also identified as feathering or gradient. Toning is often used to produce the illusion of dimension, volume, and depth.

The subtle, muted tone of the photographic image on this book cover for *Zero Decibels: The Quest for Absolute Silence* is used as a visual metaphor for silence, with an intent that it can be read and understood, but just barely. The added restraint of the serif typography, with its extreme thick and thin stroke nuances, adds a quiet presence to this message.

MOTHER DESIGN
New York, New York, USA

Graduated Color Wheel

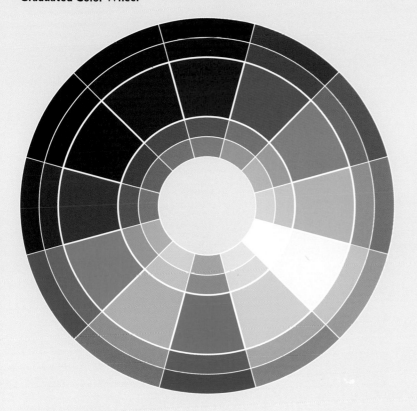

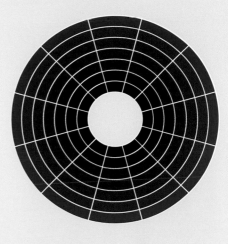

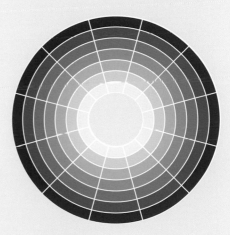

Saturation/Chroma

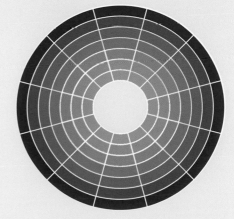

Graduated Color Wheel

Each hue is shown here in a progressive or graduated series of values (tints and shades). Note that the point of greatest saturation is the same for each hue. Yellow is of greatest intensity toward the lighter end of the scale, while blue is more intense in the darker zone. Use a graduated color wheel to look for combinations that are similar in value or saturation, and to build contrasting relationships.

Tone

These color tonal wheels demonstrate changes in saturation and value by adding or subtracting black, white, or gray. When white is added to a bright red, the value is lighter and the resulting color is less saturated. Adding black to a bright red results in a dark red closer to the neutral scale because of saturation changes. If gray is added, the saturation is lowered but the value is unchanged.

These three identity variations for the financial group Liquid Capital use a single color with related light and dark tones of that same color to further convey movement and diversity in their various organizations. Greens are used for markets, magentas for securities, and for the overall group—a range of oranges. This tonal concept is further reinforced and represented in the financial group's brand positioning photography—dynamic images that support the group's key brand messages.

JOG LIMITED
London, United Kingdom

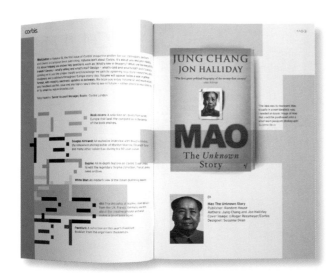

Volume magazine, a sales tool specifically designed for the image library, Corbis, to communicate with its book publishing clients, showcases recently designed book covers and publications using Corbis-based imagery. The visual diversity of this work is furthered accentuated by the framing and displaying of each cover or publication on a variety of background patterns. Each spread, activated with a different, distinct tone or shade, is actually an overscaled fragment of a custom-designed, pixilated letterform. These structured letterforms symbolize a digital age in which most publications are now designed and set electronically using pixels rather than picas.

JOG LIMITED
London, United Kingdom

LIQUID CAPITAL
SECURITIES

LIQUID CAPITAL
MARKETS

LIQUID CAPITAL
GROUP

Types and Effects

In color theory, a tint is the mixture of a color with white, increasing its lightness, and a shade is the mixture of a color with black, reducing its lightness. Mixing a color with any neutral color, including black and white, reduces its chroma or colorfulness, while its hue remains unchanged.

A tone can also be gray or what is called a midtone. It is identified as achromatic and is mixed from black to white. Tones can range from light to dark values in a gray scale. Grays can flatten and minimize the brilliance of any pure color or hue. Darker grays also affect color or hue in a way similar

A variety of subtle tones are used in this promotional poster for a jazz ensemble performance titled "A Tribute to Kind of Blue" at American University. The poster's composition, as well as its use of different color tints and shades, reinforces the identity and meaning of jazz in American culture as a diverse, multifaceted, multilayered, musical experience.

CHEMI MONTES DESIGN
Falls Church, Virginia, USA

A range of light- and dark-colored tonal values and layers on these notebook covers provides a strong visual dynamic, spatial depth, and kinetic movement to these swirling, curvilinear color compositions.

ADAMSMORIOKA INC.
Beverly Hills, California, USA

le théâtre la Roulotte présente
LES AVENTURES DE
LAGARDÈRE
d'après *LE BOSSU* de *Paul Féval*
librement adapté et mis en scène par FRÉDÉRIC BÉLANGER

École nationale de théâtre
du Canada   Montréal   Québec

to black; lighter grays affect color or hue in a way similar to white. For example, a tone mixed with yellow produces a rich, colorful, earth tone that resembles ochre and umber.

Monochromatic tone is a single color mixed with either a tint, shade, or tone. This type of color scheme can effectively simulate the presence of other colors or hues through use of tone and its effects on individual and distinct colors.

In theory, there are an almost infinite number of value gradations between true black and true white. The contrast between these two extremes is mitigated by midtones, from the palest to the darkest of grays.

It is due to these primary factors that tone is a valuable conceptual and compositional element in visual communications.

Line illustration and hand lettering for this poster, *Les Aventures de Lagardére*, are further strengthened by the effective use of a monochromatic color palette—an intense, vibrant red paired with a darker tone of the same color. Here tone simulates the presence of another color, thereby adding volume and depth to the overall composition.

LAURENT PINABEL
Montreal, Quebec, Canada

The identity and branding for the Microsoft Store, a square divided into four smaller squares, uses tones or tints of quadratic colors—red, green, yellow, and blue. This reliance on tints provides this symbol with depth, dimension, and visual activity. Variations on this same monochromatic theme of color and tone are used in environmental graphics and promotional elements, reinforcing the visual language of this program, as well as symbolizing the diversity of the company in a retail environment.

COLLINS
New York, New York, USA

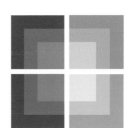

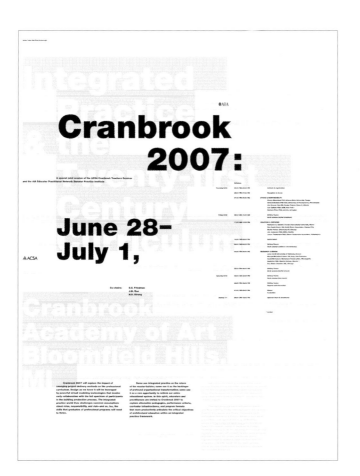

Intense color and tone is effectively used as a secondary informational layer to this poster announcing a series of educational programs at the Cranbrook Academy of Art. Sans serif typography set in various scales and contrasting colors, paired with figure-ground, allows the reader to change focus in an immediate manner, allowing easy access to layers of information.

JACK HENRIE FISHER
Brussels, Belgium

con·trast \ˈkän-ˌtrast\ *n*
1 a: juxtaposition of dissimilar elements (as color, tone, or emotion) in a work of art

19

"There are dark shadows on the earth, but its lights are stronger in the contrast."

CHARLES DICKENS (1812-1870), *British, Author*

Contrast is a visual principle that fundamentally provides the eye with a noticeable difference between two things or objects—large and small, red and green, light and dark, or hot and cold. In visual communications, contrast is the perceptible difference in visual characteristics that makes

These notebook covers effectively use the design principle of contrast to present a graphic message that is powerful, and immediate. The bold use of pure geometric shapes, textures, figure-ground, and letterforms, further strengthen this concept.

ADAMSMORIOKA INC.
Beverly Hills, California, USA

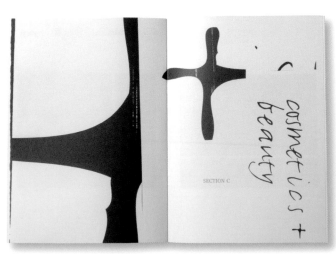

an object (or its representation in an image) distinguishable and distinct from other objects in a composition as well as its surrounding background. Contrast in a composition is the opposite of visual harmony.

It can be achieved by exaggerating the visual differences in size, shape, color, and texture between compositional elements, thereby enhancing and making a message more immediate and understandable to a viewer. Contrast can draw and direct attention, create a mood or emotion, and create hierarchy and emphasis in complex information in any visual message.
(continued on page 192)

The extreme scale, cropping, and juxtaposition of these fluid, calligraphic letterforms, placed in counterpoint to formal serif typography and articulated in a stark black-and-white palette, provide dynamic contrasts that create tension, movement, and visual impact to each and every one of the spreads in this promotional brochure for Colour Cosmetica.

VOICE
Adelaide, Australia

1967

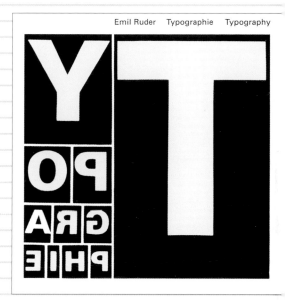

Emil Ruder   Typographie   Typography

Emil Ruder: Typography Book Cover
EMIL RUDER
Basel, Switzerland

EMIL RUDER (1914–1970) was a Swiss typographer, graphic designer, author, and educator instrumental in starting the Allegmeine Gewerbeschule (Basel School of Design), as well as developing the International Typographic Style or the Swiss School.

As a young man, he studied in Paris and trained as a typesetter in Zurich. In 1929, at the age of fifteen, he began a four-year compositor's apprenticeship and attended the Zurich School of Arts and Crafts.

In 1948, Ruder met the artist-printer Armin Hofmann, and they began a long period of collaboration and teaching that achieved an international reputation by the mid-1950s.

Ruder was also a writer and published a basic grammar of typography titled *Emil Ruder: Typography*, which was published in German, English, and French in 1967. This groundbreaking book helped spread and propagate the International Typographic Style and became a basic text for graphic design and typography throughout Europe and the United States.

The International Typographic Style was defined by sans serif typefaces and employed a rigorous page grid for structure that produced asymmetrical layouts. Its philosophy and tenets evolved directly from the de Stijl movement, the Bauhaus, and Jan Tschichold's New Typography.

In Ruder's work, as well as in his teachings, he called for all graphic designers to find an appropriate balance in contrasts between form and function. He believed that typography loses its function and communicative value when it loses its narrative meaning. He further believed that typography's primary role in any visual composition is legibility and readability. A careful and critical analysis of visual contrasts, or the contrast of macro and micro, was essential to understanding both of these parameters—the negative, or white, space of the page and the negative, or white, space of letter and word forms, such as counters, letter spacing, and word spacing.

Ruder stated, "Typography has one plain duty before it and that is to convey information in writing. No argument or consideration can absolve typography from this duty."

He also promoted an overall, systematic approach to the design of page layout and the use of complex, structured grids to bring all compositional page elements into a unified, cohesive whole while still allowing for contrasting variations in narrative and visual and content.

Emil Ruder and Typographie

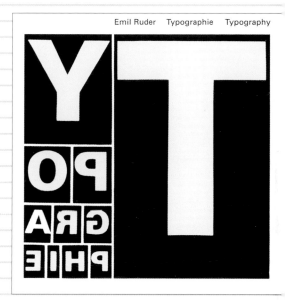

These Eastern European-inspired labels and packaging for Slavko, an alcoholic beverage line, was created using contrasts in color, scale, typography, and graphic form. Bold, inline letterforms layered with high contrast, posterized imagery, and bright, saturated colors all give increased visual emphasis, weight, and prominence to this branding program.

LG2BOUTIQUE
Montreal, Quebec, Canada

Comparative Relationships

Contrast is the comparative relationship between light and dark. Many other types of contrast in visual communications refer to comparative relationships or juxtapositions between two or more compositional elements. These juxtapositions can be positive and negative, geometric and organic, organized and chaotic, smooth and rough, static and kinetic, and large and small.

Contrasting relationships can be further articulated by combining elements to achieve variety and unity. Here, the ultimate challenge is to create a composition made up of disparate elements that work together as one orchestrated whole. Contrasting size,

Contrast between black-and-white letterforms and handwritten script, as well as contrast in scale of graphic forms and textures, provides visual drama and excitement to this poster promoting a performance by the world-renowned mime Marcel Marceau. The emblematic use of a simple black-and-white palette, the dynamic cropping of the graphic hands as if they were moving beyond the edges of the poster, and the pure representation of the performer's face as a visual anchor and frame for the title of the performance all add to this series of visual contrasts found in this active and impactful composition.

TAKASHI KUSUI, Student
KEVIN BRAINARD, Instructor
School of Visual Arts
New York, New York, USA

weight, direction, value, color, texture, and form can all add effective and meaningful visual interest by allowing one element to contrast and complement the other.

For example, a serpentine curve appears more curvilinear when it is close to an extremely orthogonal and straight element. A color such as red will always appear redder when it is adjacent to or surrounded by its complementary color—green.

Characteristics and Functions

Contrast can create emphasis by establishing juxtaposition with compositional elements to stress their visual differences. For example, bright colors juxtaposed with dark colors,

Solid black fields layered over existing textural elements and intense colors of a tabloid newspaper create a highly distinctive contrast for this publication celebrating the ten-year anniversary of a contemporary art museum in Bregenz, Austria. Large-scale, sans serif letterforms and blocks of narrative text are knocked out of these black fields, allowing existing backgrounds of the newspaper to show through and provide ample contrast for immediacy and readability of specific information.

SAGMEISTER INC.
New York, New York, USA

The promotional materials for the AIGA Boston Twenty-Fifth Anniversary use a subtle ornamental background pattern, composed of fragmented decorative and typographic elements set against a silver metallic, highly reflective, foil-stamped version of the event's logotype. In this context, contrast is used in both a restrained and obvious manner, to achieve surface variation, nuance, and an immediate visual impact.

STOLTZE DESIGN
Boston, Massachusetts, USA

angular shapes with curvilinear shapes, and minuscule elements with monumental elements can create visual excitement and emphasis, as well as direct attention to focal points in a composition and organize hierarchal orders in a visual message.

Contrast creates emphasis, importance, weight, or dominance for an element of a composition. A composition lacking contrast may result in visual monotony, neutrality, and even confusion.

Types of Contrast

Contrast effectively uses opposing design elements such as tone, color, and shape in a composition to produce an intensified, visual effect. For example, chiaroscuro (Italian for "light-dark") in fine art and photography is characterized by strong tonal contrasts between light and dark. It is also a technical term used by artists and art historians for using contrast of light and dark or tone to achieve a sense of volume in modeling three-dimensional form such as the human body.

Since we live in a world of color, using it as a contrasting force can immediately be understood by the viewer when conveying or emphasizing differences among visual

The visual branding program of Casa Lever, a restaurant located in a modernist New York City architectural landmark, uses warm colors, bold shapes, and simple geometry to evoke the spirit of Italian modernist work. Graphic contrasts can be found throughout the visual characteristics of this contemporary program—in its typographic form, two-tone color palette, informational scale and hierarchy, as well as in its logotype, packaging, and website.

MUCCA DESIGN
New York, New York, USA

This logotype for Terence Higgins Trust's **HIV** campaign in the United Kingdom draws visual attention with the effective use of extreme contrast. A vibrant red symbolizing the potential nature of a person's **HIV** status is set against flanking monolithic black letterforms, creating a dramatic focus to the powerful impact of **HIV** throughout our society.

FELTON COMMUNICATION
London, United Kingdom

THIVK®

In this promotional poster for a symposium on "impure architecture" held at the Guggenheim Museum in New York City, the fundamental design principle of contrast is used as a conceptual and visual cue for the design and composition of the entire poster. An unconventional, angular axis is used to organize and display typographic information that varies in content, scale, character, figure-ground, alignment, and texture.

SUPERMETRIC
New York, New York, USA

Simple, obvious contrasts of large and small, black and white, and serious and playful are all evident in the interpretive graphics for a Tim Burton retrospective exhibition at the Museum of Modern Art in New York City. For example, Burton's hand lettering is juxtaposed with formal san serif typography used for an introductory career timeline, and a large-scale, spiraling floor graphic directs itself onto an introductory entry wall while simultaneously underlining the exhibition title **Tim Burton**, shown in his own smaller-scale, restrained hand lettering.

JULIA HOFFMANN
New York, New York, USA

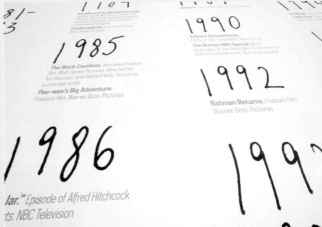

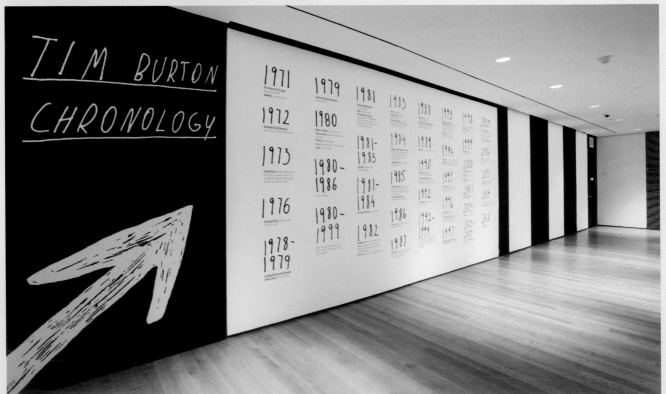

This memorable poster celebrating Fritz Gottschalk's seventieth birthday is a study in graphic simplicity, visual immediacy, and linear contrast. A segment of the crisp, evenly continuous outline of the universal cross symbol found in the Swiss flag is abruptly ragged and irregular, reconfigured to create a letterform. The designer literally tore off the left side of the cross and recomposed it into an *F* for Fritz. Here, the simple transformation of graphic form is further realized with contrasts in line, shape, color, and letterform.

CARBONE SMOLAN
AGENCY
New York, New York, USA

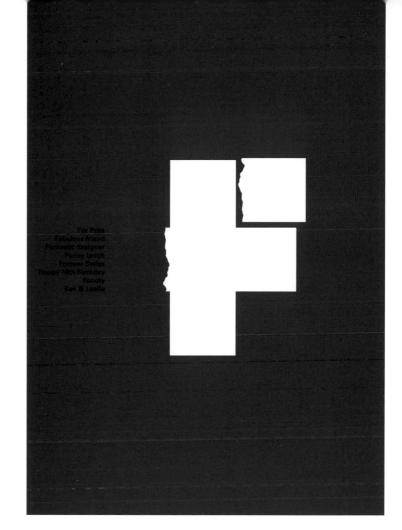

For Fritz
Fabulous friend
Fantastic designer
Funny laugh
Forever Swiss
Happy 70th Birthday
fondly
Ken & Leslie

elements in a wide variety of messages and compositions. Distinct, contrasting shapes can also produce striking reactions from the viewer. For example, a conventional shape appears more conventional and normal when an irregular, nonconventional shape is present in the same composition.

Contrast can exist on many obvious and subtle levels in a composition. The human eye can simultaneously detect contrasts in scale, value, shape, direction, and surface. It can also clarify and strengthen any visual message by providing stability and clarity to the cohesiveness of a composition, draw the eye's attention to a specific area, and affect a figure–ground relationship by maximizing or minimizing its visual immediacy.

In this editorial spread titled "Ashamed to be Asian?" dynamic contrasts appear between its compositional elements—the figure–ground of black and white; the free-form character of letterforms and the sharp, cutout lines of illustrations; the intense and muted colors of the figurative illustration; and the scale of large and small elements.

TAMMI CHAN, Student
CHRISTOPHER
AUSTOPCHUK, Instructor
School of Visual Arts
New York, New York, USA

fig·ure–ground \ˈfi-gyər ˈgraund\ *n*
1 a: relating to or being the relationships between the parts of a perceptual field which is perceived as divided into a part consisting of figures having form and standing out from the part comprising the background and being relatively formless

20

"Everything we see hides another thing; we always want to see what is hidden by what we see."

RENE MAGRITTE (1898-1967), *Belgian, Painter*

Figure-ground is primarily the visual relationship between the foreground and background of a composition. This relationship between figure and ground is one of the primary principles of visual perception and visual communications. Related design elements of shape and contrast have a critical

The symbol for "Peace One Day," a public awareness campaign for global cease-fires and nonviolence, relies upon an ambiguous figure–ground relationship between a dove's wing and a profile of a person's face to further reinforce that we are directly connected to one another and ultimate peace in the world. In this compositional relationship, the symbol's positive figure—a silhouette of a dove with an outstretched wing—and its negative ground, a side profile of a person's face, are one and the same.

JEANELLE MAK
New York, New York, USA

direct effect on how a figure and its ground interact with one another. Figure–ground relationships also refer to the optical phenomenon that occurs when specific design elements in any composition appear to move forward or recede. For example, the page that you are currently reading contains typographic text and images that constitute "figure," and the book's white paper constitutes "ground." How and to what degree these two compositonal elements interact, creating either tension or harmony, is fully determined by the graphic designer and ultimately will contribute to the success or failure of this *(continued on page 202)*

This circular symbol for **APA Technologies,** a manufacturer of watches that monitor ultraviolet rays, uses figure–ground to create a dual visual effect. Lines radiate from the symbol's center representing the Sun, as well as create narrow triangular shapes that move inward bringing attention to the product name.

WINK
Minneapolis, Minnesota, USA

Kunstgewerbemuseum Exhibition Poster
MAX BILL
Zurich, Switzerland

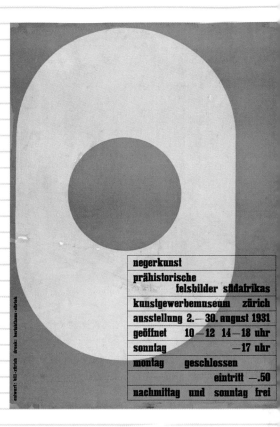

MAX BILL (1908–1994), born in Winterthur, Switzerland, was an architect, painter, typographer, industrial designer, engineer, sculptor, educator, and graphic designer.

Bill was initially a student at the Kunstgewerbeschule and apprenticed as a silversmith before beginning his studies in 1927 at the Bauhaus in Dessau, Germany, with teachers such as Wassily Kandinsky, Paul Klee, and Oskar Schlemmer.

He permanently settled in Zurich, Switzerland, in 1929, and in 1937 became involved with a group of Swiss artists and designers named the Allianz. The Allianz group advocated the concrete theories of art and design and included Max Huber, Leo Leuppi, and Richard Paul Lohse.

In 1950, Max Bill and Otl Aicher founded the Ulm School of Design (Hochschule fur Gestaltung-HfG Ulm) in Ulm, Germany, a design school initially created in the tradition of the Bauhaus and that later developed a new design education approach integrating art and science. Bill served as the school's director from 1951 to 1956. Ulm is notable for its inclusion of semiotics, the philosophical theory of signs and symbols, as a field of study. Faculty and students included Tomas Maldonado, Josef Albers, Johannes Itten, John Lottes, Otl Aicher, Walter Zeischegg, and Peter Seitz.

Bill was the single most decisive influence on Swiss graphic design or the International Typographic Style, beginning in the 1950s with his theoretical writing and progressive work. He said, "It is possible to develop an art largely on the basis of mathematical thinking."

From 1967 to 1971, he was a professor at the Staatliche Hochschule fur Bildende Kunste in Hamburg and chair of environmental design.

As a graphic designer, he fully and enthusiastically embraced the tenets and philosophical views of this modernist movement. The majority of his graphic work is based solely on cohesive visual principles of organization and composed of purist forms—modular grids, san serif typography, asymmetric compositions, linear spatial divisions, mathematical progressions, and dynamic figure–ground relationships.

His powerful use of figure–ground relationships is never more evident than with his exhibition poster, designed in 1931, for the Kunstgewerbemuseum in Zurich, Switzerland. The poster's figure–ground is its primary compositional principle; its bright white figure is asymmetrically located and set against a muted-tone background. The pure geometry of the figure's inner circle is a powerful focal point further offset by the pure linear square containing information on the exhibition.

Max Bill and Swiss Modernism

This assignment is a study of unit, structure, pattern, and figure–ground created in the repetition of a single, cropped letterform. Students start with a basic compositional exercise involving a black letterform on a white surface, cropping away pieces of the letterform within a 20 cm (7.8-inch) square. These initial letterform compositions are used to generate patterns of four and then sixteen units within a predetermined grid system. Attention is given to the complexity of figure-ground relationships within each pattern. Color is introduced in the final stage of the assignment as students explore further means to enhance pattern, rhythm, and figure-ground relationships.

ERINI FAHIM, SEHYR AHMAD, OMAR MOHAMED, Students
AMIR BERBIC, RODERICK GRANT, Instructors
*American University of Sharjah
Sharjah, United Arab Emirates*

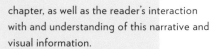

chapter, as well as the reader's interaction with and understanding of this narrative and visual information.

Definition of Elements

Design elements in any composition are perceived as either figure (objects or focus) or ground (the remaining background or the rest of the perceptual compositional field).

It is also critical to remember that ground, or the space surrounding a figure, is also a shape. Shapes can exist independently as well as overlap each other, depending on the specific figure–ground relationship of a composition.

Figure is also considered a positive compositional element, while the space, or ground, around it is considered opposite and a negative compositional element. Each is dependent upon the other—it is impossible to change one without affecting the other. Creating dynamic relationships between positive and negative is the cornerstone of well-resolved visual compositions.

Figure is a compositional element to which we pay attention. It is also identified as a positive shape in a visual composition. It is defined as the outline, form, or silhouette of

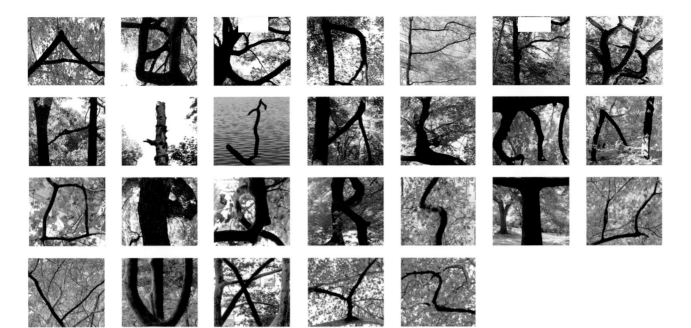

a positive shape in a visual composition. It is defined as the outline, form, or silhouette of an object. It refers to an active, positive form revealed against a passive, negative ground. In the simplest visual compositions there may be only one figure that the viewer needs to pay attention to. In more complex visual compositions, there may be multiple figures. Familiar, figurative, and representational objects are easy to see and assimilate as figure.

Ground is the surrounding space of an object or compositional element. It is also defined as the negative space in a composition, as well as everything else that is not a figure. As attention shifts from figure to fig-

ure, the ground also shifts so that an object can go from figure to ground and back.

Types of Figure–Ground

There are three basic types of figure-ground compositions and relationships:

Simple

A simple figure–ground can be created when a coherent, independent object is juxtaposed in a space that functions as its surrounding ground. The ground can be compressed or shallow, or convey an illusion of depth. In a simple figure–ground composition, the figure is positive and active, whereas its ground is always negative and passive. In this composi-

This set of arboreal-based letterforms is the outcome of a student's thorough photographic exploration of letterforms found in nature. It is also a primary representation of a simple figure-ground relationship, one in which the figure's, or in this case the foreground's, darker branches and limbs are positive and active, whereas its ground, or in this case the background's, green textures in the surrounding woodlands are negative and passive.

TAKASHI KUSUI, Student
JI LEE, Instructor
School of Visual Arts
New York, New York, USA

This public awareness campaign's logotype for Terence Higgins Trust's HIV Program in the United Kingdom— "Get It On"—uses the exaggerated negative space or counter of its lowercase *n* for the figure–ground reversal of a symbolic condom.

FELTON COMMUNICATION
London, United Kingdom

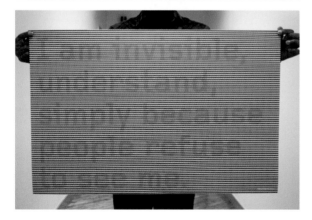

This promotional poster, titled *Stealth* and developed for New York City's Studio Museum in Harlem, is an exploration of identity through the use of figure–ground, visual texture, and three-dimensional form. Despite the poster's ultimately becoming a dynamic physical object, its essential message is revealed in its form and is based on a quote from Ralph Ellison's *Invisible Man*–"I am invisible, understand, simply because people refuse to see me." When flat, it reveals this almost invisible typographic statement through the illusion of figure–ground. When folded, the poster's form is evocative of a stealth bomber (hence its name).

THE MAP OFFICE
New York, New York, USA

tional relationship, the figure is clearly visible and separate from its background.

Reversal
A figure–ground reversal can be created when a figure functions as a ground and ground as figure. This graphic inversion is caused by shapes that form in the spaces located between the parts of the figure, creating the reversal. This type of figure–ground composition can be a dynamic means to activate neutral white space in a visual composition. In a simple figure–ground composition, the borders are perceived as limitless, whereas a figure–ground reversal

This symbol, based on a simple figure-ground relationship, clearly illustrates green trees and brown mountains. However, when arranged as shown, the symbol's white "negative" space framed by the upper and lower "positive" figures create a negative or ground that reads as a *w* for Mountain Woods, a community in rural Colorado.

WINK
Minneapolis, Minnesota, USA

Bold, all-cap sans serif letterforms juxtaposed with delicate handmade letterforms composed of branches and flowers create a dramatic and memorable composition, as well as a simple figure-ground reversal for this brochure cover for the Fort Worth Opera Festival.

THE MATCHBOX STUDIO
Dallas, Texas, USA

Ambiguous

An ambiguous figure–ground composition is created when the graphic relationship between a composition's figure (or object) and ground (or space) is undetectable, yet fully comprehensible. With this type of figure–ground relationship, a pair of objects share the same edge or profile. A classic example of an ambiguous figure–ground relationship is Rubin's vase, developed by psychologist Edgar Rubin. In this image, the black positive space forms two profiles of a human face that appear to be ready to kiss, and the inverse negative space forms a vase. Visually, the eye's concentration on either the black or white alternates between the faces and the vase.

Characteristics

The principle of figure–ground is one of the most basic in visual communications because it refers to our ability to visually separate elements based on contrast—dark and light, black and white, and positive and negative. In the simplest terms, the figure is what we notice and the ground is everything else we tend to not notice.

FORT WORTH OPERA FESTIVAL 2009

An effective and perceptible figure–ground relationship occurs when the eye can identify a figure as an object distinct and separate from its ground or compositional background. This perception is dependent solely on the design principle of contrast.

A composition's figure–ground relationship is clear and stable when the figure receives more attention and immediacy than the ground. When a figure–ground relationship is unstable, the relationship is ambiguous; therefore, the compositional elements can be interpreted in different ways.

Balanced and effective figure–ground relationships animate any composition, adding visual impact and power to its message.

However, when a figure dominates its ground, the effect can be clear but potentially boring. Locating a clearly defined object in the center of a composition leaves no doubt about the subject, but its presentation may lack visual nuance and power.

Ultimately, figure–ground is one of the most important design principles to consider when creating any visual communication. In doing so, graphic designers can further guarantee that the work they are producing will be effective, communicative, memorable, and highly meaningful to the viewer.

This wall mural is an integral storytelling element of the overall visitor exhibit experience at the WTC Tribute Center located fewer than 50 feet (15 m) from Ground Zero directly across from the World Trade Center (WTC) site. Most New Yorkers remember how extraordinarily blue the sky was the morning of 9/11. This 80-foot (24 m) long wall begins as an expanse of blue, appearing like the sky that day, then gradually filling with missing-person posters, stretching from floor to ceiling at the far end of the gallery. This collagelike figure–ground treatment invokes the iconic image of walls all over lower Manhattan covered with posters for weeks after the disaster, as families looked for their missing loved ones.

POULIN + MORRIS INC.
New York, New York, USA

This series of book covers for Albert Camus' *The Stranger*, *The Plague*, and *The Fall* are seminal studies in simple figure–ground relation-ships fully articulated using fundamental design elements such as point, line, and shape, as well as a stark black-and-white color palette.

JOHN GALL
New York, New York, USA

frame \\'frām\ *n*

1: a closed, often rectangular border of drawn or printed lines

21

"Art consists of limitation. The most beautiful part of every picture is the frame."
G. K. CHESTERTON (1874-1936), *British, Author, Essayist*

In basic terms, a frame is an enclosure to a visual image. It is a fundamental element of visual communications and can be used to separate, organize, unify, contain, and distinguish, as well as increase visibility and immediacy in any visual message. Like an actual picture frame, it can take various

The graphic identity for the Toledo Museum of Art uses frame as a graphic representation for the institution as well as an icon that has been an integral element to the presentation and viewing of fine art for centuries. The four words that make up the museum's name help define the edges of the frame's form. The frame also provides views inside the institution by serving as a visual stage for its collections, exhibitions, and cultural activities. Typography anchors and activates the inside perimeter of the frame and is knocked out of it to create a stronger visual dynamic and figure–ground when incorporating and framing other visual elements such as fine art details or images of the exhibitions. The sign system uses the logotype's frame to focus attention on either landmark historic and contemporary architecture or sculpture.

C+G PARTNERS LLC
New York, New York, USA

graphic forms and can be found virtually everywhere. In the familiar world, a frame can set off a work of art from the wall on which it is being displayed and simultaneously bring visual attention to it. In the broadest definition of the word, a frame can be many things and have many functions. It can be a proscenium stage for a theatrical event, an exhibition vitrine for displaying an artifact, or an architectural molding surrounding an entrance door. Frames can be obvious or implied. They can be realized as a border to a page or as an inset solid surface within a page composition.

Characteristics and Functions

As a compositional element, a frame can have a variety of visual characteristics and functions. It can appear simple or decorative, subtle or obvious, flat or modeled. It can be a container for another element as well as act as a transition element from active compositional space to passive compositional space. Its presence in a composition can be subtle, thereby becoming more integrated to its visual content, or it can have extreme graphic presence, ultimately setting content apart in a composition.

(continued on page 212)

A fluid, serpentine linear frame, evocative of ornamental ironwork, captures the fluid hand lettering on this wine label for Calea Nero d'Avola, vintage 2007. The integral graphic relationship of frame to letterform in this composition creates a visual unity that further strengthens the delicate, subtle graphic quality of this wine's brand and identity.

LOUISE FILI LTD.
New York, New York, USA

1955

The Man with the Golden Arm Poster
SAUL BASS
Los Angeles, California, USA

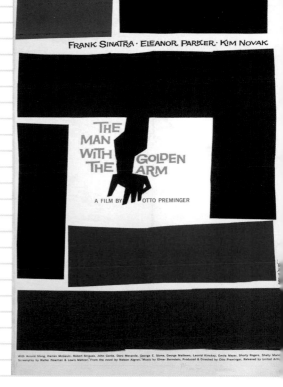

SAUL BASS (1920–1996) was a graphic designer and Academy Award–winning filmmaker who received global recognition for his work in graphic, film, industrial, and exhibition design but was best known for his animated film-title sequences.

During his forty-year career, he worked with some of Hollywood's greatest filmmakers, including Alfred Hitchcock, Otto Preminger, Stanley Kubrick, and Martin Scorsese. His work included the epilogue for *Around the World in Eighty Days* (1956), his direction and editing of the racing sequences for *Grand Prix* (1966), the shower sequence for *Psycho* (1960), and the prologue for *West Side Story* (1961).

Among his most famous film-title sequences are the kinetic typography racing up and down a high-angle view of the United Nations building façade in *North by Northwest* (1959) and the disjointed typography that raced together and then pulled apart for *Psycho*. His later work for Martin Scorsese allowed him to move away from conventional optical techniques he had pioneered earlier and work with computerized titles for films such as *The Age of Innocence* (1993) and *Casino* (1995).

Bass was born in New York City and studied at the Art Students League and then at Brooklyn College with Gyorgy Kepes. He initially began his time in Hollywood designing print advertisements for the film industry, until he collaborated with director Otto Preminger on the design of the poster for the film *Carmen Jones* (1954).

Preminger was so impressed with Bass's work, Bass was asked to produce the title sequence for the film as well. This was Bass's first opportunity to design more than a conventional title sequence and to create something that would ultimately enhance the audience's experience and further contribute to the mood and theme of the film.

Bass was one of the first designers to realize the creative potential of the opening and closing credit sequences of a film, all contained within a fundamental design element—frame. He believed that film-title sequences could "set the mood and the prime underlying core of the film's story, to express the story in some metaphorical way. I saw the title as a way of conditioning the audience, so that when the film actually began, viewers would already have an emotional resonance with it."

His first popular success, for which he became widely known, was with Otto Preminger's film *The Man with the Golden Arm* (1955). The film was about a jazz musician's struggle to overcome heroin addiction, a taboo subject in the 1950s. Here he uses the addict's arm, jagged and distorted, as the central, iconic image. The film's poster is a study on how a frame can be used to bring focus, tension, contrast, and balance to an image that is extremely dynamic and powerful. The film's title sequence featured an animated, black-paper cutout of the same arm used for the poster. As expected, the sequence caused a sensation and became a memorable benchmark for the design of future title sequences.

A continuous, bold, magenta frame surrounding this poster for the National Theatre School of Canada maintains a visual order and focus to the varied, free-form, and highly expressive illustrative elements used in its composition.

LAURENT PINABEL
Montreal, Quebec, Canada

A frame typically functions as a containment element for an image, setting it apart from its background to give the image more prominence, as well as increase its visibility within a composition. It can also have other functions, such as dividing, cropping, fragmenting, and distorting elements.

In either extreme, a frame can be used effectively to emphasize or deemphasize the content of any visual message.

Related Forms and Functions

A frame can be considered as a margin in a traditional page layout, such as in a book or magazine. Margins influence the way a reader interacts with narrative and visual content of a page, such as a block of typographic text or a group of photographic images, by providing passive or open space around these compositional elements. A more pronounced margin provides visual emphasis and immediacy to images or a block of typographic text. The opposite result occurs when a margin is minimal and narrow, creating an effect where images or blocks of text appear larger than they actually are, as if they were expanding beyond the limitations of the compositional page.

A simple frame surrounding
the title *Mao* and articulated
in the same line weight or
stroke thickness as the title's
three letterforms brings
this book cover literally into
focus, while the overall image
remains out of focus.

MUCCA DESIGN
New York, New York, USA

A consistent-weight linear
frame that matches the
stroke thickness of the
"Heath" typography further
unifies this logotype, especially when it is integrated
and layered with other visual
elements such as stationery,
sales catalogs, brochures,
website, and advertising.

VOLUME INC.
San Francisco, California, USA

Multiple graphic framing
of this project name and
location, "Prospect New
Orleans," creates a structured, integrated pattern
similar to brick coursing,
further communicating
strength, connection, team-
work, and community.

PURE + APPLIED
New York, New York, USA

The packaging and label design for Soto, an organic skincare product line, embodies an ingredient table, an effective use of color, and an alpha-based product identification system as its core idea. Bold, brightly colored frames used as the primary graphic device contain single san serif letter product identifiers that are immediate and eye-catching.

LANDOR
Paris, France

Another form of frame—in this case, margin—also provides a "safe" area in a composition, such as a publication, for specific elements such as folios (page numbers), headers, and footers. While these page conventions are usually located in a nominal space, a page margin can also be more pronounced to contain other elements such as images, captions, and sidebars, when needed.

A frame can also act as a border. A border clearly and concisely demarcates where an image ends and its surrounding background begins. It can be an obvious edge to an image or composition that may lack a definitive perimeter or outline, or it can be used to visually emphasize an outer edge, or frame, as well as separate a section of an image or information within an overall composition. A border can be graphically articulated with line, shape, and texture, realized with simple and restrained visual characteristics or more detailed and complicated ones.

The framing of elements in a composition is called cropping. Cropping can alter the size and shape of any image, as well as directly impact an image's content and meaning. For example, a vertical image can be cropped to become a square, circle, or

In this poster, frame is used to contain and accentuate the film festival title—Japanese Cinema Festival '09—as well as separate and organize in individual graphic frames a wide range of information such as programs, screenings, dates, times, and locations. As a visual metaphor, frame is this context is also evocative of film frames, shoji screens, and tatami mats.

RYOTA IIZUKA, Student
SIMON JOHNSTON, Instructor
Art Center College of Design
Pasadena, California, USA

such, each time taking on new proportions and potential meaning. Cropping in on a specific element or detail of an overall image can alter the focus of that image, giving it a new identity and visual presence.

The visual representation of a frame is not limited to compositional elements such as line, shape, color, texture, or tone. It can also be articulated with type and letterform.

Even in the virtual world of websites and electronic interfaces, a frame is a ubiquitous element with a multitude of appearances and functions. It is the literal and physical frame around a computer monitor, and it appears on a computer's desktop on

A singular graphic frame, equal in visual prominence and weight to this public awareness campaign's logotype for Darfur, allows this typographic element to stand apart and maintain its visual immediacy when layered on a variety of photographic images and graphic textures.

VOLUME INC.
San Francisco, California, USA

A subtle, tinted frame is used to bring immediate attention to this restaurant's restrained, sans serif logotype "SĪNO," an Asian-inspired Chinese restaurant and lounge. When layered on a variety of different color fields, textures, and images, this frame maintains a visual immediacy and focus to this identity program.

PUBLIC INC.
San Francisco, California, USA

The cookbook cover has a sophisticated visual character, capturing the warmth, personality, and elegance of the restaurant Chanterelle, while at the same time communicating the gracious service found in this family-run establishment. The composition of the cover is also evocative of a fine art book, with a centered white field framing the book title's classic serif typography as well as bridging and connecting the two distinct photographic images, further unifying the cover as a cohesive whole.

MUCCA DESIGN
New York, New York, USA

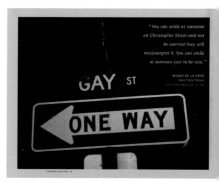

numerous windows that contain a hierarchy of information such as controls, icons, and other types of navigational information.

A frame can be a functional, as well as an aesthetic element within a composition. It can strengthen and reinforce the viewer's understanding of information as well as appear solely as a decorative element. With either of these functions, it is the responsibility of the graphic designer to determine the appropriate use of frame.

Graphic variations on a literal frame and bracket are used extensively throughout this branding program and annual report for "The 1%." A bold, effective use of color, proportion, and figure–ground all enhance depth and dimension without illustrating the literal nature of these visual qualities and characteristics.

MENDE DESIGN
San Francisco, California, USA

Frame takes on a series of varied graphic forms throughout *This Book Is Not Pink*, as represented in these spreads, which maintains a consistency and continuity for the reader as a means to bring further focus and grounding to the varied visual elements and narrative content of each spread.

ANDREW LIM, Student
MICHAEL IAN KAYE, Instructor
School of Visual Arts
New York, New York, USA

pro·por·tion \prə-ˈpȯr-shən\ *n*
3: the relation of one part to another or to the whole with respect to magnitude, quantity, or degree

proportion

22

"Without proportion there can be no principles in the design of any temple; that is, if there is no precise relation between its members, as in the case of those of a well-shaped man."

VITRUVIUS (80-70 BC), *Roman, Architect, Author, Engineer*

Proportion is the systematic relationship of one thing to another in any given composition. In visual communications, it is an essential design principle defined as the integral relationship of sizes within a composition. These integral relationships are transparent and function as an underlying

VOTE

Good design makes choices clear.

framework for all compositional elements. Proportion also represents the critical relationship between one part of a composition and another or between the whole of a composition and its size, quantity, or degree. Generally the goal of any proportional system is to produce a sense of coherence, harmony, and integrity among the elements.

Historical References
Proportion has shaped our visual world throughout history—it is an intrinsic part of the Parthenon, da Vinci's *Mona Lisa*, and Michelangelo's *David*.

(continued on page 222)

This poster, sponsored by AIGA and promoting the get-out-the-vote campaign for national elections, presents a simple, evocative, and intriguing image and message. Posed in front of bold, sans serif typography that spells "vote," an enigmatic figure is wrapped and bound, ultimately raising questions about freedom, identity, self-expression, change, and power—and their opposites. The vertical proportion of this poster's format, married with the monumental proportion of the wrapped, bound figure and its vertically proportioned letterforms, further creates a seamless and integrated visual composition.

ALFALFA STUDIO
New York, New York, USA

This book's proportional format, as well as its interior layout, is derived from the Brooklyn Botanic Garden's overall plan designed by the Olmsted Brothers and based on the golden section or rectangle. This proportional formula is also graphically articulated as a continuous series of hairline borders and frames that contain, isolate, and highlight a wide range of photographic, illustrative, and narrative content throughout the book.

POULIN + MORRIS INC.
New York, New York, USA

Univers Family of Typefaces
ADRIAN FRUTIGER
Paris, France

39 univers				

45 univers	46 *univers*	47 univers	48 *univers*	49 univers

53 univers	55 univers	56 *univers*	57 univers	58 *univers*	59 univers

63 univers	65 univers	66 *univers*	67 univers	68 *univers*

73 univers	75 univers	76 *univers*

83 univers

ADRIAN FRUTIGER (B. 1928) is one of the most prominent typographers of the twentieth century and the designer of one of the most notable typeface families ever to be created—the sans serif Univers.

As a young boy, he experimented with invented scripts and stylized handwriting as a negative response to the formal, cursive penmanship being enforced at the Swiss school he was attending. At the age of sixteen, he began a apprenticeship as a compositor with an Interlaken printer. During this apprenticeship, he also learned woodcutting, engraving, and calligraphy.

Between 1949 and 1951, Frutiger studied at the Kunstgewerbeschule (School of Applied Arts) in Zurich. In 1952, Charles Peignot recruited Frutiger for Deberny & Peignot, one of the world's foremost type foundries in Paris. At that time, Deberny & Peignot was using a new phototypesetting process and wanted Frutiger to adapt typefaces for it, as well as design a large, matched typeface family of different weights. During this period, he began to design the Univers family.

The twenty-one variations of the Univers typeface family have five weights and four widths. At its center is Univers 55, the equivalent of a standard "book" weight. Frutiger also proposed to abandon imprecise terms such as *condensed, extended, light, bold, roman,* and *italic,* and instead use a reference numbering system that illustrated the proportional relationships between each variation. At the time, it was a revolutionary concept of how typefaces and their related families could be described.

He also created a visual "periodic table" for the Univers family—its vertical axis identifies different weights, and any variation beginning with the same number is of the same weight. Its horizontal axis identifies perspective shifts, from extended to condensed with italic variations. Any weight ending with an even number is italic. Roman variations are designated with an odd number, oblique variations with an even number.

With the design of Univers, Frutiger also started a trend in type design toward a larger x-height with lowercase letters proportionally more similar to their ascenders, descenders, and capitals. The sizes and weights of its capitals are also closer in size and weight to its lowercase letters, ultimately creating a page of text with visual harmony and ease for the reader.

The Univers family of typefaces is known for its remarkable visual uniformity, which enables a graphic designer to use all twenty-one fonts together as a flexible, integrated typographic system.

In 1986, Adrian Frutiger was awarded the Gutenberg Prize for technical and aesthetic achievement in typography.

Adrian Frutiger and Univers

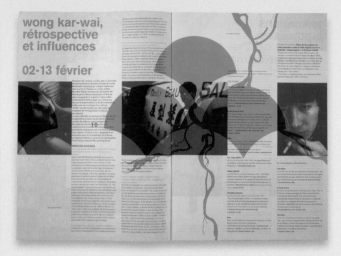

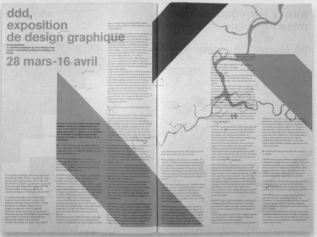

The three-column page grid of this publication for Lux, a regional theater and arts center in southern France, is fully integrated to, as well as based on, the proportional design principle of the golden section. The use of this proportional page relationship further guarantees visual cohesiveness and continuity throughout this publication, as well as related posters, announcement cards, and collateral print material that is diverse and varied with narrative and visual content.

HELMO
Montreuil, France

Euclid, the famous Greek mathematician, was the first to put the theory of proportion into words and images. He divided a line into two sections in such a way that the ratio of the whole line in relation to the larger part is the same relationship as the larger part is to the smaller.

Vitruvius defined proportion in terms of unit fractions, the same system used by the Greeks in their orders of architecture.

One of the most universal images representing the visual theory of proportion is Leonardo da Vinci's famous drawing *Vitruvian Man,* which first appeared in the 1509 book, *Divina Proportione,* by Luca Pacioli. It was here that daVinci attempted to codify proportion based on his studies of the human form, as well as his numerous observations and measurements of proportions for all its parts. He referred in these notebooks to the works of Vitruvius. Many artists of the Renaissance subsequently used proportion as a primary design principle in their work.

In the fifteenth century, Albrecht Dürer determined what characteristics of the human body were visually balanced and beautiful by accurately measuring and documenting the proportions of its parts.

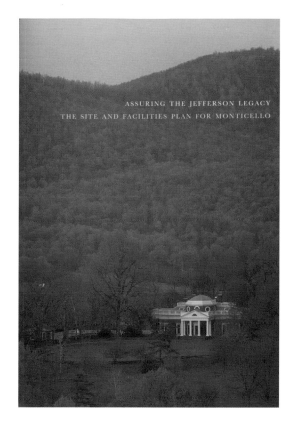

Basic Relationships

Not obvious, and not hidden, the principle
of proportion can be simply conveyed. In
Priya Hemenway's *Divine Proportion: Phi in
Art, Nature, and Science*, she states, "The
whole is to the larger in exactly the same
proportion as the larger is to the smaller."
Proportion lends insight into the process of
design and gives visual coherence to composition through visual structure.

In basic proportional relationships,
the outer dimensions determine the format
of a two-dimensional design and are its
most basic proportion. A square, a vertical
rectangle, and a horizontal rectangle are all
formats with unique proportions that affect
particular characteristics of a composition.
Outer proportions or dimensions can have
an integral relationship to internal divisions
and alignments. Outer dimensions affect the
viewer's orientation and are often dictated by
the composition's ultimate proportion.

The relationship between outer dimensions and internal divisions also provides the
graphic designer with a system for managing
design decisions. Proportional systems have
been used for centuries in architecture and
art, and are based on ratios—a comparison
of one set of sizes with another. Although
ratios are commonly expressed in mathematical terms, they also can be expressed as
visual relationships. For example, the golden
section or rectangle is a ratio that dates back
to the ancient Greeks, and its proportional
properties have both aesthetic beauty and
structural integrity.

The Golden Ratio

The golden ratio is the ratio between two
segments or elements of an object such
that the smaller (*bc*) segment is to the larger

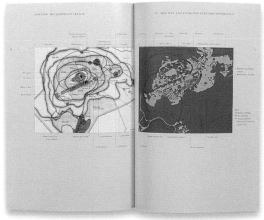

The format and page design
of *Assuring the Jefferson
Legacy: The Site and Facilities
Plan for Monticello* is fully
influenced by the design and
planning principles used by
Thomas Jefferson in all of his
work. These visual principles
are reflected in the book's
layout, typography, and color
palette. They are also evident
in the overall proportion of
the book, which is based on
the golden ratio, furthering
Jefferson's ideal of harmony
found in nature as well as in
the built environment.

POULIN + MORRIS INC.
New York, New York, USA

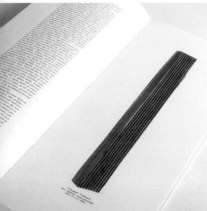

segment (*ab*) as the larger segment (*ab*) is to
the sum of the two segments (*ac*), or *bc/ab* =
ab/ac = 1.618.

It can be found throughout nature, as
well as throughout the history of visual
and applied arts. This proportional ratio is
evident in natural forms such as pinecones,
nautilus shells, seed patterns in the center
of sunflowers, and the human body. It is
constructed through a series of extended
relationships with a strong aesthetic harmony,
since the interior proportions relate in scale
to the proportions of the original square and
its extensions.

The golden ratio can also be extended
to construct the golden rectangle, which the
Greeks used as the basis for the majority of
their city planning and architecture, including
the Parthenon. Renaissance artists used it to
create overall harmony and balance in works
of painting and drawing. Stradivarius used it
in the design and construction of his violins.
It has also been used in the planning and
design of the Great Pyramid at Giza, Stone-
henge, Chartres Cathedral, the LCW chair
designed by Charles Eames, and the Apple
iPod. Even today, contemporary graphic
designers use the golden ratio as an optimal

format for print and digital media. This proportional relationship has also been identified in many other ways over the centuries,
including the golden mean, golden number,
golden section, golden proportion, divine
proportion, and section aurea.

Visual communication is partly an
experience of visual balance—of the relationship of parts to the whole. Perceiving it as
anything else is missing its most fundamental
component. Painting, sculpture, architecture,
music, prose, or poetry are also organized
and methodically balanced around a hidden
sense of true proportion.

Most of what we perceive as pleasing to
the eye, as well as balanced and harmonious,
has some relationship and connection to the
rules of proportion.

How to Construct the Golden Section Rectangle

Step One

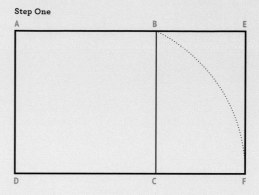

Step Two

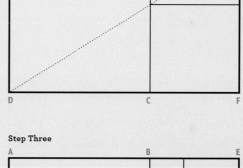

Step One
Draw a perfect square, *ABCD*.

With the midpoint of *DC* as a center, draw an arc with a radius equal to the length of a line drawn from the midpoint of *DC* to *B*.

Step Two
Draw a line from *D* to *E* to divide the rectangle into smaller divisions.

Step Three

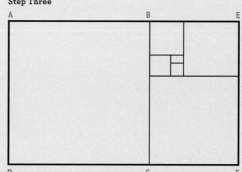

Step Three
To continue, draw a line between opposite corners of the rectangle. For example, a line from *F* to *B*.

Step Four
This is the proportion recognized as the golden section or rectangle.

A golden rectangle is one whose side lengths are in the golden ratio, $1:\frac{1+\sqrt{5}}{2}$ or 1:1.618.

Step Four

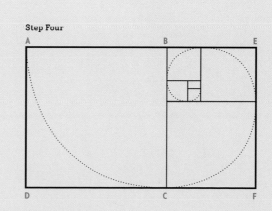

im·age \'i-mij\ *n*
2 b: a visual representation of something:
as (1): a likeness of an object produced
on a photographic material (2): a picture
produced on an electronic display
(as a television or computer screen)
6: a vivid or graphic representation
or description

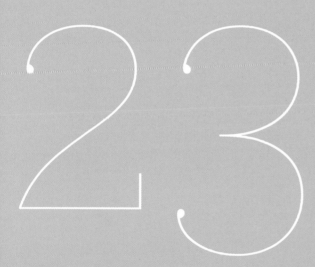

23

"A picture is a poem without words."
HORACE (65–8 BC), *Roman, Poet*

An image is an artifact usually defined as a two-dimensional picture, idea, or impression of a person or physical object. A powerful and memorable image can make or break any visual communication. Photography, illustration, and other types of image forms can communicate a specific idea or

emotion, gain a viewer's attention, further a reader's imagination, and ultimately enhance and enrich any visual message.

Characteristics

In visual communications, a graphic designer can consider numerous forms and methods when undertaking the act and process of image making—glyph, pictogram, symbol, drawing, illustration, painting, photography, and even typography can all be described as forms of image. While they all have distinct and varied visual characteristics and functions, they also have potential as meaningful and obvious counterpoints to narrative form. *(continued on page 230)*

A variety of illustration styles is used in provocative and meaningful ways, creating a memorable and highly communicative series of covers for these public awareness brochures for the Scripps Research Institute.

MIRIELLO GRAFICO
San Diego, California, USA

This singular photographic image of a rich, lush landscape is used to communicate a series of performances titled *Promenades* at a regional theater and arts center located in southern France. The subtle, yet dynamic, use of a figurative cutout from the same background image and then juxtaposed is eye-catching and extremely engaging. The **incorporation of hand-drawn lettering is secondary and supportive of this powerful photographic composition.**

HELMO
Montreuil sous Bois, France

1959

Common Sense and Nuclear Warfare Book Cover
IVAN CHERMAYEFF
New York, New York, USA

Bertrand Russell
Common Sense and
Nuclear Warfare

BROWNJOHN, CHERMAYEFF & GEISMAR

Simon and Schuster

$1.00

In the 1960s, American paperback book publishers and American graphic designers started working together for the first time with a collective, creative objective. At the forefront of this new collaborative movement was a group of visual pioneers and designers such as Paul Rand, Alvin Lustig, Roy Kuhlman, Rudolph de Harak, Tom Geismar, and Ivan Chermayeff.

IVAN CHERMAYEFF (b. 1937), with his partner, Tom Geismar, have created some of the most memorable and recognizable images of the twentieth century.

In his formative years, Chermayeff worked as a record album cover designer as well as an assistant to Alvin Lustig in the early 1950s. He studied at Harvard University, Illinois Institute of Technology (IIT), and Yale University School of Art and Architecture. Following his graduation in 1960, Chermayeff and fellow classmate Geismar moved to New York City to join with already-established Robert Brownjohn to start their own design consultancy firm.

It was during the early 1960s that Brownjohn, Chermayeff, and Geismar established themselves as one of the few progressive and innovative groups of image makers in American graphic design. They were masters in combining their background and training in modernist ideals with the streetwise visual language of the times. Their early work explored a remarkable integration of type and image combined with expressive, intelligent, and literate storytelling. Their numerous book covers produced at the time combined images and symbols to further convey and brand the essence of a book's subject matter. They were powerful signs that grabbed the attention, as well as sparked the imagination, of the reader.

Chermayeff's cover design for Bertrand Russell's *Common Sense and Nuclear Warfare* is a high-contrast, photomontage of two black-and-white photographs—a mushroom cloud superimposed on the back of a man's head. These powerful visual metaphors act as a counterpoint and provide the reader with an unnerving and fearsome idea about mankind's vulnerability to nuclear war, even before opening the book. It is a seminal example of the marriage of image, symbol, and word to create powerful and meaningful visual communications.

He says, "Great images, to be great, must be original and memorable. Occasionally a designer recognizes a commonality between two separate visual images and pins them together, making one new, powerful, and provocative form. Finding connections, large and small, is what the design process is all about."

Ivan Chermayeff and Thomas Geismar were awarded the prestigious American Institute of Graphic Arts (AIGA) Gold Medal in 1979.

Ivan Chermayeff and the Modern American Paperback

09
soulpepper

THE GUARDSMAN
FERENC MOLNÁR
TRANSLATED BY FRANK MARCUS

**AUGUST 31 —
OCTOBER 24**

416.866.8666
SOULPEPPER.CA

09
soulpepper

AWAKE AND SING!
CLIFFORD ODETS
JUNE 6 — JULY 31

416.866.8666
SOULPEPPER.CA

09
soulpepper

CIVIL ELEGIES
DENNIS LEE
CREATED BY MIKE ROSS & LORENZO SAVOINI
ORIGINAL MUSIC BY MIKE ROSS

DECEMBER 3 — 24

416.866.8666
SOULPEPPER.CA

09
soulpepper

WHO'S AFRAID OF
VIRGINIA WOOLF?
EDWARD ALBEE
**AUGUST 29 —
OCTOBER 24**

416.866.8666
SOULPEPPER.CA

09
soulpepper

TRAVESTIES
TOM STOPPARD
**FEBRUARY 12 —
MARCH 21**

416.866.8666
SOULPEPPER.CA

09
soulpepper

GLENGARRY
GLEN ROSS
DAVID MAMET
APRIL 2 — MAY 9

416.866.8666
SOULPEPPER.CA

Character-driven themes, such as for these three plays— *The Guardsman*, *Travesties*, and *Glengarry Glen Ross*, provide any graphic designer with a multitude of image challenges and opportunities. This poster series for the Soulpepper Theatre uses dynamic and provocative imagery that is composed of photography, illustration, line art, and a layering combination of styles. All provide a highly interpretive and communicative visual story directly related to each of the play's themes.

SANDWICH CREATIVE
Toronto, Ontario, Canada

An image can be two-dimensional or virtual, such as a photograph, an illustration, or a screen display; or it can be three-dimensional, such as a sculpture or statue. An image can be captured by an optical device such as a camera, mirror, lens, telescope, or microscope, as well as by natural objects and phenomena such as the human eye or the reflective surface of water.

The word *image* is also used in the broader sense of any two-dimensional figure such as a map, graph, pie chart, or abstract painting. Images can be rendered manually, such as through drawing, painting, or carving, or rendered automatically through conventional printing or digital technology.

Classifications

Images vary greatly in media and content. The extensive choice of image types available today can be organized as follows:

Volatile
A volatile image exists only for a short period of time. This image type may be a reflection of an object in a mirror, a projection of a camera obscura, or a scene displayed on a cathode ray tube or video monitor.

Fixed
A fixed image, also called a hard copy, is an image that has been recorded on a material or object, such as paper or textile, by a photographic or digital process. A laser print, photographic print, and a large-scale digital wall mural are all types of fixed images.

Still
A still image is a single static image, as distinguished from a moving image. This term is used in photography, visual media, and the digital world.

Moving
A moving image is typically a movie (film) or video, including digital video. It can also be an animated display such as a zoetrope. In addition to conventional film, moving images can be captured with digital cameras, laptops, webcams, and cell phones.

Graphic Forms

An image is a potentially powerful element in visual communication because it is one of the few forms that can represent an emotional experience and be immediately understood and embraced by the viewer.

The Penguin Classics imprint is more than a half-century old and is recognized around the world for its offerings of world-class literature. In the these three book covers for Robertson Davies' novels, four-color photographic imagery is used as bold, iconic storytelling vehicles for each of the book's fictional themes. The imagery also has distinct, memorable, and relevant characteristics from each narrative due to the unconventional and unorthodox vantage points and interpretations taken with each photograph.

SOAPBOX DESIGN
COMMUNICATIONS
Toronto, Ontario, Canada

This set of book covers is part of an branding campaign based on the illustrative reinterpretation of classic book covers directed toward junior high school students. Dynamic, textural, and highly emotional line illustrations engage the young reader, giving them an immediate and meaningful connection to each book and its themes. Vibrant and intense color palettes, hand-drawn letterforms, and reductive and representational visual elements are collectively used to unify this diverse series.

MIKEY BURTON
Philadelphia, Pennsylvania, USA

Images can be stylized and take many graphic forms, such as an icon, sign, symbol, supersign, or logotype. Photography and illustration are forms of image that are broad based in content, compositions, and style, each affording the designer a specific visual language or dialect. Both forms can be realistic representations or interpretive expressions depicting a wide range of visual narratives. Each of will have a direct impact and influence on the ultimate meaning in a visual message.

Type (letterform, narrative form) is also a form of image that can have meaningful qualities for effective visual communications.

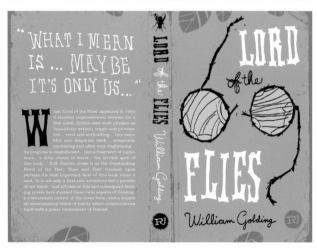

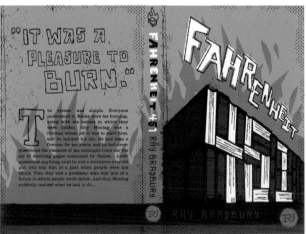

This class assignment is an exploration of addition, subtraction, transformation, and substitution relationships created with photographic form. Students start with two photographic images—one of architecture and one of a landscape. These images are first printed, then cut to a 4 cm (1.5-inch) grid and flush mounted to black kraft paper. This process involves a substitution of sixteen landscape squares into the architecture image, and then sixteen architecture squares into the landscape image. The goal is to achieve the greatest transformation with each substitution. This process is also informed by the composition of each image, not only in terms of the overall arrangement of visual elements, but also in the formal qualities of each unit in the imposed structure or grid. The substitution Is defined and governed by such design principles as contrast, continuity, rhythm, juxtaposition, similarity, and difference. The ultimate objective is for each student to develop new relationships of photographic form that did not exist previously.

SARAH AL GROOBI. Student
AMIR BERBIC,
RODERICK GRANT,
Instructors
American University of Sharjah
Sharjah, United Arab Emirates

The presentation and representation of any image can span a broad spectrum defined at one end by realism and at the other end by abstraction. Between these two visual extremes are a myriad of possibilities for the graphic designer to choose from—the more realistic, the more direct and immediate the image; the more abstract, the more restrained and interpretive the image.

Functions

Images can function in a multitude of roles within any visual communication. They can provide a meaningful counterpoint to narrative text, engage the reader with enhanced visual interest, bring clarity and organization to complex information, and communicate emotions grounded in the human experience.

They can visually represent a specific person, place, event, or reference in narrative text, as well as provide a counterpoint to it. An image can be literal, representational, metaphorical, or abstract. They can also immediately alter the meaning of words, just as words can change the meaning of any image.

Combining image and narrative form is challenging for any graphic designer. These distinct visual forms can be combined

Michelangelo Buonarroti **RIME**
prefazione di Vinicio Capossela

Gustave Flaubert **DIZIONARIO DEI LUOGHI COMUNI**
prefazione di Michele Serra

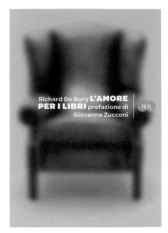

Richard De Bury **L'AMORE PER I LIBRI** prefazione di
Giovanna Zucconi

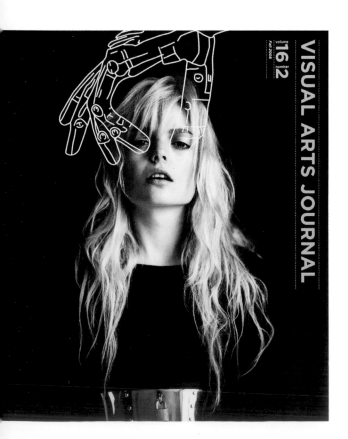

to establish more meaningful relationships or contrasting counterpoints between the two forms and simultaneously strengthen the collective message.

When deciding to use photography versus illustration, a graphic designer needs to consider that the most people will respond and engage more immediately with a photograph because they perceive this image type as the closest form of their own objective reality, as opposed to illustration that is traditionally seen as an artist's (or designer's) visual inter-pretation of a subjective reality. One form is immediate, intuitive, powerful, and persuasive; the other, less so.

The juxtaposition of line art and photography, scale and texture, horizontal and vertical orientation all provide additional visual impact and presence to the figurative images used on this cover for the *Visual Arts Journal*, a bi-annual publication featuring work from School of Visual Arts students and alumni, as well as perspectives on the latest art trends.

VISUAL ARTS PRESS
New York, New York, USA

Bright, saturated colors and iconic photographic images with an out-of-focus appearance create a visual power and immediacy for each of these book covers. Additionally, bold, sans serif typography combined with open-space kerning allows the typography to be visually perforated, creating more immediacy and connection for the viewer.

MUCCA DESIGN
New York, New York, USA

The visual immediacy of this book cover for *Killing the Buddha* is solely dependent on the fundamental element of image. The calming soft blue sky with a white cloud combined with an iconic, overscaled red *X* implies the violence of this book's theme and cover concept without relying on literal typography or imagery.

THE OFFICE
OF PAUL SAHRE
New York, New York, USA

Ultimately, there are many methods to communicate meaningful messages and ideas with image. The possibilities are endless for any graphic designer to create rich, communicative, and memorable visual experiences for the viewer. The only limitation is the graphic designer's imagination.

pat·tern \ˈpa-tərn\ *n*

3: an artistic, musical, literary, or mechanical design or form

24

"Pattern, the fruit of design, can be seen as the measure of culture."

WILLIAM FEAVER, *British, Art Critic, Author*

Like texture, pattern is a fundamental design principle that helps define the visual quality of surface activity. The visual characteristics of any pattern help us see distinctions between one object and another. Pattern is a specific type of visual texture and is traditionally derived from a defined and

Soft, muted tones of color, pattern, and typography are used as figurative textures to further enhance the identity program for Odun, a Mexico City restaurant featuring Asian cuisines. The overall identity, as well as its array of tones, colors, and patterns, was inspired by a diversity of influences, flavors, scents, and spirits found throughout Asian cultures.

BLOK DESIGN
Mexico City, Mexico

repeated compositional structure always appearing in an organized and regimented graphic manner.

The visual elements of point, line, and shape are the basis for creating pattern throughout history. Combining pattern with the organizational design principle of the grid, graphic designers can create an infinite variety of end results. By utilizing a singular element in different organizations, configurations, and compositions, patterns can be realized with endless variations either subtle or obvious, all built around a singular common graphic denominator.

(continued on page 240)

AZUERO
EARTH
PROJECT

A carefully composed pattern of natural leaf forms, varied in scale, color, profile, and orientation, creates the fluid form and body of a monkey symbolizing the Azuero Earth Project. Its mission is to preserve the ecosystem of the Azuero Peninsula, protect biodiversity, and promote healthy 'green' communities.

SAGMEISTER INC.
New York, New York, USA

1911

Hermann Scherrer Poster
LUDWIG HOHLWEIN
Munich, Germany

LUDWIG HOHLWEIN (1847–1949) was trained and practiced as an architect until 1906, when he became interested in graphic design and the visual arts.

During the 1890s, he lived in Munich, where he was part of the United Workshops for Arts and Crafts, an avant-garde group of artists and craftsmen dedicated to the tenets and principles of the Arts and Crafts movement. Hohlwein moved to Berlin in 1911 and started working as a graphic designer primarily designing advertisements and posters for the men's clothing company Hermann Scherrer.

Hohlwein's most creative phase of work and a large variety of his best-known posters were created between 1912 and 1925. It was during this critical period that he developed his own unique visual style. By 1925, he had already designed 3,000 different advertisements and became the best-known German commercial artist of his time.

Poster historian Alain Weill comments that "Hohlwein was the most prolific and brilliant German posterist of the twentieth century. . . Beginning with his first efforts, Hohlwein found his style with disconcerting facility. It would vary little for the next forty years. The drawing was perfect from the start, nothing seemed alien to him, and in any case, nothing posed a problem for him. His figures are full of touches of color and a play of light and shade that brings them out of their background and gives them substance."

Hohlwein's work relied mostly on strong figurative elements with reductive qualities of high contrast, intense flat color, and bold patterns of geometric elements. This is evident in his iconographic poster for Hermann Scherrer. The figurative element of the man is optically centered in the field of the poster with no apparent horizon line. The well-dressed gentleman and his riding accessories, as well as his pure-bred dog, are all represented in a reductive, stark manner combined with vivid color and an abstract, black-and-white checkerboard pattern. Here, Hohlwein treats this distinctive pattern as a two-dimensional plane. It is in extreme contrast to the surrounding three-dimensional compositional elements, creating a strong and memorable focal point for the poster.

His adaptation of photographic images was based on a deep and intuitive understanding of visual design principles. His creative use of color and architectural compositions dispels any suggestion that he used photographs as the basis of his creative output. Additionally, his use of high tonal contrasts, interlocking shapes, and distinctive graphic patterns made his work instantly recognizable and memorable.

Aside from Lucian Bernhard, Ludwig Hohlwein was one of the most successful and celebrated designers of the Plakatstil and Sachplakat modes or "poster" and "object poster" styles in Germany during this time period.

Ludwig Hohlwein and the Hermann Scherrer style

The branding program for Nizuc, an upscale resort and residential community in Mexico, was inspired by the site's Mayan history. The project's figurative symbol, also evocative of Mayan carvings and bas-reliefs, is the base element of graphic patterns used throughout this visual program.

CARBONE SMOLAN
AGENCY
New York, New York, USA

Historical Influences

Throughout history, an abundance of pattern making has occurred in practically every culture around the world. Patterns have been evident not only in the graphic arts, but in fine and applied arts, such as textiles, pottery, wallpaper, apparel, furniture, interiors, metalwork, ceramic tiles, mosaics, and stencils, as well as new and innovative digital experiments by contemporary artists and graphic designers.

Artists and graphic designers have also developed a wide range of styles, forms, and motifs. For example, early twentieth-century innovators of pattern making include William

The Street Sweets graphic identity and branding program uses a combination of pattern, typography, and color. For example, a dense arrangement of verbs and adjectives such as *delightful*, *bliss*, *love*, *fresh*, and *delicious* form a dynamic, structurelike pattern that is used as a typographic backdrop in a variety of large and small-scale applications— business cards, food packaging, shopping bags, and food truck graphics.

LANDERS MILLER
New York, New York, USA

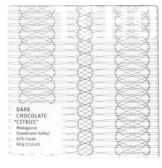

Morris (British), Koloman Moser (Austrian), Anni Albers (German), Fortuny (Italian), Alvin Lustig (American), Ray Eames (American), and Alexander Girard (American) up to contemporary designers such as Richard Rhys (British).

In the early 1900s, with the advent of the modernist movement in the visual and applied arts, a preference for minimalist surfaces and textures became the norm; ornate patterning and overtly decorative surfaces were avoided. This trend has now been tempered, and a far wider palette of choices is now evident and appreciated worldwide.

Basic Structures and Forms

A pattern can be a theme of recurring events or objects, sometimes referred to as elements of a given set. These events, objects, or elements always repeat themselves in a predictable and organized manner.

Pattern has a strong relationship to geometry, since it is an organized and regimented texture in which singular elements are composed on a defined and repeated structure. It is due to this underlying structure that patterns are always synthetic, manmade, and mechanical, and never organic.

TCHO is a San Francisco-based luxury chocolate manufacturer and uses a broad palette of pattern as functional and interpretive elements in its visual branding program. Its graphic influences are derived from Aztec culture, where chocolate was used as a form of currency. Contemporary line variations on currency patterns, representing the six flavor-driven product lines—chocolaty, nutty, fruity, floral, and citrus—are used as decorative product identifiers. Each pattern is framed within a square and is the base element connecting all packaging, collateral, and visual communication material. The brand's color palette extends from dark brown to bright magenta, orange, and yellow, reflecting the flavors as well as the high-tech modernist values of the product line.

EDENSPIEKERMANN
Berlin, Germany

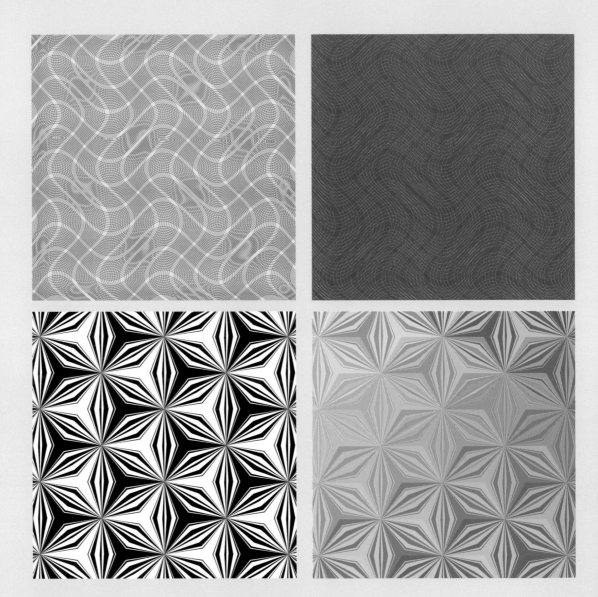

This assignment requires students to analyze the potential of pattern in relationship to color and composition. Using abstract shapes and fundamental graphic elements, students initially develop a 10 X 10-inch (25.4 X 25.4 cm) square complex pattern based on an assigned piece of music. The final pattern is to visually represent the music (or a portion of it) in some visual manner. This pattern is then modified into seven color variations—black and white, monochromatic, analogous, complementary, split complementary, triadic, and tetradic.

ALETA CORBOY, Student
ANNABELLE GOULD, Instructor
University of Washington
Seattle, Washington, USA

Brown, Juana Francisca's Kitchen is a confectionery located in Bogotá, offering a delicate selection of gourmet sweets. Their packaging system uses kraft board boxes, a series of preprinted tag cards, and rubber stamps with decorative motifs and patterns that carry information about what's inside the box. The repetitive dot and line motifs and patterns are evocative of decorative icing used on confections and small baked goods.

LIP
Bogotá, Colombia

The most basic patterns are composed through repetition and are considered a repeat of any visual element such as point, line, shape, form, or color. A single element is combined with duplicates of itself without change or modification. For example, a checkerboard is a simple pattern based on alternating squares of black and red.

Patterns can also be based on familiar elements, such as in simple decorative patterns of stripes, zigzags, and polka dots. Other patterns can be more visually complex and can be found in nature, art, and the built environment. These include arabesques, branching, circulation, fractals, helixes, lat-

This entrance to Brooklyn Botanic Garden comprises two 12-foot (4 m) high curved walls rising on both sides of the entrance and sheathed in stainless steel with an etched cherry tree leaf pattern. The actual entrance gates are the same material; however, the leaf pattern here is water-jet cut, creating a stainless steel grille for viewing into the garden when it is closed.

POULIN + MORRIS INC.
New York, New York, USA

Decorative geometric patterns are layered in vellum; the outer layer represented graphically in stark black and white, the other revealing the same pattern in a rich, vibrant, multicolored palette. This pattern layering device is a metaphor for the dual undertone themes of these classic Jane Austen novels—*Sense and Sensibility* and *Emma*.

ISABELLE RANCIER, Student
TRACY BOYCHUK, Instructor
School of Visual Arts
New York, New York, USA

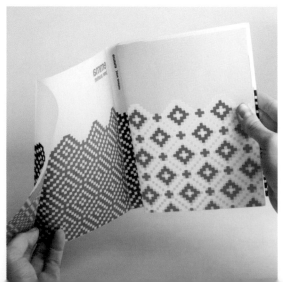

Kinetic and energetic line patterns are used for a series of notebook covers developed, designed, and marketed by this California-based design firm. The juxtaposition of two patterns for each notebook, and the use of a broad range of intense, vibrant color palettes throughout, add a visual power and vibrancy to each of these cover combinations.

tices, meanders, nests, polyhedra, spheres, spirals, symmetry, volutes, and waves. A recurring pattern in fine art and architecture is referred to as a motif.

Moirés are also a form of pattern first used after World War II, when graphic designers began to exploit and experiment with the conventional methods and attributes of process reproduction and offset printing. Moiré patterns revealed to the viewer the layered tints and enlarged halftones of these processes, creating dynamic and unexpected visual effects of color and texture that had not been visually experienced before this time period.

Today, digital software is an easily accessible and immediate means by which the same visual pattern effects can be achieved.

Both labels for "Il conte" use a common base pattern comprising geometric form triangles and vine leaf elements that function as a frame and iconic backdrop for each wine name—*Montepulciano d'Abruzzo* and *Pinot Grigio*. This pattern is further enhanced and articulated with color, red or warm white, depending upon which wine type is identified.

ty·pog·ra·phy \tī-ˈpä-grə-fē\ *n*
2: the style, arrangement, or appearance of typeset matter

25

"Typography at its best is a visual form of language linking timelessness and time."

ROBERT BRINGHURST (B. 1946), *Canadian, Author, Poet, Typographer*

Typography is designing with type. Type is the term used for letterforms—alphabet, numbers, and punctuation—that when used together create words, sentences, and narrative form. The term *typeface* refers to the design of all the characters mentioned above, unified by common visual

Bold, sans serif letterforms, slanted back in perspective to imply movement, speed, and direction, are the primary visual characteristics of the new logotype for the Van Nuys FlyAway, a part of the Los Angeles World Airports' system of regional satellite bus depots that service Los Angeles Airport (LAX) via a park-and-ride bus system. As part of the recent renovation and expansion of the facility, the new logotype was designed to look and feel like an extension of a modern airport and applied extensively to architectural and wayfinding signs, environmental graphics, and bus fleet graphics.

SUSSMAN/PREJZA
& COMPANY
Culver City, California, USA

elements and characteristics. Typography is also a unique principle in a graphic designer's vocabulary because it has dual functions. It can function on its purest level as a graphic element such as point, line, form, shape, and texture in a visual composition. However, its primary function is verbal and visual. It is to be read. When typography has a relationship only to its verbal meaning, its communicative character can lack visual impact. When typography reflects a treatment that enhances both its verbal and visual meaning, it is perceived on multiple levels, not only intellectually but also sensually and emotionally.

Typography, of course, is all around us. In graphic design, the goal of the designer is not to just place typography on a page but rather to understand and use it effectively in visual communications. The selection and choice of typography, size, alignment, color, and spacing all are critical.

Historical References

Since the beginning of mankind, we have needed to communicate our lives to our fellow man. Before we learned to "speak" verbally, we spoke "visually" by leaving crude
(continued on page 250)

U&lc cover
HERB LUBALIN
New York, New York, USA

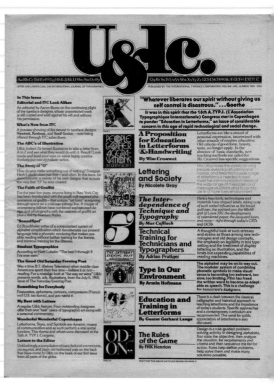

HERB LUBALIN (1918–1981) was a legendary art director, designer, and typographic master who brought humor, sensuality, and a modernist flair to every letterform and typographic element in his work.

Born in Brooklyn, New York, he attended Cooper Union, where he began his love affair with calligraphy, letterform, and formal typography. Immediately following his graduation in 1939, he joined the advertising agency of Sudler & Hennessey (later Sudler, Hennessey & Lubalin) as an art director.

In 1964, he left the agency to start his own design firm, where he ultimately worked in a broad range of areas including advertisements, editorial design, trademarks, typeface design, posters, packaging, and publications.

During this time, he became discontent with the rigid limitations of metal type and began to experiment with cutting and reassembling his own type proofs. Here, he was able to explore typography in a detailed and intimate manner that he had never experienced before. He manipulated type by hand—compressed it into ligatures, enlarged it to extreme sizes, and ultimately transformed it by giving it added meaning. It was also during this period that he produced some of the most memorable and dramatic typographic work of the decade.

In 1970, Lubalin joined with phototypography pioneer Edward Rondthaler and typographer Aaron Burns to establish the International Typeface Corporation (ITC). From 1970 to 1980, ITC designed, produced, and licensed thirty-four fully developed typeface families and approximately sixty display typefaces. Characteristics of ITC type families included an emphasis on large x-heights as well as short ascenders and descenders, allowing for tighter line spacing—a prevalent typographic style of the time.

During this same period, ITC published a typographic magazine, *U&lc*, which showcased its various type families and display typefaces to the design community. Because of its extraordinary combination of typographic design, illustration, and editorial content celebrating the virtues of well-designed typography, it was avidly read by type enthusiasts worldwide. Lubalin, as design director, gave this tabloid-size newsprint publication a complex, dynamic, and expressionistic style that had a major impact on publication design of the 1970s.

Throughout his career, he always considered space and surface his primary visual communication tools. One designer noted that Lubalin's work reminded him of a Claude Debussy quote that said "music is the space between the notes."

Lubalin embraced typographic characters as both visual and communicative forms—forms that were meant to invoke, inform, and ultimately engage the viewer. Rarely have complex typographic arrangements been so dynamic and so unified. The traditional rules and practices of typography were always abandoned for a more nontraditional and humanistic approach that made him a typographic master.

Herb Lubalin and *U&lc*

Bold, black, oversized letterforms are used on this set of textbook covers for *Written Language and Power* and *Introduction to Linguistics* to create iconic, singular, and immediate identifiers for each publication.

CASA REX
São Paulo, Brazil

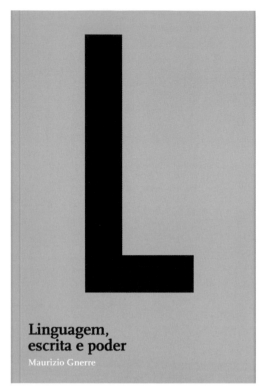

Linguagem, escrita e poder
Maurizio Gnerre

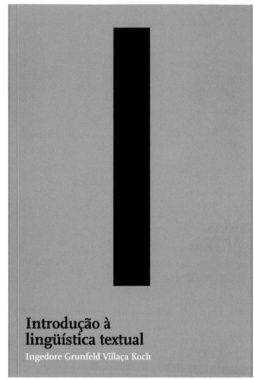

Introdução à lingüística textual
Ingedore Grunfeld Villaça Koch

marks on walls and surfaces. From prehistoric cave paintings and Egyptian hieroglyphics to Roman inscriptions and medieval crests, communicating experiences to one another has been a common human denominator for telling our stories at any given time. Man has discovered how to make the word and the image become one. As our world has become more complex, so has the means by which we communicate those stories in their many forms. The most universal means throughout our collective history has been, and will continue to be, typography.

Anatomy of Letterforms
To better understand and recognize the similarities and differences between typefaces, an effective graphic designer needs to be familiar with the anatomy of letterforms. Each typeface has a distinct appearance with fundamental characteristics and features that provide distinguishing details to group or set typefaces apart from one another.

Form Variations
Typographic form varies only in case, weight, contrast, posture, width, and style. The extensive choices of individual typefaces or

fonts, available today share the following six common characteristics with only subtle alteration and variation:

Case
Each letter in any alphabet comprises two case forms—uppercase and lowercase.

Weight
The weight of a letterform is defined by the overall thickness of its stroke in relation to its height. Common weight variations include light, book, medium, bold, and black.

Contrast
The contrast of a letterform is determined by the degree of weight change in its stroke.

Posture
The posture of a letterform is its vertical orientation to a baseline. Upright and perpendicular letterforms to a baseline are roman; slanted or angled are italic.

Width
The width of any letterform is based on how wide it is in relation to its height. A letterform's standard width is based on a square

Ā f M g R x

Apex · Ascender · Crossbar · Bracket · Vertex · Ear · Counter · Descender · Stem · Leg · Joint · Serif

Cap height · x-height · Baseline

K b s S fj Q o Q

Arm · Spur · Bowl · Spine · Terminal · Ligature · Vertical Stress · Inclined Stress · Tail

Cap height · x-height · Baseline

Apex
The outer point where two diagonal stems or strokes meet, as at the top of an *A* or *M* or at the bottom of an *M*.

Arm
A projecting horizontal or upward diagonal stem or stroke not enclosed within a character, as in an *E*, *K*, or *L*.

Ascender
The stem or stroke of a lowercase character located above the x-height, as in *b*, *d*, or *k*.

Baseline
A line on which the bottom of characters without descenders sit or align.

Bowl
A curved stem or stroke that encloses a counter, as in a *b*, *p*, or *O*.

Bracket
A curving joint between the serif and a stem or stroke; also known as a fillet.

Cap height
The distance from a baseline to the top of a capital character.

Cicero
A European typographic unit of measurement approximately equal to the British or American pica, or 4.155 mm.

Counter
An area enclosed by a bowl or a crossbar.

Crossbar
A horizontal element connecting two vertical or diagonal stems or strokes, or crossing a stem or stroke, as in an *A*, *H*, *f*, or *t*; also known as a bar or cross stroke.

Descender
The stem or stroke of a lowercase character located below the baseline, as in a *g*, *p*, or *y*.

Ear
A small projecting stroke sometimes attached to the bowl of a *g* or the stem of a *r*.

Joint
The angle formed where two strokes meet or intersect, as is a *K* or *R*.

Leg
A projecting diagonal stem or stroke extending downward, as in a *R* and *K*; also known as a tail.

Ligature
A stem or stroke that connects two characters together creating a ligature or tied character.

Link
The stem or stroke that connects the bowl and the loop of a *g*.

Loop
The descender of a *g* when it is entirely closed.

Pica
A typographic unit of measurement where 12 points equal 1 pica (1/16 inch or 0.166 inch) and 6 picas equal 1 inch (0.996 inch).

Point
The smallest unit of typographic measurement; one point is equal to 1/72 inch or 0.0148 inches or 0.351 mm.

Serif
The beginning or end of a stem or stroke, arm, leg, or tail drawn at a right angle or at an oblique to the stem or stroke.

Shoulder
The portion of a curved stroke, but not the hairline, connecting two vertical strokes or stems.

Spine
The diagonal portion or main curved stroke of an *S* or *s*.

Spur
A small, pointed projection from a stem or stroke, sometimes found on the bottom of a *b*, *t*, or *G*.

Stem (or Stroke)
The principal vertical or oblique element(s) of a character, as in an *A*, *B*, *L*, or *V*; except for curved characters where they are called strokes.

Stress (or Axis)
The inclination suggested by the relationship of thin and thick stems or strokes in a character, which can be an inclined or vertical stress or axis.

Swash
A flourished terminal, stem, or stroke added to a character.

Tail
The short stem or stroke that rests on a baseline, as in a *K* or *R*; or extending below a baseline, as in a *Q* or *j*. In a *K* and *R*, also known as a leg.

Terminal (or Finial)
A stem or stroke ending other than a serif.

Vertex
The angle formed at the bottom of a character where the left and right strokes meet or intersect, as in a *V* or *x*.

x-height
The distance from the baseline to the top of lowercase *x*.

The graphic and packaging design for Mrs. Meyer's Clean Day, a line of aromatherapeutic household cleaners, uses no-fuss, no-frills, utilitarian, sans serif typography that is functional with a subtle hint of visual style, character, and flair. This typographic approach is appropriate in this context since the product line is designed to represent the same work ethic.

WERNER DESIGN WERKS
St. Paul, Minnesota, USA

proportion. Exaggerated widths with narrower proportions are identified as condensed or compressed; ones with wider proportions are identified as extended or expanded.

Style
The style of letterforms refers to the two basic categories of serif and sans serif, as well as its historical context and classification.

While there have been many different approaches to typographic design over the centuries, whether driven by societal needs or technological advances, basic typographic characteristics such as the ones referenced above are still used today. Well-designed typographic forms transcend history, culture, and geography.

Descriptions and Classifications
How does a graphic designer decide, among the thousands of typefaces available, which font or font family might fulfill a specific design need? While most typefaces are classified into three categories, namely serif, sans serif, and script—it is a limited and somewhat shortsighted classification system. One method for familiarizing yourself with typefaces and their unique characteristics and

This series of theatrical production posters for Edward
Albee's *The Goat, or Who
Is Sylvia?* uses typographic
overlays as interpretive
representations of the play's
themes and explorations of
morality and identity. The
effective use of bold typographic forms and collage, as
well as the overlay blocking,
fragmenting, and revealing of
alternative representations

of "Goat" and "Sylvia," forces
the viewer to immediately
question and further consider
who these two characters are.

ADRIANA URIBE, Student
PAUL SAHRE, Instructor
School of Visual Arts
New York, New York, USA

attributes, as well as understanding their
historical development and potential applications, is to use a more detailed and accurate
system of typeface classification.

The following classification system is
a simplified, practical reference tool for any
graphic designer:

Old Style
Typefaces classified as Old Style are primarily based on roman proportions. They do
not have strong contrasts in stroke weights,
the stress of curved strokes is noticeably
oblique, a smaller x-height defines their
lowercase letters, terminals are pear shaped,
and lowercase counters are small. Bembo,
Centaur, Garamond, Jenson, and Goudy are
Old Style typefaces.

Transitional
Typefaces classified as Transitional primarily
have greater stroke contrast in comparison
to Old Style typefaces. Their serifs are
sharper, a larger x-height defines their lowercase letters, and the stress of curved-stroke
letterforms is vertical or nearly so. Basker-
ville, Bell, Bulmer, Fournier and Perpetua are
Transitional typefaces.

Perricone MD's branding campaign includes packaging, website, advertising, and promotional sales collateral that reflect a modern visual interpretation of a traditional apothecary—understated, small-scale serif typography, scientific photography, frosted amber glass— all organized and composed in an asymmetrical, balanced manner. In this application, asymmetrical serif typography, while restrained and small-scale in relationship to the detail photograph of the bottle, is clean, crisp, immediate, and highly visible.

MONNET DESIGN
Toronto, Ontario, Canada

The purity and simplicity of these all-cap letterforms used in this identity program for the retailer Walrus creates a strong and impactful visual message that is immediate, direct, and memorable due to the sensitive and effective use of sans serif typography.

MERCER CREATIVE GROUP
Vancouver, BC, Canada

Modern
The most prominent characteristic of Modern typefaces is their extreme contrast in stroke weights. Serifs are thin and completely flat, displaying little if any bracketing. The stress of Modern typefaces is almost invariably vertical. Bodoni, Didot, Melior and Walbaum are classified as Modern typefaces.

Sans Serif
The distinguishing feature of sans serif typefaces is their lack of serifs (sans means "without" in French). Stroke weight is even and uniform, and their stress is vertical. The italic versions of san serif typefaces often appear as slanted romans or obliques. Akzidenz Grotesk, Franklin Gothic, Futura, Meta and Univers are classified as sans serif typefaces.

Slab Serif
Slab serif typefaces are uniform in stroke weight and their stress is vertical. Their serifs are usually the same weight as the stem of the letterforms. Slab serif typefaces are also identified as Egyptian. Cheltenham, Clarendon, Egyptienne, Lubalin Graph, Memphis, Rockwell, Serifa and Stymie are classified as slab serif typefaces.

Graphic
This category of typefaces includes unique and idiosyncratic type families that have graphic and illustrative characteristics such as script, cursive, brush, display, decorative, and blackletter.

The graphic character of any typeface communicates a purely visual message as well as a narrative one. It may have a distinct physical presence on the page and also convey obvious or implied meanings such as young or old, feminine or masculine, aggressive or timid. While everyone may not understand or connect with the designer's intent with any given typeface used, it is the sole responsibility of the graphic designer to carefully evaluate his or her own typographic decisions in the context of the message and the audience.

Optical Issues
The graphic character of a typeface also has a direct relationship to the perception of its size. For example, a typographic line set in the same point size with two visually distinc-tive type styles will appear to be different sizes. This optical discrepancy is due to a graphic, as well as measured, difference

Poster 1 (dark)

AGDA

How Can Graphic
Design Help Save
The Planet?

Designer
Dinner #3

AUGUST

Deus Ex Machina
Opening Doors
Colour Trends

SEPTEMBER

OCTOBER

Ken Cato

Designer
Dinner #4

NOVEMBER

David Pidgeon
Xmas Party

DECEMBER

Poster 2 (light)

AGDA

Trivia

Designer
dinner #1

MARCH

Inspired by design
Business focus

APRIL

Tobias
Frere-Jones

Designer
dinner #2

MAY

The other forty
one minutes

JUNE

Inspirational
spaces

JULY

Landor · S.H.BENNETT

Proudly supported by AQUENT

Both of these promotional posters for the Australian Graphic Design Association function as an announcement for a series of member programs and offerings. The visual power and dynamic character of typographic form—in this case, Futura—is used as a visual common denominator in both poster compositions. Left and right justification of each program listing, as well as the use of horizontal hairlines located between each listing, further organize and isolate information reinforcing a visual hierarchy. Bold, graphic contrast with black and white and saturated colors of red and yellow are used effectively to further engage the viewer.

LANDOR
Paris, France

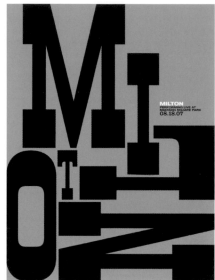

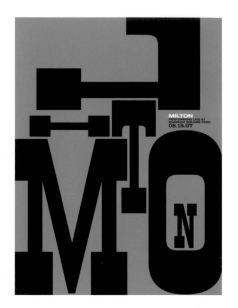

Old, wood-type, slab serif letterforms are the inspiration, as well as the primary imagery, for these posters promoting the band Milton's public concert in Madison Square Park in New York City. This bold, black typography is organized in a playful composition and set off by vibrant color backgrounds.

STEREOTYPE DESIGN
New York, New York, USA

between the actual x-heights of both type styles. Sans serif x-heights tend to be larger in relationship to their cap heights than serifs, which tend to be smaller in relationship to their cap heights. The difference in graphic and measured sizes can vary as much as two to three points, depending on the typeface. For example, a sans serif typeface such as Frutiger or Gill Sans may be legible and comfortable to read at 8 points, but an Old Style typeface such as Bembo or Garamond at the same size will be illegible and impossible to read with any level of comfort or ease.

Alignment Formats

Typography can be organized in several different compositional formats called alignments. A flush left alignment is set so that multiple typographic lines (or text) begin at the same point along a left-hand vertical edge. A flush right alignment is set in the same manner with all text beginning at the same point along a right-hand vertical edge. A centered alignment is set so that all text shares the same center axis with the width of the paragraph. Additionally, there are two alignment options with a centered composi-

tional format. A centered alignment is set so that all text lines are varied lengths, centered above one another, and share the same center axis with the width of the paragraph. A justified alignment is set so that every text line is the same length and aligning on both the left- and right-hand vertical edges. A justified alignment is the only alignment where all text lines are the exact same length.

When text is set flush left, flush right, or centered, the varied lengths of these text lines create an uneven textural edge(s) called a "rag."

Alignments also can have an effect on typographic spacing within a body of text. When text is set flush left rag right, word spacing is uniform and even. The same effect occurs with flush right rag left and centered alignments. In a justified alignment, word spacing varies because the width of the paragraph is fixed and the words on every line need to align with both vertical edges, no matter how many words are on each line.

With justified alignments, variations in word spacing are the most challenging issue for any graphic designer to resolve properly and effectively. The result of ineffective justified alignments is an overabundance of

The textured letterforms used in these two posters for **UCLA School of Architecture's "Double Edge" lecture series** function as visual metaphors and identifiers for each architect's style, aesthetic, and individual approach to their discipline and craft. A two-column grid provides maximum scale and visibility, allowing the viewer to immediately connect with the subtle visual nuances appearing in each typographic treatment. Color, contrast, and figure-ground also reinforce these subtle textural distinctions and characteristics in both posters.

THE MAP OFFICE
New York, New York, USA

Brawer & Architects Hauptman

This logotype for Brawer & Hauptman Architects is unified and singular in appearance due to the use of layered and integrated letterforms—a ligature created with the ampersand and *c* in the word *Architects*, and the lower serif of the *A* in *Architects* registered with the crossbar of the *e* in *Brawer*.

PAONE DESIGN
ASSOCIATES, LTD.
Philadelphia, Pennsylvania, USA

This visual identity system for an exhibition titled Graphic Design in China relies solely on the fluorescent light installations evident in each exhibition venue that spell out the names of each designer and disciplines represented in the exhibition. These custom, stencil-like letterforms used in the exhibition, as well as in smaller-scale, print applications such as this promotional poster, are all derived from lines representing fluorescent tube fixtures used throughout the light installations.

SENSE TEAM
Shenzhen, China

"rivers"—arbitrary negative spaces that occur and visually connect from line to line within the body of the typographic text. One of many methods to solve this issue is to identify the optimum flush-left alignment width for the type size being used prior to creating a justified alignment.

Typographic Color

Typography is a reality as well as an abstraction in visual communications. While we think of typography primarily as elements used together to form words and sentences, it also has an inherent function purely as a visual form. As such, typography can function in the same way as other basic graphic design elements such as point, line, shape, form, color, texture, contrast, and pattern in any visual composition.

It has rhythmic, spatial, and textural characteristics, identified as typographic color. Typographic color is similar to a color's hue—such as yellow, red, or blue—as well as its variations in density, contrast, texture, and value. Effective typographic color in any visual communication is determined by variations in weight, spacing, kerning, leading, mass, and texture.

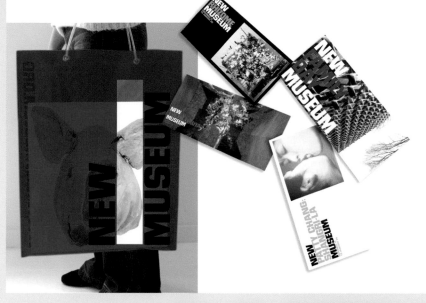

A change in typographic color immediately influences not only the spatial and textural appearance of typography but, more importantly, its meaning. A typographic color change allows a designer to highlight structure and invigorate a page. An effective use of typographic color in graphic composition and verbal clarity is directly related to the success of any visual communication.

Ultimately, a graphic designer's use of typography as an effective and communicative design element is solely dependent upon their technical expertise and historical knowledge, as well as a thorough understanding of the functional and aesthetic characteristics of letterform and typographic composition.

NEW
235 BOWERY
NEW YORK NY
10002 USA
MUSEUM

New York City's New Museum of Contemporary Art is the city's only museum dedicated exclusively to showcasing contemporary art. Its branding program, as well as its bold, sans serif logotype, is based on the premise of "new art and new ideas" as well as the act of self-renewal. The designer's first step with this program was to simplify the institution's name to "New Museum" and to loosen up the visual feel of the museum itself. The logotype changes and takes on new visual forms when used in a variety of print and digital applications that rely upon a full spectrum of colors, images, and other related visual elements.

WOLFF OLINS
New York, New York, USA

grid \\'grid\ *n*

2 b: a network of uniformly spaced horizontal and perpendicular lines (as for locating points on a map)

"**The grid system is an aid, not a guarantee . . . . But one must learn how to use the grid; it is an art that requires practice.**"
JOSEF MÜLLER-BROCKMANN (1914-1996), *Swiss, Author, Designer, Educator*

Fundamentally, a grid is composed of a series of horizontal and vertical lines that provide alignments and intersections for the graphic designer to use in an obvious or subtle manner. It is a primary design principle for all visual communications. Similar to many other design elements and

principles in this book, a grid's functions are limitless. It can provide order and visual unity as well as enhance the rhythm and pacing of any visual message. A typographic page grid is a two-dimensional organizational framework used to structure content. It is an armature for the graphic designer to organize narrative and visual content in a rational, aesthetic, and accessible manner.

Historical References

Whenever there has been a need to build an object, divide an area, or decorate a flat surface, some form of a grid has been used. The (continued on page 264)

A three-column page grid, based on a square planning module, is used as an effective organizational tool for the layout and design of this annual report for Media Trust, an organization that works in partnership with the media industries throughout the United Kingdom in building effective communications for charities and nonprofit organizations. This type of page grid provides maximum flexibility and continuity, allowing for a variety of types of narrative and visual information to be treated in a meaningful and accessible manner for the reader. Different-scale typographic elements and blocks of narrative text are set flush left, ragged right, and hang from a set of integral grid datums throughout the report, giving it a more active and varied presentation yet still providing a unified visual voice.

FORM
London, United Kingdom

1971

The Herald Newspaper
MASSIMO VIGNELLI
New York, New York, USA

In 1960, after completing his architectural studies in Milan and Venice, **MASSIMO VIGNELLI** (b. 1931) moved to the United States as cofounder and design director of Unimark International, at the time one of the largest design-consulting firms in the world. During the 1960s, Unimark and Vignelli designed many of the world's most recognizable corporate identities and public information systems for clients such as American Airlines, Ford Motor Company, and Knoll International, as well as the iconic sign program for the New York City subway system.

Unimark's philosophy was based on a disciplined and systemized approach for creating effective and rational mass communications for their clients; solutions that provided the means by which an individual could implement any aspect of a program in an efficient and effective manner.

The primary tool for achieving this objective was the grid, ultimately standardizing graphic communications for the majority of their corporate clients including Alcoa, JCPenney, Memorex, Panasonic, Steelcase, and Xerox.

In 1971, following the closing of Unimark's New York offices, Vignelli cofounded Vignelli Associates with his wife, Lella. It is a multidisciplinary design consultancy firm whose philosophy and approach is firmly grounded in the modernist tradition and on simplicity through the use of fundamental elements and principles in all of their work. The firm's broad range of work and interests, including furniture, tableware, apparel, showrooms, interiors, posters, publications, and corporate identity programs, is based on a simple belief, Vignelli says: "If you can design one thing, you can design everything."

While Vignelli's typographic range expanded beyond the sole use of Helvetica for Unimark's clients to now include classical typefaces such as Bodoni, Century, Garamond, and Times Roman, he retained and strengthened a rational use of grid systems and an emphasis on clear, precise, and objective visual communications.

One primary example of this philosophy was evident in the early 1970s with the design of the *Herald* newspaper. Prior to this time, newspapers and tabloids were one of the most neglected areas of visual communication. In 1971, Vignelli Associates was given the opportunity to design the *Herald*, a new weekly newspaper for the New York City tristate area. the *Herald* was structured on a page grid of six columns with sixteen modules per column. One typeface, Times Roman, was used throughout the publication, with one type size for all running, narrative text, two type sizes for titles and subtitles, and italic for captions and decks. Every page or two constituted a section of the whole paper, and all pages were structured with clear horizontal bands, which provided a strong, easy-to-read accessibility to the paper's editorial content. Reliance on a fully articulated page grid, as well as a unified set of design specifications, further indicated that the paper would be equipped for fast production and quick turn-around.

Unfortunately, the newspaper folded in less than a year due to union and distribution problems. However, use of the grid as an organizational, design, and production principle proved to be successful and was subsequently used by designers and publishers as an effective tool for the redesign of numerous newspapers and tabloids in the coming years.

Massimo Vignelli and *The Herald*

This information-based data poster titled *The Shape of News*, documents the designer's analysis of newspaper title pages and their various content. The overall composition is arranged according to the U.S. states and provides the viewer with insight into the way public opinion was formed during the Iraq War. This study uses various colors to express **a multivariate mapping of news interests and coverage such as local, national, and international; the wars in Iran and Afghanistan reveal the tenor of regional reporting over a period of two months. The actual use of newspaper page grids as the poster's primary communication device further conveys the use and type of information in a familiar manner.**

CHRISTINA VAN VLECK
Lexington, Massachusetts, USA

grid has been relied upon as a guiding organizational principle by Renaissance artists as a method for scaling sketches and images to fit the proportion of murals, by cartographers in plotting map coordinates, by architects for scaling drawings and plotting perspective views, and by typographers in the design of letterforms and the printed page.

Prior to the invention of movable type and printing by Johannes Gutenberg in the fifteenth century, simple grids based on various proportional relationships were also used to arrange handwritten text on pages. While the grid evolved and developed over the next five hundred years, it primarily remained the same in structure and use.

Evolution of the Modern Grid
In the early 1950s, European designers such as Emil Ruder and Josef Müller-Brockmann, influenced by the modernist tenets of Jan Tschichold's *Die Neue Typographie (The New Typography)*, began to question the relevance and use of the conventional grid.

The result was the development of the modern typographic grid that became associated with the International Typographic Style or Swiss Design, which provided

CITY OF MELBOURNE

designers with a flexible system for achieving variations of the printed page. A seminal reference book on this subject, *Grid Systems in Graphic Design*, written by Müller-Brockmann, helped propagate the use of the modern page grid, first in Europe, and later throughout the world.

Functions

Visual communication carries its message and meaning through the organization and arrangement of disparate design elements. The clarity and immediacy of any message is further achieved with visual unity by the use of the grid. It is a useful and purposeful tool for any graphic designer. A page grid provides a framework for composition through its network of horizontal and vertical intersecting lines that organize and divide the page into field and interval, thereby creating a guide for establishing proportional relationships between the composition's design elements.

The grid is an invaluable principle of a graphic designer's vocabulary, as well as an essential tool that can be used in the increasingly complex production of print-based and digitally based visual communications.

The identity and branding program for the city of Melbourne is based on a triangular grid and fully expresses the multifaceted spirit of the city as a creative, cultural, and sustainable urban center. An iconic *M* is the central element of this program and has been constructed from the same triangular element of the program's organizational grid.

This grid's triangular base module is also used as an interpretive visual element that is articulated in a diverse palette of colors, patterns, textures, and images.

LANDOR
Paris, France

The inventive use of a flex-ible, four-column page grid with alternating narrow and wide columns, when needed, provides Yale's "A Guide to Yale College" with a rhythmic pacing and unexpected varia-tion from spread to spread. Full color, photographic images of different scales are allowed to invade columns and bleed beyond the de-lineated format of the page grid, while a thoughtfully considered hierarchy of type weights and sizes contributes to a unified whole.

PENTAGRAM
New York, New York, USA

An asymmetrial columnar grid provides clear organiza-tion, flexibility, and compositional diversity for the navigation, narrative information, and photogra-phic elements of this website for Gotham Construction, a New York City-based construction company.

SUPERMETRIC
New York, New York, USA

It can be used to compose, organize, separate, enlarge, reduce, and locate visual elements. Grid construction can be loose and organic or rigorous and mechanical. When used correctly and appropriately, a grid pro-vides simplicity, clarity, efficiency, flexibility, economy, continuity, consistency, and unity to any visual communication.

A grid, like any other element in the design process, is not an absolute. It should be used with flexibility and, when necessary, be modified or even abandoned for a more intuitive solution. It can be developed as a simple framework that has an obvious and integrated relationship to its narrative and visual content or it can be composed of more complex forms and proportions that provide more varied and nuanced results.

Müller-Brockmann maintains that "the grid system is an aid, not a guarantee. It permits a number of possible uses, and each designer can look for a solution appropriate to their own personal style. But one must learn how to use the grid: It is an art that re-quires practice." As a counterpoint, Charles-Édouard Jeanneret-Gris (aka Le Corbusier), a pioneer of modernist architecture and the International Style, in his comments about his

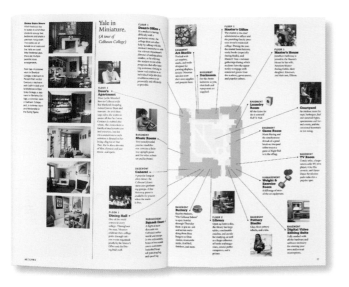

grid system called "Le Modulor" points out: "I still reserve the right, at any time, to doubt the solutions furnished by the Modulor, keeping intact my freedom which must depend on my feelings rather than my reason."

The use of an underlying organizational grid can enhance the clarity, legibility, and balance of any visual communication. When multiple pages are involved, as in a book or website, it guarantees continuity and unity.

Applications

A grid can be used to solve a wide range of design problems and is an effective organizational framework for newspapers, magazines,

A purely utilitarian, organizational grid used in this poster is composed of forty-eight equally proportioned modules and functions as a visual identity for this water table communicating the effects of Hurricane Katrina in the Gulf of Mexico. Stenciled letterforms are used solely to identify each of the neighboring states—Mississippi, Alabama, Louisiana, and Florida—that

were affected by flooding, intermittently interrupted by the letters SOS as a further identifier for the urgency of the message. The contrast of warm and cool colors further reinforces the seriousness of this message.

STEREOTYPE DESIGN
New York, New York, USA

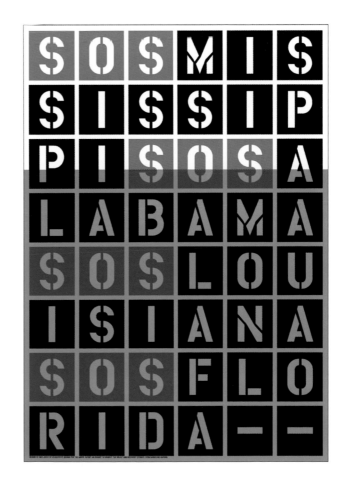

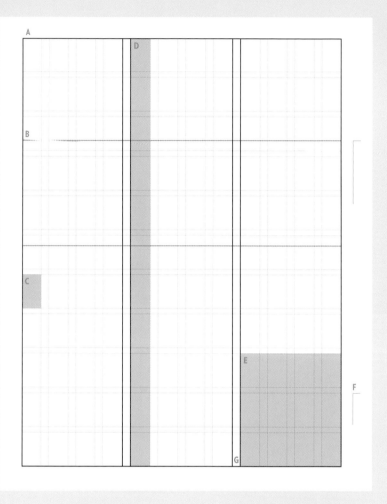

A

Margins are the borders or negative spaces surrounding the page's format and content. They define the live area of the page where type and image are located and composed. Proportions of margins are also a critical consideration since they assist in establishing the overall balance and tension in the page composition. Margins are also used to bring focus and attention to content, create respite for the reader's eyes, and function as an area for supporting page information.

B

Flow lines are horizontal alignments that organize content into defined areas, assist in guiding the reader's eyes across the page, and used to imply additional start and stop points for type or images on the page.

C

Modules are individual units of space within the grid separated by regular intervals that, when repeated across the page, create columns and rows.

D

Columns are vertical alignments of type that create vertical divisions between the page margins. There can be any number of columns; sometimes they are all the same width or are different widths corresponding to specific types of information.

E

Spatial zones are groups of modules that form distinct fields on the page for containing or displaying similar or alike information, such as groups of images or multiple columns of text.

F

Markers are graphic indicators for supporting page information, such as running headers or footers, folios or page numbers, or any other element that occupies only one location on a page or spread.

G

Gutters, also known as alleys, are vertical spaces located between columns of type.

* The page grid illustrated here is the page grid used throughout this book.

books, annual reports, brochures, catalogs, sign systems, corporate identity and branding programs, and websites.

As a flexible compositional tool, a grid can assist the graphic designer in creating either static, symmetrical compositions, or active, asymmetrical ones. The construction of any grid can be orthogonal, angular, irregular, and circular. It can be an invisible and functional layer of a composition or it can be an obvious and active visual element of a composition.

The structure of a grid should always be based on a thorough understanding and analysis of the visual and narrative material to be used. This will allow a considerable degree of flexibility when composing and arranging disparate elements, such as typographic text and images, on a grid and ultimately the page, be it two-dimensional, three-dimensional, or virtual.

A grid can be visible or invisible, an implied framework or an obvious design element. It is also an essential design principle for organizing and presenting complex, multifaceted information in a systematic manner. Publications, websites, sign systems, advertising campaigns, and corporate communica-

Both of these informational data-based posters use the same articulated grid to organize and structure relational statistics in a meaningful and informative manner. Imaginary visual landscapes are built from the intersection and interplay of data formulated in both of these studies on people living in selected cities.

LORENZO GEIGER
Bern, Switzerland

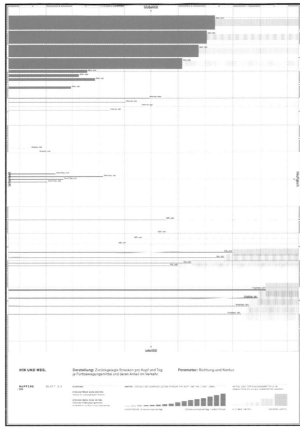

tions are all made up of multiple pages—each requiring a slightly different composition due to their varied content.

If a grid is well planned and conceived, it provides the graphic designer with an efficient way to create multiple layouts while maintaining visual consistency, continuity, and cohesiveness.

The development of the grid has been an evolutionary process. No one artist or designer can be identified as its sole creator or inventor; however, many creative minds have contributed to its development and will continue to influence its further refinement over time.

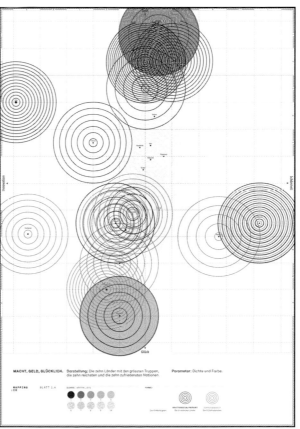

abstraction
the visual simplification, distortion, or rearrangement of a recognizable image

analogous colors
colors created from adjacent colors on a color wheel, with minimal chroma differences

apex
the outer point where two diagonal stems or strokes meet, as at the top of an *A* or *M* or at the bottom of an *M*

arm
a projecting horizontal or upward diagonal stem or stroke not enclosed within a character, as in an *E, K,* or *L*

art nouveau
French for "new art"; also known as Jugendstil, German for "youth style"; an international movement and style of art, architecture, and applied art that was popular from 1890 to 1905 and characterized by organic, floral, and plant-inspired motifs

Arts and Crafts movement
an international movement that originated in Great Britain during the late 1800s through the writings of William Morris (1834–1896) and John Ruskin (1819–1900) and was characterized by simple form and a medieval style of decoration

ascender
the part of a lowercase letter that rises above the body of the letter, or x-height, as in a *b, d, f, h, l,* and *t*

asymmetry
a state of visual balance (also known as informal or dynamic balance) in which compositional elements are not identical but are perceived as visually balanced

axonometric
a drawing projection method where a form is viewed from a skewed direction to reveal more than one of its sides in the same picture plane

balance
a state of equilibrium in which visual forces of equal strength pull in opposite directions

baseline
a line on which the bottom of characters without descenders sit or align

bowl
a curved stem or stroke that encloses a counter, as in a *b, p,* or *O*

bracket
a curving joint between the serif and a stem or stroke; also known as a fillet

cap height
the distance from a baseline to the top of a capital character.

chiaroscuro
a technical term for achieving strong contrasts of light to create a sense of volume in modeling three-dimensional objects

chroma
the amount of colorant in a pigment

cicero
a European typographic unit of measurement approximately equal to the British or American pica, or 4.155 mm

closure
a principle of visual perception in which the human eye visually completes an unfinished shape or form through the memory of that shape or form

color
a visual property of an object that depends on a combination of reflected and absorbed light from the spectrum, as well as inherent hues found in light and pigment

column
vertical alignments of type that create horizontal divisions on a page grid

complementary colors
any two colors found directly opposite one another on a color wheel

Constructivism
an art movement, originating in Russia in 1919, that rejected the idea of "art for art's sake" in favor of art as a practice directed toward social purposes and needs

contrast
a visual principle in which differences in light, value, texture, and color create the illusion of depth

counter
an area enclosed by a bowl or a crossbar

crossbar
a horizontal element connecting two vertical or diagonal stems or strokes, or crossing a stem or stroke, as in an *A, H, f,* or *t*; also known as a bar or cross stroke.

cubism
a twentieth-century avant-garde art movement, pioneered by Pablo Picasso and Georges Braque, characterized by objects that are broken up and reassembled in abstract forms

descender
the part of a lowercase letter that falls below the body of the letter or baseline, as in *g, j, p, q,* and *y*

de Stijl
a Dutch art movement (also known as neoplasticism) founded in 1917 and characterized by pure abstraction, as well as essential reduction of form and color

ear
a small projecting stroke sometimes attached to the bowl of a *g* or the stem of an *r*

expression
a principle of visual perception concerning the emotional, cultural, and social content of a visual message

figure-ground
the relationship of foreground and background in a two-dimensional composition

figure-ground reversal
a visual effect where a figure can function as a ground and a ground as a figure

flow line
horizontal alignments that organize content into defined areas on a page grid

form
three-dimensional derivatives of basic shapes, such as a sphere, cube, or pyramid

gestalt
the perception of the whole image as opposed to its individual parts or elements

glyph
a simplistic form or element of writing

golden ratio
also known as the divine proportion, golden section, and golden rectangle; proportional relationship defined as the whole compared to a larger part in exactly the same way that the larger part is compared to a smaller one; its mathematical expression is the number 1.618

grid
a module system composed of a set of horizontal and vertical lines used as a guide to align type and image and create a uniform composition

gutter (or alley)
vertical spaces located between columns of type on a page grid

hierarchy
an arranged, established visual order of importance, emphasis, and movement given to elements in a composition

hue
a fundamental property of color defined in its purest form

International Typographic Style
a graphic design style developed in Switzerland in the 1950s and characterized by clean, readable, asymmetric layouts and use of the page grid and san serif typefaces; also known as the Swiss School

isometric
a drawing projection method where three visible surfaces of a form have equal emphasis, all axes are simultaneously rotated away from the picture plane at 30 degrees, all lines are equally foreshortened, and angles between lines are always at 120 degrees

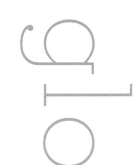

joint
the angle formed where two strokes meet or intersect, as is a *K* or *R*.

leg
a projecting diagonal stem or stroke extending downward, as in an *R* and a *K*; also known as a tail

ligature
a stem or stroke that connects two characters together creating a ligature or tied character

light
electromagnetic radiation of wavelengths visible to the human eye and used to create contrast, depth, brightness, and illumination

line
a fundamental element that consists of a number of points located next to one another in one direction

link
the stem or stroke that connects the bowl and the loop of a *g*

loop
the descender of a *g* when it is entirely closed

margin
border or negative space surrounding a page's format, grid, and content, and defining the live area of the page where type and image are located and composed

marker
graphic indicators for supporting page information, such as running headers or footers, folios or page numbers, or any other element that occupies only one location on a page or spread

module
individual units of space within a page grid separated by regular intervals that, when repeated across, create columns and rows

monochromatic colors
colors with varying values of a single color, created by adding white or black to a color

movement
a principle of visual perception that moves the viewer's eye through a two-dimensional space

pattern
the combination of lines, shapes, and/or colors in a consistent, orderly, or repetitive motif

pica
a typographic unit of measurement where 12 points equal 1 pica (1/16 inch or 0.166 inch) and 6 picas equal 1 inch (0.996 inch)

Plakatstil
an early poster style of art that began in the early 1900s and originated in Germany

point
an abstract phenomenon indicating a precise location; also defined as the smallest typographical unit of measure; one point is equal to 0.0148 inches

primary colors
yellow, red, and blue are pure in color composition and cannot be created from other colors

proportion
a comparison of two ratios; includes an indication of how the two ratios are related

quadratic colors
created from colors located in the corners of a square or rectangle juxtaposed on a color wheel

radial balance
a state of visual balance (also known as rotative symmetry) in which visual forces of equal strength radiate or extend out from a central point

rhythm
an alternating repetition of shape and space or a planned movement of visual elements in a composition

saturation
a fundamental property of color defined by intensity, or the brightness or dullness of a color

scale
the relationship of size or a composition of size from one element to another

secondary colors
colors created by combining two of the three primary colors

semiotics
the study of sign processes or the significance and communication of signs and symbols

serif
the beginning or end of a stem or stroke, arm, leg, or tail drawn at a right angle or at an oblique to the stem or stroke

shade
a fundamental property of color defined by the amount of black in a color

shape
the external outline or contour of an object, figure, or mass

shoulder
the portion of a curved stroke, but not the hairline, connecting two vertical strokes or stems

space
an element of design that indicates area and depth on a two-dimensional plane

spatial zone
groups of modules that form distinct fields on a page grid for containing or displaying similar or alike information, such as groups of images or multiple columns of text

spine
the diagonal portion or main curved stroke of an *S* or *s*

spur
a small, pointed projection from a stem or stroke, sometimes found on the bottom of a *b, t,* or *G*

stem (or stroke)
the principal vertical or oblique element(s) of a character, as in an *A, B, L,* or *V,* except for curved characters where they are called strokes

stress (or axis)
the inclination suggested by the relationship of thin and thick stems or strokes in a character, which can be an inclined or vertical stress or axis

Suprematism
a Russian abstract art movement that focused on fundamental geometric forms such as the circle and the square

swash
a flourished terminal, stem, or stroke added to a character

symmetry
a state of visual balance (also known as formal balance or reflective symmetry) in which compositional elements are identical, equally balanced, and can be divided into two equal parts that are mirror images of each other

tail
the short stem or stroke that rests on a baseline, as in a *K* or *R*; or extending below a baseline, as in a *Q* or *j*. In *K* and *R*, also known as a leg

tension
a principle of visual perception in which the forces of balance or imbalance, stress, action, and reaction exist between the elements of any composition

terminal (or finial)
A stem or stroke ending other than a serif

tertiary colors
colors created by combining one primary color with one secondary color

texture
a design element that creates or implies the tactile quality and characteristics of a surface

tint
a fundamental property of color defined by the amount of white in a color

tone
a visual characteristic, also known as value or shade, based on the degree of light or dark apparent on the surface of an object

triadic colors
colors created from other colors that are equidistant from one another on a color wheel

typography
the arrangement and aesthetics of letters and letterforms

value
a fundamental property of color defined by the lightness and darkness of a color

vertex
the angle formed at the bottom of a character where the left and right strokes meet or intersect, as in a *V* or *x*

x-height
the height of the body of lowercase letters, exclusive of ascenders and descenders

Books

AdamsMorioka and Stone, Terry. *Color Design Workbook: A Real-World Guide to Using Color in Graphic Design*. Beverly: Rockport Publishers, 2006.

Albers, Josef. *Interaction of Color*. New Haven: Yale University Press, 1963.

Arnheim, Rudolf. *Art and Visual Perception: A Psychology of the Creative Eye*. Berkeley: University of California Press, 1971.

Arntson, Amy E. *Graphic Design Basics*. New York: Rinehart and Winston, 1988.

Blackwell, Lewis. *20th Century Type*. New Haven: Yale University Press, 2004.

Bringhurst, Robert. *The Elements of Typographic Style*. Vancouver: Hartley and Marks, 2005.

Cohen, Arthur A. *Herbert Bayer: The Complete Work*. Cambridge: MIT Press, 1984.

Dondis, Donis A. *Primer of Visual Literacy*. Cambridge: MIT Press, 1973.

Drew, Ned, and Sternberger, Paul. *By Its Cover: Modern American Book Cover Design*. New York: Princeton Architectural Press, 2005.

Elam, Kimberly. *Geometry of Design: Studies in Proportion and Composition*. New York: Princeton Architectural Press, 2001.

Elam, Kimberly. *Grid Systems: Principles of Organizing Type*. New York: Princeton Architectural Press, 2005.

Elam, Kimberly. *Typographic Systems*. New York: Princeton Architectural Press, 2007.

Eskilson, Stephen J. *Graphic Design: A New History*. New Haven: Yale University Press, 2007.

Evans, Poppy, and Thomas, Mark A. *Exploring the Elements of Design*. New York: Thomas Delmar, 2008.

Gertsner, Karl. *The Forms of Color: The Interaction of Visual Elements*. Cambridge: MIT Press, 1986.

Goethe, Johann Wolfgang Von. *Theory of Colours*. Cambridge: MIT Press, 1970.

Hofmann, Armin. *Graphic Design Manual: Principles and Practice*. Switzerland: Niggli Verlag, Sulgen, 1965.

Igarashi, Takenobu. *Igarashi Alphabets*. Zurich: ABC Verlag Zurich, 1987.

Itten, Johannes. *The Art of Color*. New York: Van Nostrand Reinhold, 1970.

Kandinsky, Wassily. *Point and Line to Plane*. New York: Dover Publications, 1979. Originally published in 1926.

Leborg, Christian. *Visual Grammar*. New York: Princeton Architectural Press, 2004.

Lupton, Ellen. *Thinking with Type: A Critical Guide for Designers, Writers, Editors, and Students*. New York: Princeton Architectural Press, 2004.

Lupton, Ellen, and Phillips, Jennifer C. *Graphic Design: The New Basics*. New York: Princeton Architectural Press, 2008.

McLean, Ruari. *Jan Tschichold: A Life in Typography*. New York: Princeton Architectural Press, 1997.

Meggs, Philip B. *A History of Graphic Design*. New York: John Wiley & Sons, 2005.

Mount, Christopher. *Stenberg Brothers: Constructing a Revolution in Soviet Design*. New York: Museum of Modern Art, 1997.

Mouron, Henri. *A. M. Cassandre*. New York: Rizzoli International Publications, 1985.

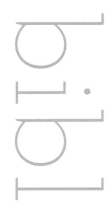

Müller-Brockmann, Josef. *The Graphic Artist and His Design Problems*. Teufen AR, Switzerland: Verlag Arthur Niggli, 1968.

Müller-Brockmann, Josef. *Grid Systems in Graphic Design*. Niederteufen: Verlag Arthur Niggli, 1981.

Rand, Paul. *Paul Rand: A Designer's Art*. New Haven: Yale University Press, 1985.

Remington, R. Roger. *Lester Beall: Trailblazer of American Graphic Design*. New York: W. W. Norton & Co., 1996.

Remington, R. Roger, and Hodik, Barbara J. *Nine Pioneers in American Graphic Design*. New York: W. W. Norton & Co., 1989.

Ruder, Emil. *Typography*. New York: Hastings House, 1971,

Samara, Timothy. *Making and Breaking the Grid: A Graphic Design Layout Workshop*. Beverly: Rockport Publishers, 2002.

Samara, Timothy. *Typography Workbook*. Beverly: Rockport Publishers, 2004.

Spencer, Herbert. *Pioneers of Modern Typography*. Cambridge: MIT Press, 1983.

Spiekermann, Erik, and Giner, E. M. *Stop Stealing Sheep and Find Out How Type Works*. Mountain View: Adobe Press, 1993.

Vignelli, Massimo. *Vignelli: design:*. New York: Rizzoli International Publications, 1990.

Von Moos, Stanislaus, Campana, Mara and Bosoni, Giampiero. *Max Huber*. London: Phaidon, 2006.

William Purcell, Kerry. *Josef Müller-Brockmann*. New York: Phaidon, 2006.

Wong, Wucius. *Principles of Two-Dimensional Design*. New York, John Wiley & Co., 1972.

Periodicals

Heller, Steven. "When Paperbacks Went Highbrow—Modern Cover Design in the '50s and '60s," *Baseline*, No. 43, 2003, pg. 5–12.

Heller, Steven. "Paul Rand Laboratory: The Art of Bookjackets and Covers," *Baseline*, No. 27, 1999, pg. 17–24.

Nunoo-Quarcoo, Franc. "Bruno Monguzzi—Master Communicator," *Baseline*, No. 30, 2000, pg. 25–32.

Doubleday, Richard B. "Jan Tschichold at Penguin Books—A Resurgence of Classical Book Design," *Baseline*, No. 49, 2006, pg. 13–20.

Friedman, Milton, ed. "LA 84: Games of the XXIII Olympiad," *Design Quarterly 127*, 1985

Books (*continued*)

Rand, Paul. *Paul Rand: A Designer's Art*. New Haven: Yale University Press, 1985.

Remington, R. Roger. *Lester Beall: Trailblazer of American Graphic Design*. New York: W. W. Norton & Co., 1996.

Remington, R. Roger, and Hodik, Barbara J. *Nine Pioneers in American Graphic Design*. New York: W. W. Norton & Co., 1989.

Resnick, Elizabeth. *Design for Communication: Conceptual Graphic Design Basics*. Hoboken: John Wiley & Sons, 2003.

Ruder, Emil. *Typography*. New York: Hastings House, 1971.

Samara, Timothy. *Design Evolution: Theory into Practice. A Handbook of Basic Design Principles Applied in Contemporary Design*. Beverly: Rockport Publishers, 2008.

Samara, Timothy. *Making and Breaking the Grid: A Graphic Design Layout Workshop*. Beverly: Rockport Publishers, 2002.

Samara, Timothy. *Typography Workbook*. Beverly: Rockport Publishers, 2004.

Spencer, Herbert. *Pioneers of Modern Typography*. Cambridge: MIT Press, 1983.

Spiekermann, Erik, and Giner, E. M. *Stop Stealing Sheep and Find Out How Type Works*. Mountain View: Adobe Press, 1993.

Vignelli, Massimo. *design: Vignelli*. New York: Rizzoli International Publications, 1990.

Von Moos, Stanislaus, Mara Campana, and Giampiero Bosoni. *Max Huber*. London: Phaidon, 2006.

William Purcell, Kerry. *Josef Müller-Brockmann*. New York: Phaidon, 2006.

Wong, Wucius. *Principles of Two-Dimensional Design*. New York, John Wiley & Co., 1972.

Periodicals

Doubleday, Richard B. "Jan Tschichold at Penguin Books—A Resurgence of Classical Book Design," *Baseline*, No. 49, 2006, pg. 13–20.

Friedman, Milton, ed. "LA 84: Games of the XXIII Olympiad," *Design Quarterly 127*, 1985

Heller, Steven. "Paul Rand Laboratory: The Art of Bookjackets and Covers," *Baseline*, No. 27, 1999, pg. 17–24.

Heller, Steven. "When Paperbacks Went Highbrow—Modern Cover Design in the 50s and 60s," *Baseline*, No. 43, 2003, pg. 5–12.

Nunoo-Quarcoo, Franc. "Bruno Monguzzi—Master Communicator," *Baseline*, No. 30, 2000, pg. 25–32.

Page numbers in italic indicate figures.

About the Author

Richard Poulin is cofounder, design director, and principal of Poulin + Morris Inc., an internationally recognized, multidisciplinary design consultancy located in New York City.

His work has been published in periodicals and books worldwide, is in the permanent collection of the Library of Congress, and has received awards from the American Institute of Architects, American Institute of Graphic Arts, *Applied Arts*, *Communication Arts*, *Creative Review*, *Graphis*, *ID*, *Print*, Society for Environmental Graphic Design, Society of Publication Designers, Type Directors Club, and the Art Directors Clubs of Los Angeles, New York, and San Francisco.

Richard is a fellow of the Society for Environmental Graphic Design (SEGD), the organization's highest honor for lifetime achievement; and past president and board member of the New York Chapter of AIGA, He is also a recipient of a research grant in design history from the Graham Foundation for Advanced Studies in the Fine Arts.

Since 1992, he has been a faculty member of the School of Visual Arts in New York City and was formerly an adjunct professor at The Cooper Union. He has also taught and lectured at Carnegie-Mellon University, Maryland Institute College of Art, Massachusetts College of Art, North Carolina State University, Simmons College, Syracuse University, University of the Arts, and University of Cincinnati.

He lives in New York City and Clinton Corners, New York, with his partner of twenty-one years.

DEDICATION

This book is dedicated to the two most important and influential people in my life:

Muriel Poulin, who has always inspired me and taught me "to know is nothing at all . . . to imagine is everything."
—*Anatole France, French Novelist, 1881.*

And, above all, to

Doug Morris, for giving me the time, freedom, love, and support to pursue my dreams.

ACKNOWLEDGMENTS

This book would not have been possible without the support and contributions of all the designers who shared their work with me. Going through this process has truly reminded me of the incredible community that I am a part of and the great work my colleagues are producing all around the world. A special thanks to Sean Adams, Michael Bierut, Ivan Chermayeff, Richard Doubleday, Steff Geissbuhler, Allan Haley, Takenobu Igarashi, Bruno Monguzzi, Roland Mouron, Deborah Sussman, Massimo Vignelli, and Catherine Zask for their assistance, cooperation, and contributions to this book.

To Steve Heller for recommending me to Rockport Publishers as a potential author for this volume.

To everyone at Rockport Publishers, especially Winnie Prentiss, publisher, and Emily Potts, acquisition editor, for their encouragement, enthusiasm, and support, as well as to David Martinell, Betsy Gammons, and Cora Hawks for collaborating with me on this book.

To AJ Mapes and Erik Herter, two of my colleagues at Poulin + Morris Inc. who have helped design this volume with a level of detail and nuance that I did not fully realize when we started this project. Their invaluable contributions and insights to the design of this book are deeply appreciated and have made it one of the truly memorable and enjoyable experiences of my career.

And to my students—past, present, and future.

IMAGE RESOURCES

15: Peter Behrens, Bildarchive Preussischer Kulturbesitz/Art Resource, New York, ©2010 Artists Rights Society (ARS), New York/VG Bild-Kunst, Bonn. *23:* Josef Müller-Brockman, © ZHdK, Museum für Gestaltung Zürich, Poster Collection. *33:* © Estate of Vladimir and Georgii Stenberg/RAO, Moscow/ VAGA, New York. *43:* Takenobu Igarashi, Photographs by Mitsumasa Fujitsuka. *51:* Herbert Bayer, Museum für Gestaltung Zürich, Graphics Collection. Photographer: Umberto Romito © ZHdK. *61:* Courtesy of Deborah Sussman, Sussman/Prejza & Company. *75:* Paul Rand, Paul Rand Papers. Manuscripts & Archives, Yale University Library. *85:* A.M. Cassandre, © Mouron Cassandre. Lic 2010-13-07-05 www.cassandre-france.com. *95:* Max Huber, © Aoi Huber Kono. *105:* Lester Beall © Lester Beall, Jr. Trust/Licensed by VAGA, New York, New York, RIT Archive Collections, Rochester Institute of Technology. *115:* Jacqueline Casey, Courtesy MIT Museum. *125:* Jan Tschichold, Reproduced by permission of Penguin Books Ltd. *133:* Jan Tschichold, © ZHdK, Museum für Gestaltung Zürich, Poster Collection. *143:* Piet Zwart, Collection of the Gemeentemuseum Den Haag. *153:* Armin Hofmann, © ZHdK, Museum für Gestaltung Zürich, Poster Collection. *161:* Courtesy of Bruno Monguzzi. *171:* Alvin Lustig, Alvin Lustig Archive, Courtesy of Kind Company. *181:* Willem Sandberg, Collection of Richard Poulin. *191:* Emil Ruder, © Niggli Publishers, www.niggli.ch. *201:* Max Bill; © ZHdK, Museum für Gestaltung Zürich, Poster Collection. *211:* Saul Bass, © Copyright Academy of Motion Picture Arts and Sciences. Courtesy of Otto Preminger Films Ltd. All rights reserved. *229:* Courtesy of Ivan Chermayeff, Chermayeff & Geismar. *239:* Ludwig Hohlwein, © ZHdK, Museum für Gestaltung Zürich, Poster Collection. *249:* Herb Lubalin, Courtesy of the Herb Lubalin Study Center of Design and Typography at the Cooper Union. *263:* Courtesy of Massimo Vignelli, Vignelli Associates.

COLOPHON

The Language of Graphic Design was designed and typeset by Poulin + Morris Inc., New York, New York. Digital type composition, page layouts, and type design were originated on Apple Macintosh G5 computers, utilizing Adobe InDesign CS3, Version 6.0.5 software.

The text of the book was set in Verlag and Archer, two typefaces designed and produced by Hoefler & Frere-Jones, New York, New York.

DEFINITIONS

All definitions used in this book are from *Merriam-Webster's Collegiate Dictionary*, Eleventh Edition, 2009.